Explore Wild

compiled, edited
and designed by

Tony Gunton

Lopinga Books

Published by Lopinga Books
Tye Green House, Wimbish, GB-Essex, CB10 2XE

Jointly with the Essex Wildlife Trust
Abbotts Hall Farm, Gt Wigborough,
Colchester, GB-Essex CO5 7RZ

First published 2008

Text & maps © Tony Gunton 2008

Front cover painting © Alan Harris 2008

Photographs © as credited

All rights reserved.

The right of Tony Gunton to be identified as the author of this
work has been asserted by him in accordance with the Copyright,
Design and Patents Act 1988

ISBN 978-0-9530362-6-4

British Library Cataloguing-in-Publication Data
A catalogue record for this book is available from the British Library

Printed by Cambridge University Press

The Nature of Essex Series No. 7

Contents

Acknowledgements

Photographers

All the photographers whose colour photographs are such an important part of this book supported the Essex Wildlife Trust and Lopinga Books by allowing us to use their work free of charge. Without this generous help the production of this book would have been impossible.

Photographers are credited on each photo caption. Some of them earn their living as wildlife photographers. Organisations wishing to contact any of them regarding use of their work in other publications can do so via the Essex Wildlife Trust or Lopinga Books.

Other important contributors

Many people have contributed to the making of this book, such as by providing information and by checking the entries for the sites under their care. We would like to thank them all for their generous support and help.

Special thanks are due to David Corke, Elaine Corke, Chris Gibson, David Harris, Bob Hills and John Thorogood for their many helpful comments on the final draft.

Wildlife conservation charities

Many of the sites in this book are owned or managed by wildlife conservation charities. Although these charities encourage visits by non-members they depend on their members to help them buy and manage their nature reserves, as well as campaign for wildlife conservation generally.

The Essex Wildlife Trust and London Wildlife Trust are local organisations (although membership is open to anyone, wherever you live). Both are part of the national Wildlife Trusts partnership

The National Trust, Royal Society for the Protection of Birds and the Woodland Trust are national organisations that work in Essex and throughout the country.

All these organisations have been supportive during the preparation of this guide book. If you enjoy visiting the places in this book, please support one or more of the wildlife charities that work for wildlife in the county. See page 3 for how to get information about these organisations and about membership.

Disclaimer

Despite all our best efforts to provide a comprehensive and accurate guide, no doubt errors remain. Information that was correct in April 2008 can also, of course, go out of date. Users of this guide are strongly recommended to make use of the telephone and website contacts, to check the latest situation before setting off on a long journey to visit a site.

The author and publishers accept no liability for loss or inconvenience resulting from any errors or omissions in this book.

The maps are designed to give visitors a good indication of what they will find when they visit a site. They must not be taken as a definitive statement of rights of way or of boundaries.

Preface to this edition

Although it has been renamed **Explore Wild Essex**, this book is really an updated and thoroughly revised edition of **Wild Essex**, published in 2000.

In the eight years that have passed since then, a great deal has changed in the Essex countryside. The pressure for development in this already crowded corner of England has increased, with three growth areas extending into it: Thames Gateway in the south, Haven Gateway in the north-east, and the M11 Corridor in the north-west.

Fortunately, in those eight years a great deal of additional land has also been set aside for wildlife. This reflects the efforts of conservation organisations, local authorities and government agencies to safeguard areas that are important for wildlife, and also a desire by the agencies driving forward development in the growth areas to compensate by providing additional green space.

A government initiative that predated the 2000 edition of Wild Essex but that has taken some time to get under way – the Thames Chase Community Forest, extending from Dagenham through Havering into Brentwood and Thurrock – has also delivered a number of new public open spaces, most of them managed by the Forestry Commission.

The net result is that the number of sites included in this edition of the book has increased dramatically compared with 2000, amounting now to 268 sites, running to almost 40,000 acres in total.

This means that it is impractical to represent all the sites on a single map, which has prompted a reorganisation of the book. Whereas the sites in **Wild Essex** were in alphabetical sequence by name or group throughout the book, with a map of Essex at the beginning, in **Explore Wild Essex** they have been separated into ten regions, with a map of the region at the start of each section.

An additional reason for separating the sites into regions is to make it easier to find the little place just up the road, or to enhance a visit to a friend or relative by stopping off somewhere *en route* or afterwards. Of course there will still be good reason to travel long distances sometimes, whether to see large numbers of birds overwintering at RSPB's new Rainham Marshes reserve, to hear the nightingales at Essex Wildlife Trust's Fingringhoe Wick, or to visit the National Trust's stunning Hatfield Forest, but hopefully this will be balanced by more trips to local or convenient sites costing less carbon emissions.

Another change is that this edition shows the long-distance footpaths, a few more of which have emerged since 2000. And for the next edition – perhaps long-distance cycle routes as well … ?

Tony Gunton
May 2008

Using This Book

What is 'Essex'?

As far as this book is concerned, Essex is the original geographical county of Essex, in other words stretching into Greater London as far as the River Lea in the west, including the London Boroughs of Havering, Barking & Dagenham, Redbridge, Waltham Forest and Newham.

What places are included?

All sites in Essex of significant wildlife interest and that are accessible to the public are included, although in many cases access is not permitted to parts of the site and/or at particular times to limit disturbance to wildlife. You may also occasionally find temporary restrictions imposed in the interests of public safety.

It is the official guide to the nature reserves of the Essex Wildlife Trust, one of the joint publishers, but also includes the nature reserves of other conservation charities, such as the London Wildlife Trust, the RSPB, the Woodland Trust and the National Trust. It also covers those of Natural Englands's National Nature Reserves that are accessible to the public, plus the country parks, nature reserves and public open spaces managed by local authorities, but excluding those of principally amenity rather than wildlife value.

Finding where to go

The book is divided into ten sections, each of which covers a geographical area, as shown on the key map on pages 4–5. (Some of these divisions coincide with local authority boundaries, but they are essentially spatial rather than administrative.) Each section is colour-coded and begins with a map of the region showing all the sites, key geographical features, urban areas, main roads, railways and long-distance footpaths. The sites follow the map in alphabetical order, except that some sites that are geographically close have been grouped. These groups are indicated by boxes on the regional map, containing the name of the group in bold and the sites within the group in italic. So, for example in the Uttlesford section, to find *Shadwell Wood* turn to Oxlip woods in the section, then look for the **Shadwell Wood** heading under that entry. An index at the end of the book lists all the sites by name, showing also their key features, such as whether they are easy to get to by public transport.

On pages 6–7 you will find a *Quick Guide*, which suggests some of the best places to go at different times of the year.

Keys to the information in the heading for each site and to symbols used on the site maps are on page 8.

Getting there

For each site directions are given for travel by road, while for travel by public transport any convenient stations and/or bus routes are listed. Because timetables and routes change so rapidly, you will need to check details of services. Call the Traveline number below or visit the web sites, which provide downloadable route maps and timetables.

Traveline call centre: 0871 200 22 33
(landline calls 10p/min; mobiles dearer).
Public transport in Essex:
www.travelinesoutheast.org.uk
Public transport in London:
www.journeyplanner.tfl.gov.uk

Species photos

Distributed throughout the book you will find many photos of particular species of animal or plant. There is an index to these photos on page 271.

Countryside Access Code

(More details at www.countrysideaccess.gov.uk/things_to_know/countryside_code.)

Be safe: plan ahead and follow any signs
Use the information in this book to decide what to expect and, if in doubt, contact the site manager in advance.

Check up on the weather (www.bbc.co.uk/essex/weather), and remember that on the coast it is usually windier and colder than inland.

Heavy machinery is used to manage many of the sites in this book, such as to cut the hay in summer, and felling of trees is a necessary part of the management of many woodlands. Please be vigilant, obey warning signs and consider the safety of children and dogs when you visit.

Leave gates and property as you find them

Protect plants and animals and take your litter home
If you see livestock or other animals in distress, don't interfere yourself but inform the land manager or contact the RSPCA – advice line **0300 1234 555** weekdays only – for guidance.

Keep dogs under close control
Remember that dogs running free may upset or injure other people, especially children; may cause serious harm to livestock; and may disturb wildlife, such as ground-nesting birds.

Additional restrictions apply at some sites, as indicated in the entries, or may apply in some areas or at some times (such as when livestock are grazing), indicated by signs asking dogs to be kept on leads or to be kept out altogether. Please observe all signs and check in advance if taking your dog.

Please always clear up after your dog and go prepared to bag up waste and either bin it or take it away with you.

Consider other people
… for example: people living or making a living near the places you visit.

Conservation charities

If you want to know more about the conservation charities whose nature reserves are included in this book or to ask about membership, please write, telephone, email or access the web sites given below. (Contact information for particular sites is given in the entries.)

Essex Wildlife Trust
Abbotts Hall Farm
Maldon Road
Great Wigborough
Colchester
Essex CO5 7RZ
☎ **01621 862960**
fax **01621 862990**
email admin@essexwt.org.uk
web www.essexwt.org.uk

London Wildlife Trust
Skyline House
200 Union Street
London SE1 0LX
☎ **020 7261 0447**
email enquiries@wildlondon.org.uk
web www.wildlondon.org.uk

The National Trust
32 Queen Anne's Gate
London SW1H 9AB
☎ **01793 817400**
email enquiries@thenationaltrust.org.uk
web www.nationaltrust.org.uk

East of England
Westley Bottom
Bury St Edmunds
Suffolk IP33 3WD
☎ **01284 747500**

Royal Society for the Protection of Birds
The Lodge
Potton Road
Sandy
Beds SG19 2DL
☎ **01767 680551**
web www.rspb.org.uk
Eastern England Regional Office
☎ **01603 661662**
South East England Regional Office
☎ **01273 775333**

The Woodland Trust
Autumn Park
Dysart Road
Grantham
Lincs NG31 6LL
☎ **01476 581111**
Membership freephone **0800 026 9650**
web www.woodland-trust.org.uk

Other organisations

Other key organisations involved with wildlife conservation in Essex, apart from local authorities, are as follows.

Natural England
Responsible for nature conservation in England, including managing National Nature Reserves and overseeing Sites of Special Scientific Interest
Enquiry service ☎ **0845 600 3078**
web www.naturalengland.org.uk

Environment Agency
Responsible for water quality; for flood warning and defence; and for recreation and conservation involving water resources
General enquiries ☎ **0845 933 3111**
Emergency hotline ☎ **0800 80 70 60**
To report all environmental incidents
Floodline ☎ **0845 988 1188**
24-hour advice and information on floods
email enquiries@environment-agency.gov.uk
web www.environment-agency.gov.uk

Forest Enterprise East Anglia
Responsible for managing Forestry Commission woods
☎ **01842 810271**

Key to sections and outline map of site

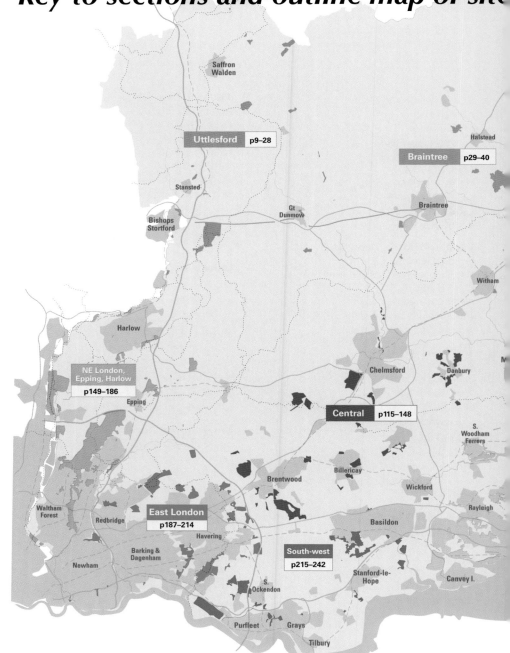

Saffron Walden

Uttlesford p9–28

Halstead

Braintree p29–40

Stansted

Gt Dunmow

Braintree

Bishops Stortford

Witham

Harlow

NE London, Epping, Harlow p149–186

Chelmsford

Danbury

M

Epping

Central p115–148

S. Woodham Ferrers

Waltham Forest

Redbridge

East London p187–214

Billericay

Brentwood

Wickford

Rayleigh

Havering

Basildon

Newham

Barking & Dagenham

South-west p215–242

S. Ockendon

Stanford-le-Hope

Canvey I.

Purfleet

Grays

Tilbury

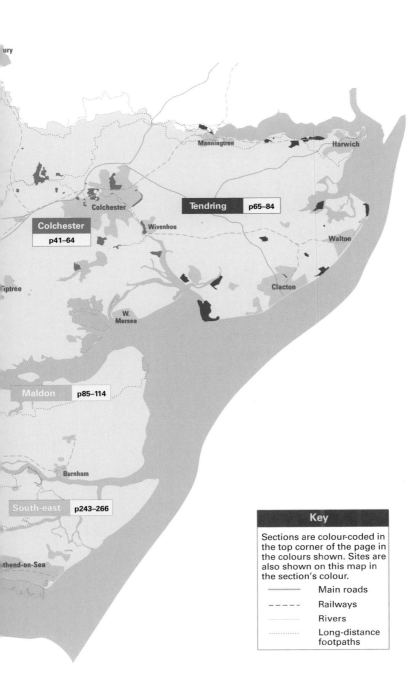

ury

Manningtree

Harwich

Colchester

Tendring p65–84

Colchester
p41–64

Wivenhoe

Walton

Tiptree

W.
Mersea

Clacton

Maldon p85–114

Burnham

South-east p243–266

thend-on-Sea

Key
Sections are colour-coded in the top corner of the page in the colours shown. Sites are also shown on this map in the section's colour.

————	Main roads
– – – –	Railways
————	Rivers
··········	Long-distance footpaths

Quick Guide: where to go when

		Uttlesford	Braintree	Colcheste
April...	The best show of woodland flowers is in early spring, before the trees put on all their leaves. At this time the woods also fill with birdsong as summer migrants join the resident birds and sing to attract mates and to mark their territories.	Birchanger Wood Oxlip woods	Broaks Wood Brookes Chalkney Wood Sandylay/Moat Woods	Hillhouse Wo Hoe Wood Welsh Wood Westhouse W
May	A different mix of breeding birds is in evidence at more open sites, where birds that nest in dense undergrowth, in reed beds or in rough grassland find a suitable niche.	Aubrey Buxton Hatfield Forest Lashley Wood Turners Spring	Loshes Marks Hall Estate	Fingringhoe Fordham Hall Friday Wood High Woods (Wivenhoe
June	Many wild flower meadows and grassland sites are at their best in June/July, before they are cut or grazed.	Onslow Green Sweetings Meadow	Brickfield & Long Meadow	
	Heath fritillary butterflies are on the wing mainly from mid-June to mid-July.			
	Saltmarsh is at its most colourful in July, with the sea lavender in flower.			Fingringhoe V
July	Wetland soils take longer to warm up so the best show usually appears in July/August, accompanied by a peak in the numbers of butterflies, dragonflies and other insects.	Rushy Mead Sawbridge-worth Marsh	Brockwell Whet Mead	Fordham Hall Roman River Valley Salary Brook Wivenhoe Ma
	High summer is the peak time for insects almost everywhere, with butterflies along woodland rides and glow-worms in scrubby sites in the south-east of Essex.		Gt Notley CP Marks Hall Estate	Hilly Fields Lexden Sergeants Orc
August	Heathlands are at their best in August with the heather in flower and many insects about.			Fordham Heat
	Swans and ducks moult ready for migration and for winter.			Abberton Reservoir
September	August sees the beginning of the autumn migration, with birds streaming down the coast on their way to their wintering grounds further south.			
	October brings autumn colours in the woods and the main flush of fungi on the woodland floor.	Hatfield Forest	Brookes Phyllis Currie	
October	Brent geese usually arrive in late September to feast on eel-grass before moving on to coastal grasslands			
	By November large numbers of water birds have settled in for the winter on inland lakes and reservoirs, while wetland birds such as bitterns and bearded tits find shelter in large reed beds.			Abberton Reservoir
...November	Many thousands of waterfowl and waders spend the winter on the estuaries and around the coast. Most arrive in September/October and leave in March/April, with numbers at a peak in January/February.			Fingringhoe W

endring	Maldon	Central	NE London etc.	E London	South-West	South-East
eras Wood Wood eyhall od	Shut Heath Wood	Blakes Wood Crowsheath Wood Norsey Wood Swan Wood The Mores Thrift Wood	Epping Forest Larks Wood Parndon Woods	Hainault Forest	Belhus Woods Mardyke Woods	Daws Heath Woods Hockley Woods Thundersley Woods
land Pits aze ness	Blue House Farm S. Woodham	Hanningfield Res. Hylands Park Thorndon Weald Park	Gernon Bushes River Lee CP	Beam Valley Claybury Park Ingrebourne Valley Wanstead Park	Chafford Gorges Langdon	Hadleigh Castle
	Oxley Meadow	Mill Meadows	Hunsdon Mead N. Weald F/M Thornwood F/M	Bedfords Park The Ripple	Horndon Meadow	
		Thrift Wood				Belfairs Park Pound Wood
	Abbotts Hall Farm Cudmore Grove					Two Tree Island
rs Ditch	Chigborough Lakes	Chelmer Valley Riverside Mid-Chelmer	Cornmill Meadows Hawksmere Spr. Harlow Marshes Roding Valley M. Walthamstow	Cranham Marsh Cranham Brickfields Fairlop Waters	Chafford Gorges Stanford Warren	
	Maldon Wick Stow Maries	Crowsheath CW Hutton CP Queens Park CP	Gunpowder Park Filter beds Harlow/Latton Commons	Bedfords Park Havering CP The Manor	Langdon Noak Bridge The Wick CP Vange Hill	Cherry Orchard CP Hadleigh Castle Magnolia NR
	Tiptree Heath	Galleywood Common	Epping Forest	Hainault Forest Tylers Common		
		Hanningfield Reservoir	River Lee CP			
Point aze	Bradwell Shell Bank				Rainham Marshes	Gunners Park Southend Foreshore
		Danbury Thorndon Writtle Forest	Epping Forest	Hainault Forest		Daws Heath Woods Hockley Woods
						Two Tree Island Southend F'shore
	Chigborough Lakes Heybridge Creek	Hanningfield Reservoir	River Lee CP	Beam Valley Ingrebourne Valley Wanstead Park	Belhus	
ord Water nd Haven ands Marsh r Stour Estuary	Blackwater Est. Blue House Farm Bradwell S/B Cudmore Grove S. Woodham				Fobbing Marsh Rainham Marshes Vange Marshes Wat Tyler CP	Lion Creek Southend Foreshore West Canvey Marshes

8

Abbotts Hall Farm

Main entries in colour; *sub-entries in* grey

700ac/280ha   **OS Ex184**   **TL 963 146**   **SSSI (part), SPA**

Size in acres and hectares   *OS Explorer map number*   *OS Grid reference*   *Designations (see key below)*   *Organisation chiefly responsible for management*

How to get there

Public transport

Opening times

Best time to visit

Facilities/notes for disabled visitors

Restrictions/arrangements for dogs

indicates livestock may be present)

Further information from...

Warnings and guidance for visitors

SSSI   Site of Special Scientific Interest
Area notified by Natural England as important and with statutory protection.

SAC   Special Area of Conservation
SPA   Special Protection Area
Areas that are strictly protected under the European Birds and Habitats Directives.

NNR   National Nature Reserve
Nature reserve of national importance, managed by or for Natural England (not always with public access).

LNR   Local Nature Reserve
Nature reserve of local importance, established by a local authority (usually with public access).

Key to maps

Vegetation
grass or heath
scrub
woodland
new woodland
marsh/fen   or
reed bed
saltmarsh
mud
sand or shingle
arable

Water bodies
fresh/brackish
salt

Site boundary

Facilities
visitor centre   **V**
museum   **M**
bird hide
information board   *i*
play area
picnic area
pub
refreshments
parking   **P**
" with fee   **£**
" informal   **P**
" inc. disabled   **P&**
toilets   **WC**
" inc. disabled   **LWC**

Paths (public rights of way shown bold)
foot only
in between†
wheelchair
bridleway/horse ride

Features
sea wall
bank & ditch
slope or cliff
church
golf course
viewpoint
building
built-up area

Entrances
vehicle
other

Roads
surfaced
other/track

† surfaced paths suitable for people with walking difficulties and possibly usable by wheelchairs, e.g. with assistance

Uttlesford

From the chalk hills in the north-west that rise to 120 metres, Uttlesford falls towards the south-east. The landscape is mainly agricultural, dominated by intensive arable cropping, but the pattern of small villages, copses and hedges dates back at least to the mediæval period. The jewel in Uttlesford's crown is Hatfield Forest, a superb mediæval hunting forest; and the region also has many fine old woods – those in the north supporting that curious plant, the oxlip – and a scattering of attractive nature reserves and village greens, including two rich marshlands on the River Stort.

Harrison Sayer

Shadwell Wood

Lt Hales Wood

Bendysh Woods

Icknield Way Path

Saffron Walden

Oxlip woods

Rowney Wood

West Wood

Harcamlow Way

Sweetings Meadow

Bustard Green

Linnetts Wood

Aubrey Buxton

Lashley Wood

Harcamlow Way

River Chelmer

Turners Spring

Birchanger Wood

Chelmer Valley Park

Gt Dunmow

Bishops Stortford

Rushy Mead

Hatfield Forest

Flitch Way

Wall Wood

Woodside Green

River Stort

Garnetts Wood

Onslow Green

Sawbridgeworth Marsh

Three Forests Way

Essex Way

Aubrey Buxton

24ac/10ha   *OS Ex195*   *TL 521 264*

Originally the pleasure park to Norman House, this Essex Wildlife Trust reserve is high woodland interspersed with grassland, on a sandy/gravel soil. It has three man-made ponds, probably about 200 years old, and three further ponds dug in the 1950s when it was a wildlife park. It was donated to Essex Wildlife Trust by Lord and the late Lady Buxton in 1976.

Cowslip, wild strawberry and common spotted orchid grow in the meadows, along with the uncommon lesser lady's mantle and adderstongue fern.

The many bird species include nuthatch, all three species of woodpecker and a number of summer visitors. There is a rookery.

22 species of butterfly have been recorded and in good years numbers can be impressive.

Black poplars have been planted to replace storm-damaged trees. This species formerly played an important part in country life, being planted to give shade to cattle and to provide firewood and charcoal for the home.

Just north of Stansted: turn east off the B1383 (Bishop's Stortford–Stansted–Cambridge) on to Alsa Street. The entrance is 200m up a private road (with white gateposts at its end) on the right.

Hourly bus service along B1383: get off at Alsa Lodge turning.

Accessible at all times.

Spring or summer.

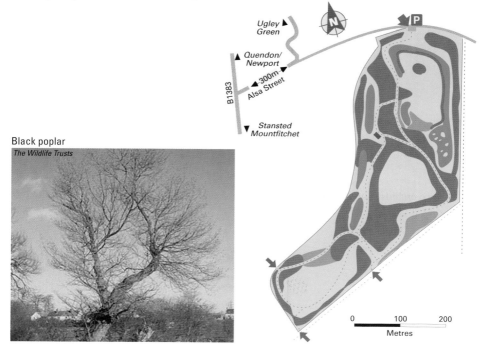

Black poplar
The Wildlife Trusts

Birchanger Wood

49ac/20ha   **OS Ex195**   *TL 503 224*

Birchanger Wood Trust

An ancient woodland on the edge of Bishop's Stortford, unfortunately bisected by the A120 bypass road. It is owned by the Birchanger Wood Trust and managed by a 'Friends' group with support from Bishop's Stortford Town Council.

It has a variety of trees, reflecting its complex geology. Oak, ash and hornbeam dominate different parts of the wood, with a scattering of hazel, field maple, wild cherry and sweet chestnut. In spring, parts of the wood are carpeted with wood anemones and bluebells.

The wood has a long history of coppicing and the Friends group has resumed coppicing here and there in the wood, creating glades full of flowering plants that are gradually shaded out as the coppiced trees regrow.

Access from Parsonage Lane in Bishop's Stortford. Follow Heath Row round to park near the water tower. The entrance is just beyond it.

Accessible at all times.

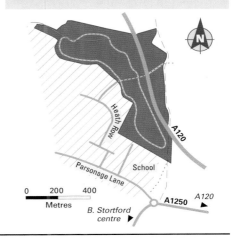

Bustard Green

12ac/5ha   **OS Ex195**   *TL 648 285*

This long narrow common is a flower-rich grassland bounded by ancient hedgerows. It is managed by local residents.

Notable plants that grow here include sulphur clover and lady's bedstraw, and occasionally bee orchids. The thick hedges provide good nesting habitat, and turtle doves – a bird in steep decline – have nested here recently. The permanent pond supports great crested newts.

From Great Dunmow head north along the B1057 to Finchingfield and turn off left into Lindsell. From Lindsell Daisyley Road leads up to Bustard Green.

Accessible at all times.

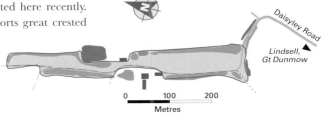

Chelmer Valley Park

**Great Dunmow
Town Council**

20ac/8ha   *OS Ex195*   *TL 633 219*

G rassland beside the River Chelmer on the north-east fringe of Great Dunmow, owned and managed by the Town Council. The river is only a stream at this point and has the distinction of holding a population of native white-clawed crayfish which, as a result of introduced foreign species, are in retreat in many of our rivers.

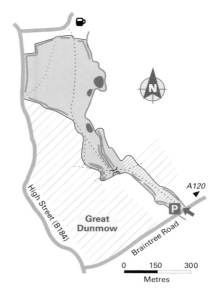

Access from Braintree Road, which links the High Street to the A120. There is a car park just east of the river.

600m from Dunmow High St, served by frequent buses from Bishop's Stortford, Braintree, Chelmsford and Stansted Airport.

Accessible at all times.

The white-clawed crayfish is Britain's only native crayfish. It has suffered a dramatic decline since the 1980s partly because of the release of non-native signal crayfish into our rivers. These larger animals compete for food, feed on white-clawed crayfish themselves and carry a lethal fungal disease called *crayfish plague*. NB: it is illegal to catch white-clawed crayfish without a licence from Natural England and Environment Agency.

Environment Agency

Flitch Way

40ac/16ha   *OS Ex195*   **TL 519 212–TL 760 227**

Essex County Council

The Flitch Way follows the route of the old railway line from Bishop's Stortford to Braintree – a distance of 15 miles. This makes it by far the longest country park in Essex! The railway was built in the 19th century and dismantled in 1969. Since then nature has taken over, with more than a little help from Essex County Council's Ranger Service.

Its name comes from the mediæval ceremony held at Little Dunmow, in which a flitch of bacon was given to couples who had not argued for a year and a day.

Sections of the line run on embankments with fine views over the surrounding countryside. In the west, for example, it runs across the northern edge of Hatfield Forest.

Other parts run in secluded cuttings, the longest of which is west of Dunmow. Here conditions are very wet, and water mint growing alongside the path scents the air.

The south-facing banks form a sun trap and are ideal for slow worms, grass snakes and lizards, which can sometimes be seen basking in the open. They also attract many butterflies and other insects.

Can be entered from a number of points along its length, including Hatfield Forest – see map. Parking at Takeley, Rayne or Braintree stations.

Trains run to Braintree from Witham. Use hourly bus service Stansted Airport–Braintree via Takeley to return.

Accessible at all times. Centre at Rayne Station open daily 9am–5pm.

May–July for wild flowers, birds and butterflies.

Call the Rangers on 01376 340262.

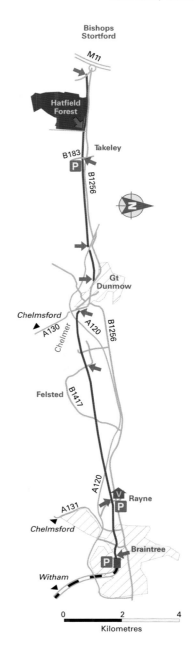

Garnetts Wood

60ac/24ha   *OS Ex183*   *TL 635 185*   *SSSI*

Essex County Council

An ancient coppice woodland owned and managed by Essex County Council. A knight was given the wood in the 12th century and in his memory there is an imposing wooden statue carved from a tree stump.

Small-leaved lime, once widespread across lowland England but now restricted to just a few woods, is the dominant tree. The wood is not as rich as Chalkney Wood nor as well restored, but it is an attractive woodland with considerable variety. There are several damp areas full of sedges and a scattering of ponds and streams.

On High Easter Road, a minor road running between Barnston and High Easter. Barnston is on the A130 2km south-east of Great Dunmow.

Bus from Chelmsford, Dunmow or Stansted Airport to Barnston, then 1 mile walk via footpaths.

Accessible at all times.

April–May for early flowers and songbirds.

Paths can be very wet in winter and spring – waterproof footwear essential.

Pendulous sedge

Wooden statue at Garnetts Wood

Tony Gunton

EWT library

Barnston

A130/ Barnston

P

N

High Easter

0   200   400
Metres

Harrison Sayer

2.5ac/1ha   *OS Ex209*   *TL 557 441*

ESSEX
Wildlife Trust

One of the few surviving areas of boulder clay grassland in north-west Essex, which otherwise is intensive arable farmland. Once part of a war-time airbase and now partially overgrown, it is nearly 106m above sea-level with fine views over south Cambridgeshire.

Flowering plants include bee orchid, wild liquorice, twayblade, fairy flax and blue fleabane. There are many blackthorn thickets – used by nesting birds – and wild roses.

On the B1052 about 3 miles north of Saffron Walden, 800m from Hadstock – identifiable from the road by the large hangar at its rear.

Accessible at all times.

Late June for roses and bee orchids.

Unsuitable for disabled visitors.

Keep out of brick structures as there may be loose masonry.

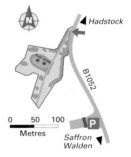

Twayblade: flowers May–July
Owen Keen

Bee orchid: flowers June–July
Pat Allen

Hatfield Forest

1049ac/420ha   OS Ex195 &183   TL 547 202   SSSI, NNR

Hatfield Forest is a working example of what a mediæval Forest must have been like. It is a landscape shaped by man's activities over hundreds, probably thousands, of years. There is certainly nothing as complete and well-preserved in Essex, and arguably in Europe.

Hatfield Forest is a compartmented forest. Open grazed areas, known as 'plains', are separated from the wooded areas by ditches and banks, once topped by paling fences designed to keep out grazing animals. Trees scattered across the plains are pollarded, in other words cut above head height where grazing animals cannot reach, while the wooded compartments are managed by coppicing, in other words trees are cut to ground level every ten years or so.

Ancient trees, and particularly ancient pollard trees, are what make Hatfield Forest so special. It has about 600 pollards in total, including not only oak and hornbeam, which

Pollard hornbeam at Hatfield Forest
Tony Gunton

can be seen elsewhere in Essex, but also many maple and hawthorn, which are rare as pollards, and just a handful of beech, lineage elm and crab apple. Nowhere else can you see such a variety of species nor such a variety of form, from gnarled, twisted old hawthorns to massive, stately oaks. It is also the stronghold in Essex of mistletoe, which is widespread on the ancient hawthorns and maples on the plains.

The coppice woods consist mainly of ash, hazel, and an unusually large number of maple. There are also some gigantic coppice stools of oak, particularly in Lodge Coppice to the west, while the west end of Street Coppice has four acres of alder on a plateau – alder is a plant of wet, flushed ground, in other words where water is moving through the soil, picking up oxygen as it goes.

The predominant woodland plant is dog's mercury but the coppice woodlands also support a very wide range of other flowers including indicators of ancient woodland such as oxlips (mainly in or near Hamptons Coppice) and herb paris (in Long Coppice).

Shermore Brook runs through the Forest from north to south, feeding into a chalky fen above the lake. Marshy areas around it are full of wetland plants and alive with insects in summer. Around the fen are a number of rare Essex plants, including tubular water-dropwort, marsh arrow-grass, marsh willowherb and marsh pennywort. Water rail are usually present here also.

A range of woodland birds breed in the Forest, including marsh tit and nightingale (decreasing), plus the odd woodcock and hawfinch. Look out for buzzards which are recolonising the county. Winter visitors include redwing and fieldfare.

B1256

Takeley Street

Great Dunmow

Bishop's Stortford/ M11

Elijah Way Country Park

Elmans Green

Old Woman's Weaver

Hamptons Coppice

Street Coppice

Estate office

Takeley Hill

Hangman Coppice

Long Coppice

Spittlemore Coppice

Elgin Coppice

Shenmore Brook

Middle Hollows

Beggar's Hall Coppice

£

Harcamlow Way

Three Forests Way

£

Round Coppice

Bush End Plain

Gravel Pit Coppice

Shell House

WC

The Warren

£

Lodge Coppice

Forest Way

Forest Lodge

Collins Coppice

0   250   500
Metres

Emblem's Coppice

Wall Wood

Turn south off the B1256 (Bishop's Stortford–Takeley) in Takeley Street, about 3 miles east of M11 junction 8.

Buses run to Takeley Street from Bishop's Stortford and Braintree/ Dunmow: get off at Green Man PH.

Open dawn to dusk daily. Refreshment room open daily 10am– 4.30pm, April to end October, otherwise 10am–3.30pm.

March to see the golden mistletoe stems on the trees in the plains; May for birdsong and spring flowers; July for butterflies in the open areas and along the rides.

Dogs on leads near livestock and around lake. Dog-free area near lake.

Call 01279 870678 or 01279 874040 (infoline) or 01279 870447 (learning).

Hatfield Forest (continued)

Follow the road and then the boardwalk from the main car park at the entrance, bear left before Shell House and follow the rides to the south-west corner of the Forest, then turn right along the road. A short distance down on the left you can enter another ancient wood and from there reach an ancient common, both owned by the National Trust.

Wall Wood

Wall Wood was one of Hatfield Forest's 'purlieu woods', which were associated with the Forest but not entirely part of it. Owned by the Essex & Puckeridge Hunt, it was given to the National Trust in 1946.

It has many ancient coppiced trees and, in the more open parts, good ground flora – carpets of dog's mercury, patches of blue-bells and a scattering of primroses.

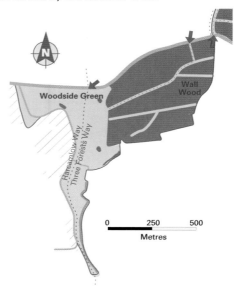

Woodside Green

Alongside Wall Wood lies Woodside Green, an ancient common consisting of open grass-land with scattered ancient trees, now grazed by cattle. It was given to the National Trust in 1935 by Major Houblon.

Hatfield Forest from the air, looking north towards Stansted Airport. The 'plains' – open areas used for grazing – run from bottom left towards the centre of the picture, partly invaded by scrub, with coppiced woodlands on either side.

David Corke

Lashley Wood

22ac/9ha   ***OS Ex195***   ***TL 655 260***

These are former grazing meadows alongside the Stebbing Brook that have been planted up with native trees – oak, hornbeam and field maple up on the slopes; ash, alder and willow in the damper area; hazel and dogwood alongside the paths. Marshy areas and clearings beside the brook have been left open. The farmer who owns the land agreed to allow public access in return for the grants that funded the planting.

On the B1057 about midway between Great Dunmow and Great Bardfield. Main entrance via a private road and public footpath to Lashley Hall between Bran End and Duck End. (Car park very wet in winter so park on the B1057 verge at the junction.)

Accessible at all times.

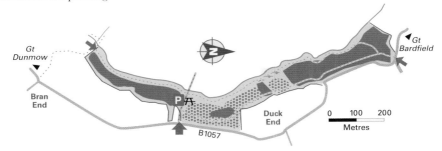

Introduced deer

Muntjac (left) are small deer no larger than a labrador dog. They are solitary, nocturnal and secretive, so rarely seen, but they do make a loud barking noise, often repeated, which gives them their alternative name of 'barking deer'. They were introduced from China in the 20th century and now are widespread across southern and eastern England, and spreading. Fallow deer were introduced by the Romans and are even more widespread in Britain. They can form large herds, sheltering in woods by day and coming out into fields at night. Both deer cause serious damage in woods, both to trees and to flowering plants like the oxlip.

Linnets Wood

12ac/5ha   **OS Ex195**   **TL 516 273**

WOODLAND TRUST

This small plantation in the village of Ugley Green, consisting of conifers with oak, cherry and hornbeam, was given to the Woodland Trust in 1992 by Rosalind 'Linnet' Latham. An additional area to the west was planted up to local residents' design in 1997 as one of the Trust's 'Woods on your Doorstep' projects.

A public footpath running from the B1383 north of Stansted Mountfitchet to the minor road from the B1383 to Ugley Green passes through the wood.

Hourly bus service along B1383: get off at Ugley Green turning.

Accessible at all times.

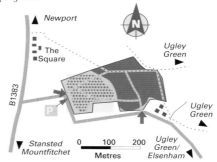

Onslow Green

2.5ac/1ha   **OS Ex183**   **TL 654 183**

ESSEX Wildlife Trust

An attractive village green with a wide marginal hedge and two ponds. It has some interesting late spring/early summer flowers, including dyer's greenweed, tormentil and a small quantity of sulphur clover.

On its margins the larger pond has yellow flag, water forget-me-not and fine-leaved water-dropwort. It attracts dragonflies and great diving beetles, and in season you may see smooth newts and the occasional great crested newt.

About one mile south of Barnston village. Approach along the A130 Chelmsford–Great Dunmow road and take the turning to Onslow Green. You will see the green on the left past a sharp left-hand bend.

Hourly or better bus services to Barnston from Bishop's Stortford, Stansted Airport and Chelmsford.

Accessible at all times.

Dyer's greenweed: flowers June–August

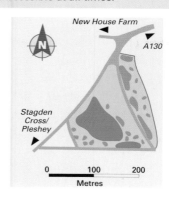

Oxlip woods

Oxlips grow almost exclusively in ancient woods and, what is more, only in ancient woods in the area where the counties of Cambridgeshire, Suffolk and Essex meet. This is an area of boulder clay soils, which are very chalky and produce woods that are unusually complex, with a wide variety of plants. The oxlip faces a number of threats, including browsing pressure from deer and rabbits, hybridisation with both native and introduced primulas, and competition from other species.

Bendysh Woods

224ac/90ha   *OS Ex195 & 209*   *TL 619 398*

Forestry Commission

These two Forestry Commission woods are ancient deciduous woods planted up with conifers which are now being removed. They have wide rides which are good for flowers: oxlips and wood anemones in March/April and later on many orchids.

They are a good place to see deer: both the native species red and roe, and the introduced fallow and muntjac.

Where the B1053 (Saffron Walden–Great Sampford) meets the B1054 at The Plough PH, take the unclassified road to Ashdon. After about 1200m turn right on to Golden Lane, then turn first left to Radwinter End, parking on the roadside just before Swan's Farm and following the footpath on the left. Footpaths also lead in from other directions.

Accessible at all times.

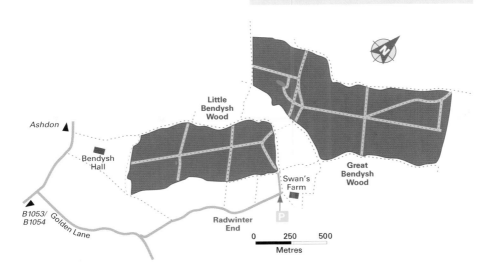

Ashdon

Bendysh Hall

B1053/ B1054

Golden Lane

Little Bendysh Wood

Swan's Farm

Radwinter End

P

Great Bendysh Wood

0   250   500

Metres

Oxlip woods Little Hales Wood

45ac/18ha   **OS Ex209**   **TL 575 406**

Forestry Commission

Compare this Forestry Commission wood with Shadwell Wood just a short distance away. This wood has been planted up with conifers, a fate that Shadwell Wood has escaped. Both woods are in an area with many deer, although in Shadwell they are fenced out of the wood. Both have oxlips, although in this wood they are eaten by deer. The small ponds just inside the wood have frogs breeding.

Shadwell Wood

17.5ac/7ha   **OS Ex209**   **TL 573 412**   **SSSI**

ESSEX
Wildlife Trust

The dominant trees in this oxlip woodland are oak and ash, with coppiced hazel and maple growing beneath them. It also has midland hawthorns, rare trees such as lineage elm and bird cherry, and *Daphne mezereum*, popular for the garden but rare in the wild.

A host of flowering plants grow on the woodland floor. Early spring brings oxlips, wood violets and wood anemones. These give way to early purple orchids, bluebells, bugle and herb paris. Summer brings common spotted orchids, meadowsweet and sanicle.

The wood is managed in the traditional manner by coppicing. This encourages many summer-visiting birds to nest, including the occasional nightingale. Fencing is used to exclude deer from the wood. Otherwise they browse the tender coppice regrowth, killing or stunting the trees, and eat the flowers.

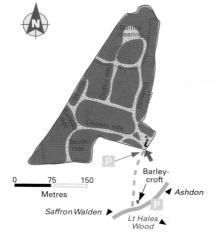

On the main road from Saffron Walden, about one mile before the village of Ashdon. Entrance to Shadwell Wood by a track at the side of 'Barleycroft' bungalow and to Lt Hales Wood on the other side of the road. Track to Shadwell Wood is difficult in wet weather. Please do not block either track.

Accessible at all times.

Spring through to early summer for flowers and migrant birds.

Unsuitable for wheelchairs. Bench at top of Chivers Ride with good views of butterflies for those who can't walk far.

Please keep your dog on a lead.

Please keep deer gates shut.

Leaflet at Shadwell Wood entrance.

Rowney Wood

204ac/82ha   *OS Ex195*   *TL 574 338*

Forestry Commission

This large ancient oxlip wood was planted up with conifers in the 1950s but has now to a large degree been returned to native deciduous woodland by the Forestry Commission. It has good ground flora (including ragged robin), white-letter hairstreak butterflies and many deer.

Turn south off the B184 (Thaxted–Saffron Walden) west of Rowney Corner and park in layby near Carver Barracks.

Hourly buses Saffron Walden–Stansted Airport serve Debden: 800m walk via Harcamlow Way.

Accessible at all times.

Circular route usable by wheelchairs in all but the worst weather conditions.

Some of the tracks get very muddy during forestry work and parallel temporary footpaths are provided.

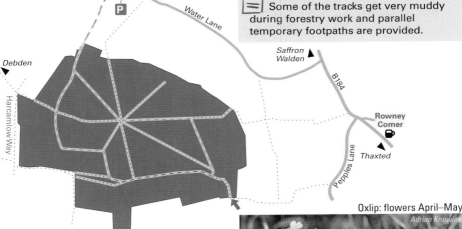

0   200   400
Metres

Oxlip: flowers April–May
Adrian Knowles

White-letter hairstreak: flies July–August
Ken Wooldridge

Oxlip woods West Wood

58ac/23ha   **OS Ex195**   **TL 624 332**   **SSSI**

This mixed deciduous wood near Thaxted is one of the finest in the area. On chalky boulder clay, it has a history of coppicing dating back to the middle ages. This ceased in the middle of the last century but was resumed by Essex Wildlife Trust when it acquired the site in 1972.

As well as oxlips it has early purple and greater butterfly orchids, and also wood barley, which is rare in Essex. Pendulous sedge grows along the rides.

The wood has a good selection of nesting birds among which are goldcrest, several species of warbler, stock dove and buzzard. It also supports good numbers of butterflies including speckled wood, brimstone and ringlet.

The wood has four ponds which have been restored and support great crested newts as well as many dragonflies and damselflies.

The wood has been returned to a coppice cycle and areas of Norway spruce have been removed. Large numbers of deer frequent the wood and precautions need to be taken to prevent them from browsing the young coppice regrowth and thus stunting or killing the trees: chestnut paling or brushwood fencing is erected around newly coppiced areas to keep them out.

Midway between Thaxted and Great Sampford, set back from the B1051. A track leads to the reserve entrance from the left-hand side of the road, one mile north-east of Thaxted. Or you can walk in along the bridleway from Tindon End.

Accessible at all times.

Early spring through to mid-summer for flowers and breeding birds; mid-spring through to early autumn for butterflies.

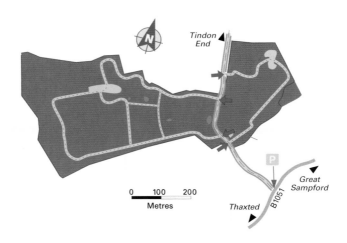

0   100   200
Metres

Tindon End

Thaxted

B1051

Great Sampford

Unusual woodland flowers

Early purple orchid: flowers May–June

Mary Smith

Broad-leaved helleborine: flowers July–August

Mary Smith

Sanicle: flowers May–July

Adrian Knowles

Yellow archangel: flowers May–June

Pat Allen

Rushy Mead

11.5ac/5ha   **OS Ex194**   **TL 497 197**

ESSEX
Wildlife Trust

The name Rushy Mead comes from an old tithe map showing the site as riverside meadows. More recently it has been occupied by a pumping station for a sewage works, which ceased operations in the 1950s. The current nature reserve was created through an agreement between the site owners, Thames Water plc, Wimpey Homes, who made a generous contribution towards running costs, and Essex Wildlife Trust, who manage it now.

The low ground has water near the surface all year, and there are good areas of sedge and reed. Their tall, dense growth provides cover for sedge and reed warbler in summer, and for snipe and water rail in winter.

The northern end of the site has developed into mature alder woodland with ash and willow. It is a particularly good area for birds, including the uncommon willow tit. Yellow iris and wild angelica are just two of the many plants that flower here in summer.

A network of drainage ditches supports a rich variety of aquatic wildlife including marsh marigold, dragonflies and water beetles.

The drier ground has areas of scrubby woodland and chalky grassland. The latter supports a good variety of wild flowers including bee orchid and wild carrot.

The main aim of management work is to maintain open water in ditches and scrape, and to control the spread of scrub and of invasive plants such as Russian comfrey.

Marsh marigold: flowers April–July

Tony Gunton

One mile south of Bishop's Stortford, lying between the A1060 road to Hatfield Heath and the River Stort. It can be entered from the A1060 or from the towpath running alongside the Stort Navigation.

800m walk from Bishop's Stortford station (BR Liverpool St–Cambridge): head south along the towpath. Hourly bus service from Bishop's Stortford station passes the main entrance on the A1060.

Accessible at all times.

Spring and summer for flowers, birds and insect life.

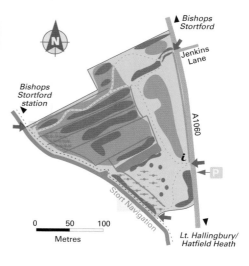

Sawbridgeworth Marsh

22ac/9ha   **OS Ex194**   *TL 493 158*   **SSSI**

This marshland nature reserve lies in the valley of the River Stort and consists of ten acres of waterlogged marsh, normally under an inch or two of water for most of the year; six acres of peaty meadow sloping up from the marsh to the eastern boundary; and a low-lying willow plantation to the south. Most of it is in Hertfordshire and a small part in Essex, so it was acquired jointly by the Essex and Hertfordshire & Middlesex Trusts when the site became available in 1970.

It contains plants which were once quite common but are now found on only a few sites in the county, such as marsh willowherb and marsh valerian. Other uncommon plants include marsh arrow-grass, southern marsh orchid and blunt-flowered rush.

It has several open drainage ditches and two ponds rich in aquatic life. The areas of sedge, reeds and tall fen vegetation provide a valuable nesting habitat for reed and sedge warblers. Other breeding birds include snipe and water rail. In summer the reserve is alive with insects.

The management regime is designed to encourage diversity of species. Enclosures are grazed by horses and parts of the marsh are cut on an annual or biennial basis. To prevent it from smothering smaller plants, the dead material is raked off and either burnt on permanent fire sites or gathered into permanent stacks which provide a valuable habitat for grass snakes and invertebrates. Periodically the willows fringing the marsh are pollarded.

To the west of the unclassified road from Sawbridgeworth to Gaston Green and Little Hallingbury. There is no car park, but there are two small lay-bys on the opposite side of the road about 200m north of the reserve entrance. Care should be taken since the road is narrow and traffic travels at high speeds.

About 800m north-east of Sawbridgeworth station: turn left outside the station then left into Hallingbury Road.

Accessible at all times.

Worth a visit at all times of the year but the spring and summer months are usually the most interesting.

Not suitable for wheelchair access because of wet conditions, narrow paths and plank bridges.

Wellingtons usually necessary.

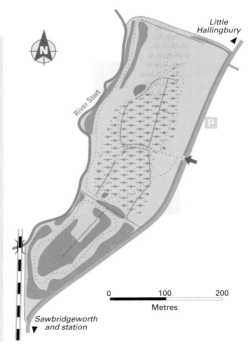

Sweetings Meadow

1.6ac/0.6ha   *OS Ex195*   *TL 632 285*

A small unimproved hay meadow on chalky boulder clay, also containing a number of fruit trees and a fine pond. It has impressive numbers of cowslips and pyramidal orchids. The many other plants include bee orchid, common spotted orchid, yellow rattle and pepper saxifrage.

About 3km south-east of Thaxted; on a minor road that links the B184 to the B1057 via Holder's Green and Lindsell. The entrance is on the south of the lane a short way west of Holder's Green.

Accessible at all times.

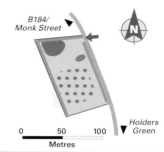

Turner's Spring

8ac/3ha   *OS Ex195*   *TL 529 243*

A mixed deciduous woodland, including a strip running alongside the Bourne Brook, plus a meadow with a central wet area of sedge beds. It was given to Essex Wildlife Trust by the Cawkell trustees in 1975.

The main wood contains oak, beech, ash and sycamore, with areas of hazel and hornbeam coppice. Spring brings a fine display of oxlips, violets, dog's mercury and herb paris, with a profusion of naturalised daffodils on either side of the central path.

Cowslip, bugle, salad burnet, agrimony and meadowsweet flower in the meadow.

The woodland strip along the Bourne Brook has carpets of violets in the spring, with some oxlips and scattered wood anemones. Where the water from the sedge beds drains into a deep depression a tufa pile has formed – pendulous sedge grows here.

Over 60 species of bird have been recorded. Butterflies are mostly limited to the commoner species but include the ringlet.

Reached via a footpath from the Stansted–Burton End road. The footpath is on the left about 600m beyond the bridge over the M11, marked by a foot-path sign beside a black-painted village pump. Cars may be parked on the road nearby.

Accessible at all times.

Spring for wild flowers.

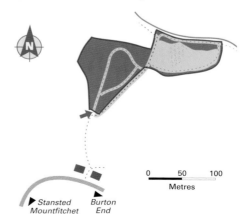

The area around Braintree, like much of Essex, is predominantly flat, lying at about 50 metres above sea level. To the north the countryside is dominated by arable farming, and as you move south it gradually becomes more urban, housing and factories predominating as you get closer to London. Its main geographical features are two river valleys – the River Pant becomes the Blackwater as it skirts Braintree itself, then flows close to Coggeshall, Kelvedon and Witham before joining the estuary at Maldon, and the River Colne flows through Halstead on its way to Colchester. It has a scattering of ancient woods, and notably a fine group of woods at Marks Hall, with Broaks Wood, Chalkney Wood and Brookes nature reserve not far away. A few new wildlife sites have been created near the urban centres of Braintree, Witham and Kelvedon, and Essex Wildlife Trust manages two nature reserves near Great Leighs and one in the far north-east.

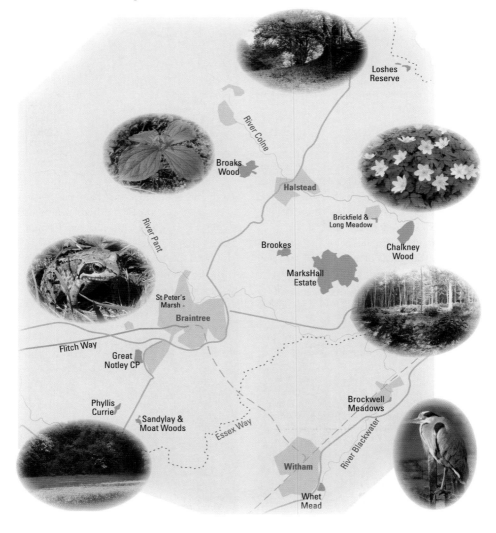

Loshes Reserve

River Colne

Broaks Wood

Halstead

River Pant

Brickfield & Long Meadow

Brookes

Chalkney Wood

MarksHall Estate

St Peter's Marsh

Braintree

Flitch Way

Great Notley CP

Phyllis Currie

Sandylay & Moat Woods

Essex Way

Brockwell Meadows

River Blackwater

Witham

Whet Mead

Brickfield & Long Meadow

10ac/3.86ha   **OS Ex195**   *TL 859 285*   **LNR**

This nature reserve near Earls Colne consists of a flower-rich former pasture, a marshy section, ponds and a former brickfield teeming with meadow ants.

It is owned and managed by its own Trust, by agreement with Braintree Council.

Access via the public footpath that leads south from Park Lane in Earls Colne, 100m. from its junction with the A1124 Halstead–Colchester road, past the school.

Hourly buses Colchester–Halstead run to Earls Colne.

Accessible at all times.

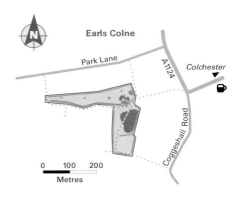

Wild service tree: found mainly in ancient woodland

Pat Allen

Opposite-leaved golden saxifrage: flowers March–July

Adrian Knowles

Broaks Wood

155ac/62ha   **OS Ex195**   **TL 784 317**

Forestry Commission

A Forestry Commission woodland, much of it ancient in origin. It is a working woodland with an average of 500 tonnes of timber harvested annually, but conservation is given a high priority. Where introduced timber trees are harvested, for example, the original native broadleaved trees are replanted or allowed to regenerate naturally. The traditional method of coppicing is used also, on species such as sweet chestnut, hazel and ash.

As a result the wood is rich in wildlife, including familar plants such as bluebells and primroses, and also some rarities. For example, it has a scattering of wild service trees and, in the stream valley to the east, opposite-leaved golden saxifrage. It is also a good place to see bats, feeding in the glades and along the rides at dusk.

The main entrance is on Hedingham Road (A1017 Braintree–Hedingham) two miles east of Halstead.

Bus service Braintree–Castle Hedingham runs along Hedingham Road.

Accessible at all times.

Spring for woodland flowers and birdsong; summer for butterflies and other insects in glades and rides.

3km waymarked nature trail (red posts). Call the ranger on 01394 450164.

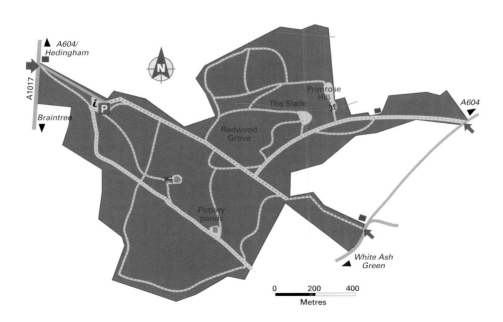

Brockwell Meadows

**Kelvedon
Parish Council**

11ac/4.4ha   *OS Ex195*   *TL 866 185*   *LNR*

An area of fen and meadow on the west bank of the River Blackwater in Kelvedon, owned and managed by Kelvedon Parish Council in conjunction with local volunteers. Cricket bat willows have been planted and also reed, to reduce water pollution.

The meadows are cut for hay and scrub is cleared on rotation.

Access off Kelvedon High St via St Mary's Road, Lapwing Drive and Teal Way. On-street parking only.

Accessible at all times.

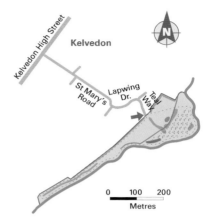

Kelvedon

0   100   200
Metres

Greater butterfly orchid: flowers June–July
Tony Gunton

Dog's mercury: flowers February–May
Tony Gunton

Herb paris: flowers May–June
Tony Gunton

Brookes Reserve

59ac/24ha   **OS Ex195**   **TL 808 268**   **SSSI (part)**

This nature reserve, owned by the Coda Wildlife Trust and managed by Essex Wildlife Trust, comprises over 40 acres of ancient woodland and some 18 acres of former arable fields, part of which has been planted up with native trees. The woods are known locally as Brooks's Woods, and the reserve is named after Thomas Brookes, the 18th-century owner.

Most of the wood is ash and hazel coppice. Areas of small-leaved lime and hornbeam add variety, and there are also more than 20 wild service trees. A network of historic green lanes, one a bridleway, crosses the woods. Thirteen ponds and the wet surface are evidence of the chalky boulder clay soil.

Bramble, pendulous sedge and dog's mercury dominate the ground flora, with primrose over large areas. Some notable species are greater butterfly orchid, twayblade, herb paris, sweet woodruff, wood small reed, hard shield fern, narrow buckler fern and at least six different varieties of sedge.

Nuthatch, treecreeper and lesser spotted woodpecker nest on the reserve along with many summer migrant songbirds. Brown hares and large herds of fallow deer are often seen.

The wood is coppiced on rotation to produce charcoal and firewood.

Between Stisted and Greenstead Green north-east of Braintree: from Greenstead Green the reserve is 2km down on the right and from Stisted 3km down on the left just past Tumbler's Green.

Hourly bus service Halstead–Braintree.

Accessible at all times. Car park may be locked at night to discourage misuse.

For songbirds, a sunny morning in April/May; a warm summer afternoon for butterflies; early October for autumn colours.

Please keep dogs on a lead.

Please do not let children play near ponds as they could be dangerous. Please keep to the paths. Waterproof footwear essential in wet weather.

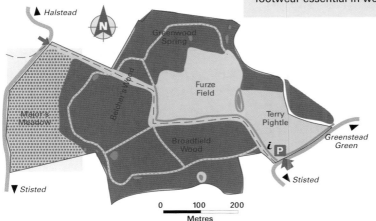

Chalkney Wood

200ac/80ha   *OS Ex195*   *TL 872 273*   **SSSI**   Essex County Council

Forestry Commission

Chalkney Wood has both great historical and great wildlife interest. It was owned from the Norman conquest until 1570 by the De Veres, Earls of Oxford. They used it to breed and rear wild boar, which were extinct in the wild at the time. There are none there now, of course, but there is still evidence of its history in features such as ancient woodbanks and the narrow tracks winding through the wood, which probably follow the same routes as in the Middle Ages.

The south-western part of the wood is owned by Essex County Council and managed as a public space. The remainder, running down to the River Colne, is owned by the Forestry Commission who have planted up much of it with conifers. As these conifers are harvested, the original native trees are being allowed to grow through and take their place.

Chalkney Wood is unusual in its great variety and in that it contains the greatest concentration of small-leaved lime trees in the county. Small-leaved lime used to be widespread

Main entrance about a mile down a minor road leaving the A1124 (Colchester–Halstead) between Earls Colne and White Colne, heading south. It can also be entered from the north via a footpath running south from the A1124 at White Colne to Chalkney Mill.

Several bus services between Colchester and Halstead run along the A1124.

Accessible at all times.

Late March through to May for spring flowers and birdsong.

Wood anemone: flowers March–May

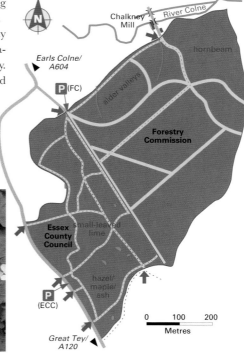

across lowland England but is now restricted to just a few woods. It has little timber value and was rarely planted, so it survives almost solely in woods that have not been reshaped by man for many centuries.

Small-leaved lime is the dominant species in much of the Essex County Council section of the wood, which is on a boulder clay soil. This gives way to London clay as the land falls towards the River Colne in the north, and as it falls so the natural vegetation contains more and more hornbeam. The southern corner contains a mix of ash, hazel, holly, field maple and wild cherry, with wild currant growing beneath them, probably because of a patch of particularly chalky soil. Along the north-western edge are a number of alder valleys fed by springs, where marsh marigold, opposite-leaved golden saxifrage and ramsons grow. Here and there are patches of aspen, a wild service tree or two, oak, sweet chestnut and elm.

The long history of coppicing is evident in the great natural richness and variety of the wood. Bluebells, anemones and primroses cover the woodland floor in different parts of the wood, especially in the areas that have been coppiced recently.

Great Notley Country Park

100ac/40ha   OS Ex195   TL 733 210

A recently created 100-acre country park alongside Great Notley Garden Village on the outskirts of Braintree. It has two lakes, several new copses planted on top of earth mounds, hay and wildflower meadows. Already skylarks and reed buntings have colonised the site, and its wildlife value can only grow as it matures.

The Discovery Centre embodies sustainable principles such as solar heating and a wind turbine, and provides interpretation and other facilities for visitors.

As this book went to press, Braintree District and Essex County Councils had agreed to manage the site and centre jointly.

On the A131 a short way south of its junction with the A120, 2 miles south-west of Braintree.

Nearest rail station is Braintree. Buses run via the station to Great Notley.

Accessible at all times.

Call 01376 347134 for latest developments and centre opening times.

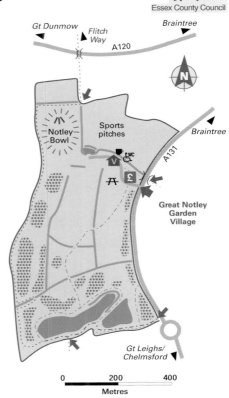

Loshes Reserve

17ac/7ha   *OS Ex196*   **TL 873 369**

ESSEX
Wildlife Trust

An Essex Wildlife Trust nature reserve on the side of an attractive valley in low hills rising from the River Stour flood plain. It was farmed until the mid-1950s then left to 'go wild' until leased by Essex Wildlife Trust in 1974.

Its main part, east of the road and south of Loshes Brook, is high woodland with a glade, thick hedgerows and a marsh. The higher ground is on a considerable depth of coarse sand; the lower on chalky boulder clay, with a high water table giving rise to spring flushes.

It has a variety of flowering plants including ramsons (wild garlic), opposite-leaved golden saxifrage, yellow archangel, nettle-leaved bell-flower and common spotted orchid.

The Hop Ground over the road has mature oaks at the top but is mostly swamp covered by hazel, alder and willow thickets. It has guelder rose, lady's smock and hemp agrimony.

Birdlife is plentiful with nightingale and grasshopper warbler among the nesting species and little egrets visiting in winter. Insects include ringlet and white-letter hairstreak butterflies. Slow worms are resident.

Three miles from Sudbury and six from Halstead. Take the Sudbury road from Halstead and, shortly after the Fox inn, take a turning signposted to Henny. After a mile this road descends a steep hill to a T-junction. Turn left and continue along a winding lane to a signpost to Alphamstone and Twinstead and turn right. The reserve is on the left at the bottom of the hill, where there is a large barn with the Trust sign outside.

Accessible at all times.

Spring and early summer.

Unsuitable for dog walking.

Children must be supervised when near stream and ponds, which have steep banks.

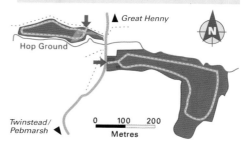

Marks Hall Estate

450ac/180ha   *OS Ex195*   **TL 841 255**

MARKS HALL

Marks Hall Estate is an ancient estate set in attractive countryside north of Coggeshall. It runs to some 2,000 acres, of which 150 are enclosed and hold an arboretum and formal gardens and a further 300 acres are accessible via footpaths. The estate was left to the nation by its last owner, Thomas Phillips Price, and is managed now by the Thomas Phillips Price Trust. It had been neglected for many years until the Trust set about the work of restoration in 1971.

Great wildlife interest can be found in the old deer park, which sadly has lost all but one of its massive ancient oaks, and in a large area of ancient woodland. Some of these woods have been planted with conifers but a great amount of the original woodland remains, containing large areas of small-leaved lime – a tree that once dominated the woods of East Anglia but now, because of long-term climate change, confined to just a few ancient woods – and a number of wild service trees.

The woods are being coppiced and this encourages flowering plants such as lily of the valley, sweet woodruff, wood sorrel and early purple orchid. The woods are frequented by deer and a wide range of woodland birds, including nightingales. Rare breed pigs are held in movable enclosures in the woods and perform the same function as wild boars used to, turning over the soil looking for food. Highland cattle graze the open grassland.

With its grassy tracks and ancient hedgerows, Marks Hall is especially good for butterflies.

Reached via a turning off the B1024 to Earls Colne north of Coggeshall: follow the brown-and-white signs from the A120.

The Visitor Centre – housed in a 15th-century barn – is normally open from Easter until 31st October except non-Bank Holiday Mondays,10.30am to 5pm, otherwise Fridays and weekends only, 10.30am to 4.30pm. Admission £3.50 adults, £1 children 5 and over. Accessible via public footpaths at all times, but permissive paths and the gardens are open during visitor centre hours. Waymarked walks of varying lengths start from the centre.

Spring for woodland flowers and birdsong; summer for butterflies.

For events and current opening times call the visitor centre on 01376 563796.

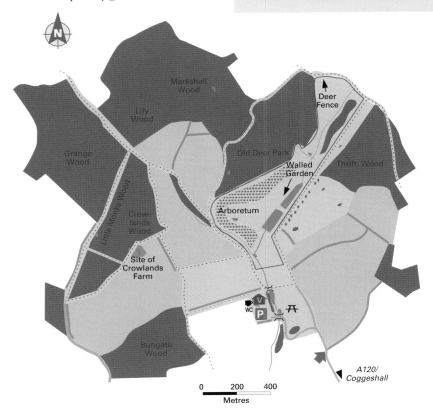

Phyllis Currie

22ac/9ha   **OS Ex183**   **TL 723 182**

ESSEX
Wildlife Trust

This nature reserve, sloping down to a tributary of the River Ter, was left to the Essex Wildlife Trust by Mrs Phyllis Currie. It is an attractive and varied landscape in its own right but what adds interest is to see how the Trust's management is increasing its value for wildlife.

The reserve is home to a wide variety of plants, birds and insects. The most attractive single feature is a lake, created in the stream valley in the 1960s. The lake, streams and ditches are valuable breeding sites for dragonflies and damselflies – 13 species have been recorded. The grassland and sheltered glades and rides provide breeding sites for butterflies – 23 species recorded. Tufted duck nest and kingfisher and grey heron are regular visitors.

A reedbed has been created, a shallow pool excavated and dams installed to raise the water level in the main stream. The Scots pine plantation is being thinned to favour broad-leaved trees. A plantation of hybrid poplar and sycamore is being felled in blocks and replanted with native tree species grown from local seed.

To help to increase wild flowers, the meadows are cut for hay and then grazed by sheep.

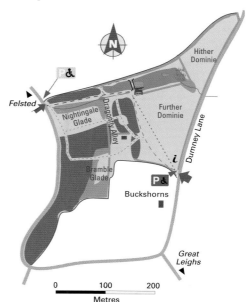

In Dumney Lane, Great Leighs. Take the road to Felsted at the St Anne's Castle PH in Great Leighs. Dumney Lane is the first right turning.

Regular buses run to St Anne's Castle PH from Braintree and Chelmsford.

Accessible at all times.

Interesting all the year round. A succession of flowers from blackthorn in February through to the last of the waterside plants in autumn is followed by the lovely colours of leaves and fruits at the end of the year, with the extra attraction of butterflies and dragonflies in summer.

Wheelchair path leading from both entrances and around the lake.

Please keep dogs on leads at all times.

Buttercups at Phyllis Currie

Roger Jiggins

Saint Peter's Marsh

0.5ac/0.2ha   *OS Ex195*   *TL 757 237*

One of the smallest nature reserves in Essex, comprising freshwater marsh fed by springs. It is a traditional frog breeding site and for this reason Essex Wildlife Trust acquired it from Essex County Council for a nominal sum. An adjoining strip of land was donated later by Messrs G. Tanner and P. O. Wicks.

To the north of St Peter's church, Bocking (close to Braintree Council offices). Entrance off St-Peter's-in-the-Fields (unadopted road).

Accessible at all times.

Dress for nettles and soft wet ground.

Sandylay and Moat Woods

18.5ac/7ha   *OS Ex183*   *TL 735 174*

These two attractive small woods next to one another were donated to Essex Wildlife Trust in 1982 by the late Mr Roland Adams and Mrs Adams. They contain a quantity of coppiced small-leaved lime, growing on boulder clay. One lime, in the middle of a ride in Sandylay Wood, is of great size and age. Sycamore and planted poplars are now being reduced in favour of other species, including small-leaved lime for coppicing; and conifer plantations are being reduced in favour of broadleaved trees.

Part of a field to the south of Sandylay Wood has been added to the reserve recently, and has been planted up with native trees.

The woods are rich in flowering plants. In spring, wood anemones are abundant by the small stream and primroses alongside the paths and rides. Other species include sweet violet, spurge laurel, early purple orchid, twayblade and stinking iris. Wood sedge is widespread, and the unusual thin-spiked wood sedge occurs also.

The reserve has many typical woodland birds, notably goldcrest around a plantation of Norway spruce, and a rich insect life.

In Great Leighs. Follow the public footpath for 400m from Mill Lane. Cars can be parked on the wide grass verge along the lane, but please do not obstruct the gateway providing access to the footpath.

Buses stop on the A131 near the Dog and Partridge PH, from where a public footpath runs east from the road to another entrance.

Accessible at all times.

Late March to May for flowering plants and breeding birds.

Whet Mead

25ac/10ha   *OS Ex183*   *TL 829 137*   *LNR*

Braintree District Council

This former rubbish tip has been restored and is now a Local Nature Reserve managed by Braintree Council. Much of it is rough meadow with a wide range of flowering plants, bordered by some scrub and young woodland and containing three linked lagoons. It attracts a good range of the commoner butterflies and dragonflies, and seed-eating birds such as skylark and goldfinch.

It is bordered on two sides by the Rivers Blackwater and Brain, which have water figwort and flowering rush growing on their banks and support water voles. Grey heron and kingfisher can often be seen feeding along the river.

Access is via Blackwater Lane which leaves Maldon Road (B1018) eastwards just north of Saul's Bridge over the River Brain and follows the river through a tunnel under the Witham bypass.

Regular Witham–Maldon buses run along Maldon Road.

Accessible at all times.

Take care when walking as tipped material may project out of the ground. Young children should be accompanied as the site is remote and river and lagoon banks are very steep.

0   100   200
Metres

Grey heron: resident

David Harrison

Flowering rush: flowers July–August

Tony Gunton

Colchester is an historic Roman town situated on the River Colne, surrounded by many fine nature reserves and country parks. Military use of the town has safeguarded large tracts of semi-natural land nearby, including Friday Wood to the south, in the valley of the Roman River.

Further south lies Abberton Reservoir, of international importance for wild birds. On the Colne Estuary to the south-east is Fingringhoe Wick, Essex Wildlife Trust's first reserve acquired in 1959, and Wivenhoe Woods and Marsh. To the west are several fine small woods and the Fordham Hall Estate, which is former farmland planted up by the Woodland Trust.

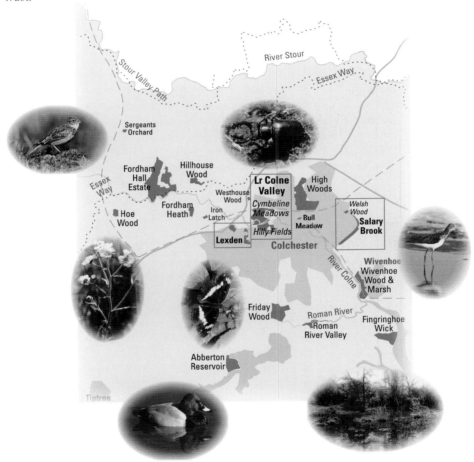

Abberton Reservoir

ESSEX & SUFFOLK WATER

1,240ac/496ha   OS Ex184   TL 963 185   SSSI, SPA

The huge expanse of Essex & Suffolk Water's Abberton Reservoir is one of Europe's top wetland sites. It is of international importance as a safe haven for wild ducks, swans and other water birds, whether resident, passing through on migration or over-wintering. It lies close to east-coast migration routes and, with its surrounding envelope of pasture and tree plantations, is a welcome sight to tired birds.

The sheer numbers of wildfowl in autumn and winter cannot fail to impress. Total numbers of the top seven species – wigeon, teal, mallard, pochard, tufted duck, coot and black-headed gull – can run to many thousands. Added to this there can be hundreds of shoveler, gadwall, goldeneye, pintail and great crested grebe.

In spring there is the unusual sight of cormorants nesting in trees, one of the few places in Britain where they do this. They began in 1981 and have continued ever since.

Late summer brings the spectacle of large numbers of swans and ducks moulting – replacing their worn-out feathers – on the reservoir. Safety is vital while they do so because they replace all their flight feathers at once, which means that for a while they are unable to fly.

In dry winters water levels fall temporarily to expose large expanses of mud. This attracts large numbers of passage waders such as ruff and spotted redshank from the coast.

The surrounding farmland, too, is of value to birds. In winter thousands of golden plover may be seen there, along with small numbers of migratory geese and swans.

For the keen birdwatcher the reservoir boasts an impressive list of rarities visiting briefly in winter or passing through on migration.

Abberton Reservoir Nature Reserve

THE
wildlife
TRUSTS

ESSEX
Wildlife Trust

118ac/48ha   OS Ex184   TL 963 185   SSSI, SPA

Essex Wildlife Trust manages this nature reserve situated on a well-protected bay of the reservoir, created in 1975 with the advice of Sir Peter Scott. A wide range of native trees and shrubs were planted which have matured into fine specimen trees and valuable hedges and thickets. A wide range of small birds nest here, particularly warblers, nightingales and finches.

The pockets of grassland provide open, sunlit sites ideal for many insects, including butterflies. In spring and summer you are likely to see small copper and green hairstreak and others such as common blue, gatekeeper and small skipper.

Around the pond good numbers of dragonflies can be seen, including the small red-eyed damselfly. With its central nesting island it attracts breeding mute swan, canada goose, mallard and moorhen in spring.

Two bird hides within the reserve give views of two floating nesting rafts for common terns, and there are two further hides on the peninsular trail around the land next to the reserve.

The visitor centre was built with the support of Essex & Suffolk Water and Colchester Council and sits right beside the reservoir. It is a birding centre *par excellence*, offering a variety of birds at different times of the year and the possibility of rarities, so interest is always high. The shop stocks one of the best ranges of wildlife books anywhere in Essex and a wide range of optics, so you can come to look at wildlife and get kitted out to improve your enjoyment at the same time.

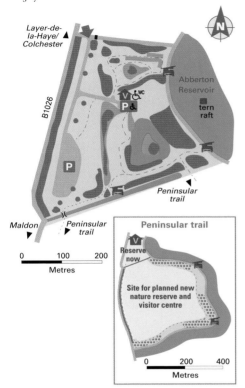

Five miles south-west of Colchester on the B1026 linking Colchester and Maldon, just outside Layer-de-la-Haye. Watch out for brown 'Abberton Reservoir Visitor Centre' signs.

Open 9am to 5pm every day except Mondays (open Bank Holiday Mondays), Christmas Day and Boxing Day: collect a permit from the centre (free to Essex Wildlife Trust members, otherwise a donation is requested). When the centre is closed, good views can be had from the two causeways which are wide enough for safe parking.

Good all the year round, but especially in winter for wildfowl; May and June for breeding birds; August for moulting swans and ducks.

A boardwalk links the centre with the hides in the nature reserve and three have low-level viewing slots.

Sorry: no dogs except guide dogs are allowed in the centre and reserve. Dogs are allowed in the car park.

The centre organises a regular programme of events for adults and children and also offers volunteering opportunities: call 01206 738172 for details. Young visitors can borrow *Wildlife Explorer bags* from the centre.

Future Plans

In 2010 Essex & Suffolk Water are hoping to commence works to raise the levels of the reservoir, to meet increased demand for water. This increase in water level means that the reserve and visitor centre will be moving to their new home, on the peninsular field.

Since 2003 new habitat has been created on the peninsular field in preparation for this move and it is hoped to open the new visitor centre, a sustainable building, around 2010. Access to the new reserve is likely to be before this date: for the latest news telephone or call in at the current centre.

Bull Meadow

22ac/9ha   **OS Ex184**   **TL 997 258**   **LNR**

Colchester

A long-established water meadow beside the River Colne in Colchester with many typical water meadow plants that are now very scarce, and many unusual insects.

Cowdray Avenue (A133)

P Leisure World

Sportsway

Riverside Walk

At the rear of Colchester Leisure World on Cowdray Avenue (A133) or via riverside footpaths. Parking at Leisure World.

Regular bus services along Cowdray Avenue

Dawn to dusk.

Fingringhoe Wick

125ac/50ha   **OS Ex184**   **TM 041 195**   **SSSI, SPA (part)**

ESSEX
Wildlife Trust

Fingringhoe Wick is Essex Wildlife Trust's flagship reserve on the west shore of the Colne Estuary, created out of disused gravel workings. From the dust and turmoil of 40 years of gravel extraction the Trust inherited a barren moonscape. But bare gravel, clay, mud and sediments are inviting seedbeds for wild plants, and today the disturbed, undulating terrain is largely buried in woodland, thickets and dense scrub. The reserve has an immense range of habitats, including patches of grassland, gorse heathland, reedbeds and – a vital wildlife feature – ponds and a large lake. There is a mixed plantation of trees, including conifers. The river frontage provides additional habitats such as saltmarsh, foreshore and inter-tidal mudflats.

Strategically placed on sloping ground overlooking the wild expanses of the Colne Estuary, The Wick offers one of the finest saltmarsh panoramas in eastern England.

Over 200 species of birds have been recorded, of which 50 species nest each year. Come in spring to hear the massed nightingale chorus and for other breeding migrants.

Watch the ponds for the darting blue flash of a kingfisher. Kestrels nest, as well as tawny owls, little grebes and sparrowhawks. Between June and September, migrant waders find the Scrape attractive. The estuary, quiet for much of the year, comes into its own in winter. Thousands of wintering waders and wildfowl rely on the expanses of mud and saltmarsh for food or for roosting. This includes up to 700 avocets, viewable from the shore hides. Sea duck can be seen in mid-river.

You will see many rabbits and grey squirrels, and maybe a fox. There are regular sightings of brown hare, stoat and weasel. Watch out for common seals in the estuary.

At least 350 species of flowering plants have been recorded, including common spotted orchids and bee orchid. The shaded, humid conditions in the thickets suit ferns, mosses and lichens. Visit in spring for tiny unobtrusive clovers, medicks and trefoils. Summer is best for colourful species, especially sea lavender on the saltmarsh, and masses of dog roses.

The Wick teems with insect life. Thirteen species of dragonfly and damselfly breed on the reserve. Many common butterflies flourish, together with the less usual green hairstreak. The sandy, eroding cliff faces are attractive to bees, ants and wasps.

Strangely, frogs are almost unknown at The Wick, although there is a tiny breeding population of toads. Common lizards, slow worms, great crested newts and smooth newts are abundant. Adders and grass snakes are reported regularly.

On a site like this an annual programme of management is essential to let in sunlight and to create areas of new young growth. Scrub must be controlled and ponds must be maintained.

Occasionally large-scale projects become necessary. For example, the Trust has re-profiled the lake shore to benefit wildfowl and has created a scrape (a shallow lake) for wading birds.

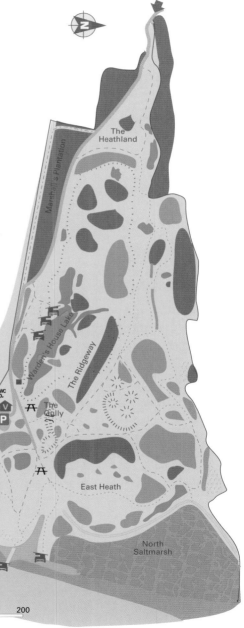

The Heathland

Marshall's Plantation

Warden's House Lake

The Ridgeway

WC

V

P

The Gully

Geedon Saltmarsh

The Scrape

East Heath

North Saltmarsh

Colne Estuary

0   100   200

Metres

Three miles south-east of Colchester. Take the B1025 from Colchester towards Mersea for three miles. After crossing the Roman River turn first left and follow the brown signs to the reserve. The lanes between Fingringhoe village and the reserve are narrow – please drive with caution.

The centre is open daily except Mondays from 9 am–5 pm and the reserve every day from 9 am–5 pm, both excluding Christmas Day and Boxing Day. Day permits must be obtained from the centre. Donations invited from non-members of the Trust: £2 for adults and £1 for children with £5 for families (2 adults and 2 children).

Worth visiting at any time of the year, but the highlights are the nightingale chorus in May and the flocks of brent geese in winter.

A short nature trail (leaflet available) is suitable for people in wheelchairs. Two bird hides that overlook the lake have concrete access paths and low-level viewing slots. A wheelchair is available in the centre on request.

Dogs are not permitted on the main nature reserve, only the signposted dog walk.

For details of a regular programme of events for adults and children or for any other information, call 01206 729678. Waymarked nature trails start from the centre.

Group visits of parties of more than ten people are welcome, but please advise in advance by calling 01206 729678.

Fordham Hall Estate

500ac/205ha   **OS Ex184**   **TL 926 277**

WOODLAND TRUST

This former arable farm surrounding the village of Fordham was donated to the Woodland Trust in 2002. Since then more than 47,000 trees have been planted to create 300 acres of new woodland, the largest woodland creation scheme in eastern England. Add to this some 15km of hedgerows, some probably ancient in origin, that have of course been retained.

Most of the remaining 200 acres adjoining the River Colne have been resown with grass and wild flowers and are being managed by cutting for hay and grazing by sheep and cattle. The River Colne runs along the southern boundary within steep banks and the meadows alongside are marshy and flood in winter. The dampest patches have colonised rapidly with wetland species such as purple loosestrife, brooklime and flag iris. Mature willows and alders grow along the river bank.

It had some 10km of public footpaths originally and the Woodland Trust has added as much again in permissive footpaths.

The wildlife potential of such a large area is considerable and the Woodland Trust has put up large numbers of bird and bat boxes to encourage colonisation. Otters occupy the river, and already barn owls are seen regularly and skylarks nest in the open fields. With skilled management it can only get better as it matures.

Turn off the A1124 (Colchester–Halstead) in the village of Fordstreet, on to Ponders Road. There is a parking area on the left shortly after you reach Fordham village.

Hourly bus service Colchester–Halstead runs through Fordstreet.

Accessible at all times.

Spring for breeding birds; summer for flying insects and wild flowers in the meadows; warm summer evenings for bats.

Skylark: resident

Alan Williams

Chappel Road

Fordham

Ponders Road

Mill Road

Fossetts Lane

Essex Way

River Colne

Halstead

A1124

Fordstreet

Colchester

0 200 400
Metres

Fordham Heath

Eight Ash Green
Parish Council

36ac/14ha   *OS Ex184*   *TL 944 263*

This is a surviving remnant of ancient wet heathland, granted to Eight Ash Green Parish Council by Act of Parliament in 1965. It is managed by the parish council with assistance from the River Colne Countryside Project.

Until the 1940s the heath was dominated by heather and gorse and was grazed by commoners' cattle, but when grazing ceased it was invaded by trees such as oak, birch, blackthorn and aspen which dominate its wooded areas today. But large open areas still remain and are being cut regularly to encourage the regrowth of the original heathland species.

Over 150 different species of wild flower have been recorded in the mosaic of rough grassland, scrub and woodland, including sneezewort, a plant typical of damp rough grassland, both of which are now very scarce.

The woodland in the northern section is being coppiced on a cycle of 12–15 years. This keeps the trees healthy and encourages a diversity of wildlife. Birds that breed here include whitethroat and nightingale.

Turn north off the A1124 Colchester–Halstead road in Eight Ash Green, about 800m north of its junction with the A12. The heath is about 400m further on.

Buses from Colchester to Fordham and Wakes Colne run past the heath.

Accessible at all times.

Paths may be wet and muddy at any time of the year.

Sneezewort: flowers July–September
Owen Keen

Friday Wood

225ac/90ha   **OS Ex184**   *TL 986 209*   **SSSI**

Friday Wood is a mosaic of woodland (some of it ancient), open areas and scrub, owned by the Ministry of Defence. It has a good range of woodland plants but is particularly important for its butterflies and moths. White admirals, now restricted to only a few Essex woods, were 'rediscovered' there in 1995 and it also has white-letter hairstreaks, whose caterpillars feed on elm. Both butterflies fly from July onwards but, unfortunately, spend much of their time in the tree canopy, so you need to work quite hard to spot them.

It is also a good place to hear nightingales.

White admiral: flies late June–mid-August
Iris Newbery

The main parking area is on a minor road that runs south from Berechurch Hall Road to Layer, parallel to the B1026 (Colchester–Maldon).

Regular bus services run along Berechurch Hall Road.

Accessible at all times.

Spring for woodland flowers and birdsong; July–August for butterflies and other insects.

Please keep to the waymarked rights of way and obey Army warning notices.

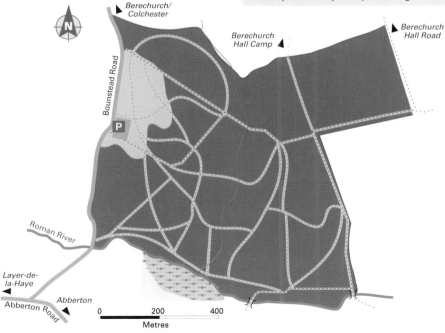

High Woods Country Park

330ac/132ha   **OS Ex184**   *TL 998 271*

Colchester

High Woods Country Park occupies land that was once part of the Royal Forest of Kingswood. Today it is a patchwork of woods, meadows, marsh and rough ground, much as our countryside must have been in the first half of the 20th century. The land was bought by Colchester Council in 1979 to save it from residential development.

The woods in the stream valley to the north, known as the Central Valley, are a remnant of Kingswood Forest. They are being coppiced and you can see the regrowth of flowering plants in the areas opened up to light. The valley floor is mainly ash and alder, with small-leaved lime and oak on the slopes. In April it is carpeted with bluebells.

The main entrance is off Turner Road, which leaves the A134 Colchester–Sudbury road north of Colchester North station.

A footpath leads into the country park starting just south of the railway bridge over the A134, right next to Colchester North station (Liverpool St line).

Car parks open from 7am to 10pm in summer, and to 7pm in winter. Visitor Centre open daily from April to September inclusive, otherwise weekends only.

April for bluebells; May/June for breeding birds in woodland and scrub; summer for wild flowers in meadow and marsh and for flying insects.

For more information telephone the Rangers on 01206 853588.

The mosaic of trees, scrub and open grassland in the eastern section suits a wide variety of insects and birds, including willow warblers, whitethroats and goldfinches. In autumn it is full of berries and wild fruit.

Friars Grove is a small ancient valley wood, surrounded by its original earth bank and ditch.

A large area of marshland has developed around the stream before it passes under the railway and this provides cover for birds such as sedge warblers and reed buntings. In summer the many insects overhead attract crowds of swifts, swallows and martins and, on warm nights, bats.

Common whitethroat: summer visitor
Alan Williams

Goldfinch: resident
Alan Williams

Hillhouse Wood

34ac/13.4ha   **OS Ex184**   **TL 945 280**

WOODLAND
TRUST

This ancient woodland in West Bergholt, near Colchester, was acquired by the Woodland Trust with help from Colchester Council and a local appeal. It is a light and open woodland with many glades and an open canopy of mainly oak and ash trees. The hazel growing beneath them is being coppiced in the traditional manner by local volunteers.

In spring the wood is carpeted with bluebells and wood anemones. Its birdlife includes all three species of woodpecker, with blackcap,

nightingale and garden warbler visiting in summer. It also has a colony of white-letter hairstreak butterflies.

The wood is reached from the end of Hall Road, which runs east from the B1508 (Colchester–Sudbury) just north of West Bergholt. There is parking space for a few cars at the end of Hall Road.

Buses between Colchester and Sudbury run along the B1508.

Accessible at all times.

Spring for woodland flowers and birdsong.

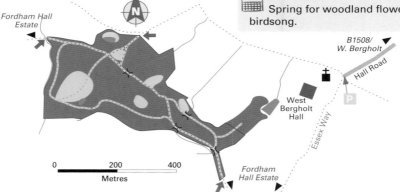

Bugs and beetles

Stag beetle: Britain's largest insect; males – with antlers – emerge in June to search for mates
EWT library

Wasp longhorn beetle: seen along hedgerows and woodland margins May–September
Tony Gunton

Hoe Wood

21.4ac/9ha   **OS Ex184**   **TL 904 263**

WOODLAND
TRUST

This is a little gem of a wood a few miles west of Colchester. It is an ancient coppice wood, and coppicing has been resumed by the Woodland Trust.

The trees are mainly hornbeam coppice with oak standards, but there are also ash, field maple, hazel, sweet chestnut, wild cherry and aspen, with a few small-leaved lime and wild service thrown in for good measure. In early spring violets, primroses and wood anemones are all over the place, and it also has a couple of ponds fringed with aquatic plants.

From the northern edge of the wood there are fine views across the Colne valley, with the Chappel railway viaduct in the centre of the scene.

Turn off the A12 at Marks Tey on to the road towards Aldham. In Aldham turn left into Tey Road by the big oak. The wood is reached via a footpath on the right about 400m down Tey Road, opposite a left turn to Hoe Farm.

The nearest railway station is Marks Tey, 2 miles south-east of the wood. Colchester–Halstead buses pass: get off at Ford Street.

Accessible at all times.

Late March–May for woodland flowers and birdsong.

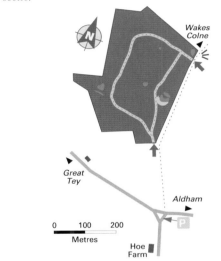

Forest shield bug: sucks the sap from plant stems; there are many different species of shield bug

Tony Gunton

Flower beetle *Oedemera nobilis*: feeds on pollen and nectar in spring and summer

Tony Gunton

Iron Latch

10.5ac/4ha   *OS Ex184*   *TL 951 261*

ESSEX
Wildlife Trust

This Essex Wildlife Trust nature reserve consists of a flower-rich meadow, plus four acres of woodland, long established and possibly ancient. It is quite wet in parts with a good selection of trees, especially ash.

When grazing ceased in the 1950s the meadow reverted to secondary woodland. This was cleared by the Trust in the early 1980s with the aim of recovering the species-rich grassland, which once held colonies of green-winged and common spotted orchids. Now it is managed by mowing and sheep grazing.

Wild and barren strawberry and birdsfoot trefoil flower in the meadow. Birdsfoot trefoil is a foodplant of the common blue and this and several other butterfly species are a special feature. Purple hairstreaks can be seen around the hedgerow oaks.

Nightingales nest in the coppiced woodland and in the managed hedgerows, and also in the neigbouring woodland that has developed on old gravel workings.

Three miles west of Colchester town centre at Eight Ash Green. It is reached by way of the unmade Iron Latch Lane which runs from the old Halstead road at TL 955 254. Cross over the railway bridge and continue along the lane with woodland on your left. The reserve lies to the right of the footpath at the end of the field on your right.

Buses from Colchester to Fordham and Wakes Colne run along Halstead Road.

Accessible at all times.

May for grassland flowers, and late summer for butterflies.

Please keep dogs on a lead near livestock.

Wild strawberry: flowers April–July

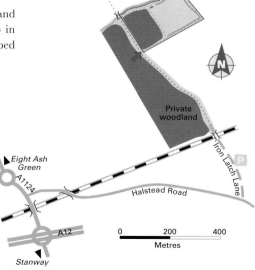

Grassland butterflies (and a day-flying moth)

Common blue (male):
flies June to September; feeds on birdsfoot trefoil

Meadow brown:
flies July to August; feeds on meadow grasses

Large skipper:
flies June to August; feeds on meadow grasses

Essex skipper (small skipper is similar):
flies July and August; feeds on meadow grasses

Gatekeeper or hedge brown:
flies July and August; feeds on meadow grasses

Narrow-bordered five-spot burnet moth:
flies late June to July; feeds on vetches and clovers

Lexden Lexden Gathering Grounds

ESSEX
Wildlife Trust

22ac/9ha   *OS Ex184*   *TL 966 253*

This was formerly a 'gathering ground' for water from constantly flowing springs and used as a water source from the turn of the century until the mid-1970s. It is owned by Anglian Water, who operate the covered reservoir and treatment works nearby, and managed by Essex Wildlife Trust.

In the 1960s parts of the site were planted with scots pine and with beech and oak. Between the woodlands lies a valley with semi-natural woodland of birch and ash on the steep slopes and a partially wooded marsh at the bottom, with a meadow beyond it.

The valley has bluebell and climbing corydalis, an uncommon plant typical of old woodland on sandy soils. The marsh has moschatel and old hazel and alder coppice. The meadow grassland is acidic with sheep's sorrel dominant over large areas.

Great spotted woodpeckers, sparrowhawks and many other woodland birds are present. Fox and badger forage on the site. In the meadow in summer you will see the commoner brown butterflies and small copper, whose caterpillars feed on sheep's sorrel.

The plantation is being thinned to improve the mix of trees and the ground flora. Rides have been widened and are kept open to help butterflies and other invertebrates. Water levels have been raised in the marsh and a pond has been dug, fed by the original springs. Shading is kept down by clearing surrounding trees and scrub.

Small copper: flies from May to October; feeds on sorrels and docks

EWT library

The entrance is on Cooks Lane off Cymbeline Way (A133), about 50m from its junction with the A12 at Lexden Road.

Bus services run along Lexden Road to the south.

Accessible at all times.

Lexden Springs

11ac/4.5ha   *OS Ex184*   *TL 973 253*   *LNR*

Colchester

This ancient meadowland with a fresh-water spring, just north of Lexden, is owned and managed by Colchester Council. Grassland like this is now very scarce and is generally rich in wild flowers. Here you will find a large colony of devilsbit scabious and also harebell and pignut.

Via Spring Lane, a turning off Lexden Road (A1124), Colchester.

Bus services run along Lexden Road.

Accessible at all times.

Phone 01206 853588.

Lexden Park

18.5ac/7ha   **OS Ex184**   **TL 973 250**   **LNR**

Colchester

L exden Park has some old parkland and mature woodland adjoining a wildflower meadow and an ornamental lake. It was declared a Local Nature Reserve in 1991 and is being managed for wildlife by Colchester Council.

The mature oaks in the south-eastern corner, probably 400 years old, are a particular feature and from near here there are also views of Lexden Dyke, an earthwork dating from the 1st century AD.

On Church Lane, Lexden.

Regular bus services run along Lexden Road to the north.

Open from 8am to dusk daily.

Facilities for people with limited mobility including level access and a modified picnic area.

Call 01206 853588 for information or help.

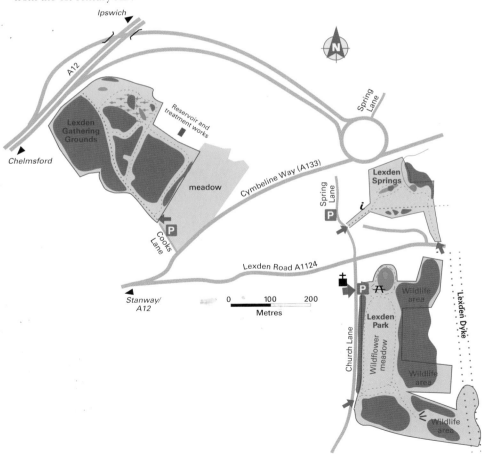

Lower Colne Valley

As it approaches Colchester from the west the River Colne meanders across a broad flood plain, forming a green space that runs almost to the centre of the town. At its heart is Cymbeline Meadows, former farmland that Colchester Council is managing much like the ancient flood meadows that used to occupy this land. Close by are other open spaces the Council manages for wildlife – Hilly Fields and Buntings Meadow.

Cymbeline Meadows

159ac/63.5ha   **OS Ex184**   **TL 980 260**

Colchester

This area bordering the River Colne has been farmed for hundreds of years and is now owned by Colchester Council. Most of it is being farmed by the Council's tenant farmer in a wildlife-friendly way, with limited use of pesticides and features such as 'conservation headlands' – strips along the edge of arable fields sown with non-invasive wild flowers that serve as reservoirs of beneficial insects.

In the north-east corner south of the railway a new wood of over 12,500 trees has been planted, known as Charter Wood. Smaller woods and copses have been planted elsewhere, including beside the Colne.

The river and its bankside meadows form a wildlife corridor running through urban Colchester and they are home to kingfishers and water voles. The river is important as a flood channel and the meadows used to flood regularly in winter, encouraging a rich flora, but in these times of changing climate this has been sporadic.

Can be reached via a public footpath from Cymbeline Way (A133) or via public footpaths leading in from the north and west.

Within easy walking distance of Colchester North station.

Accessible at all times.

A parking area for disabled visitors can be reached via Baker's Lane (Spring Lane exit from the Lexden roundabout) and a surfaced pathway leads down to the river from there.

A farm trail has been laid out starting from Baker's Lane. **i** available from the Council or phone 01206 853588.

Hilly Fields & Buntings Meadow

40ac/16ha   **OS Ex184**   **TL 984 253**

Colchester

This public open space, owned by Colchester Council, shares the ridge on which the town of Colchester developed, overlooking the flood plain of the River Colne. It is part of the Sheepen site that was an industrial and commercial area of Colchester in Iron Age and Roman times: most of it is a Scheduled Ancient Monument.

Since farming stopped about 40 years ago it has developed a mosaic of varied habitats. Much of it is grassland partially invaded by scrub and woodland, but the eastern section towards the town has very sandy soils and patches of heathland have developed, with broom and gorse patches.

At the foot of the slope against Cymbeline

Way is a marsh fed by springs. Ponds that had silted up over the years have now been restored. Noctule and pipistrelle bats feed over the ponds: visit late on a warm evening to see them.

Buntings Meadow to the west is managed particularly for butterflies and has a butterfly trail.

Accessed via Sussex Road, that runs north off Lexden Road (A1124).

Frequent bus services from Colchester Town Centre to Lexden and Stanway run along Lexden Road.

Accessible at all times.

Most paths are unsuitable for wheel-chairs because of the steep terrain.

Call 01206 853588 for information or help.

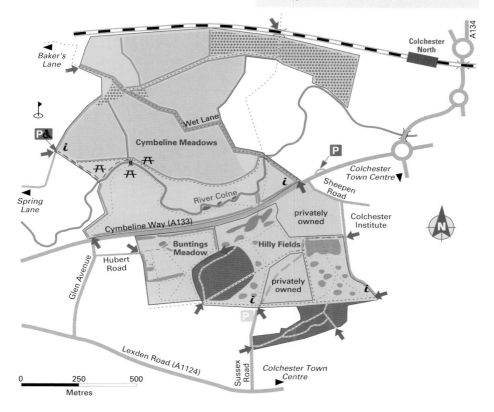

Roman River Valley nature reserve

ESSEX
Wildlife Trust

44ac/18ha   **OS Ex184**   **TL 975 211**

This fragment of traditional river valley landscape is an Essex Wildlife Trust nature reserve. The Roman River is a narrow stream at this point, and meanders through marsh and woodland, mostly old.

Small teasel: flowers July–September

Adrian Knowles

The marsh is fed by springs filtering out of glacial gravels, and is full of aquatic plants including one that is unusual – the small teasel, which has globular white flowers in late summer.

The woodland is part of Needle Eye Wood, and has a variety of trees including standard oaks, coppiced hornbeam and several old yews. Its flowering plants include yellow arch-angel and moschatel.

Birdlife includes most of the common woodland species and occasionally nightingales. Like most wetland sites it has a rich insect life as well.

Entrance on the west side of the B1026 (Colchester–Layer) just north of Kingsford Bridge, north of Layer-de-la-Haye.

Bus services from Colchester to Layer and Maldon pass the entrance.

Accessible at all times.

April–May for birdsong and early flowers; July for dragonflies and other insects.

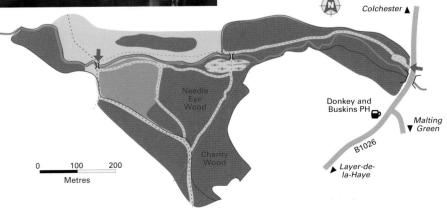

Colchester

Needle Eye Wood

Charity Wood

Donkey and Buskins PH

Malting Green

B1026

Layer-de-la-Haye

0   100   200
Metres

Salary Brook

50ac/20ha   *OS Ex184*   *TM 027 250*   *LNR*

Colchester

This secluded area of marsh, wet grass-land and ponds lies alongside Salary Brook on the eastern fringe of Colchester. It is owned by Colchester Council, who are working with local volunteers to improve access and encourage the fine wetland vegetation, which includes hemlock water dropwort and devilsbit scabious.

In the north-east of Colchester. Salary Brook can be reached via footpaths off Avon Road, which runs from the Tesco roundabout on the A133 to Bromley Road, near the Beehive PH. Welsh Wood is between the Roach Vale, Woodlands and Salary Close estates.

Bus services from Colchester run along the A133.

Accessible at all times.

May for birdsong. High to late summer for wetland flowers and insects.

Welsh Wood

7ac/2.68ha   *OS Ex184*   *TM 025 263*   *LNR*

This small fragment of ancient wood-land has a wide range of trees, including small-leaved lime, a tree characteristic of very old woodlands that used to be widespread but (probably because of long-term climate change) is now very unusual. It lies in a stream valley and is very wet, which makes for a variety of woodland flowers.

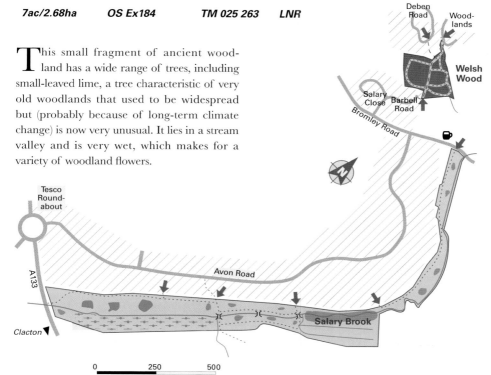

Sergeant's Orchard

8ac/3ha   **OS Ex196**   **TL 907 308**

ESSEX
Wildlife Trust

These two ex-arable fields and a 19th-century orchard were left to the Essex Wildlife Trust in 1996 by the then owner of Sergeant's Farm. Within the orchard area a wide range of old varieties of fruit tree remain, together with an old pond and the remnants of the hedges.

The orchard, the hedges and the ponds are being restored, and a new orchard has been planted on the western field using stock taken from the old varieties in the original orchard.

Between Aldham and Chappel turn off the A1124 into Vernons Road. Follow signs for Bures/Sudbury and turn right at the T-junction. There is a small pull-in at the entrance to the bridle path with a chain attached to two metal posts.

Accessible at all times.

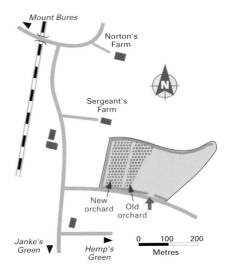

Sergeant's Orchard in winter

Westhouse Wood

7ac/3ha   **OS Ex184**   **TL 974 272**

ESSEX
Wildlife Trust

Despite its small size this wood on the outskirts of Colchester contains a wide range of trees and shrubs. Hazel is the dominant coppice species, and small-leaved lime, crab apple and rowan are scattered among fine oak and ash standards, along with sweet chestnut, holly and field maple.

As a result of coppicing, bluebells and wood anemones carpet the wood in spring, and there are fine displays of foxgloves in areas that have recently been cleared. Work has also been carried out to keep three small ponds, occupied by newts and frogs, wet throughout the summer months.

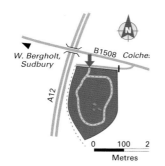

W. Bergholt, Sudbury

B1508 Colche:

A12

0   100   2
Metres

 The entrance is down a slip road on the left off the B1508 Colchester–Sudbury road, just before it passes over the A12 at Braiswick, north-west of Colchester.

Bus services from Colchester to West Bergholt, Bures and Sudbury run past the entrance.

Accessible at all times.

Wivenhoe Wood & Marsh

67ac/27ha   **OS Ex184**   **TM 034 217**   **LNR, SSSI (part)**

Colchester

Wivenhoe Wood is a fine old coppice woodland on the east bank of the River Colne near Wivenhoe, alongside grassland and scrub that once belonged to Lower Lodge Farm and a section of tidal foreshore with saltmarsh.

It is likely that the sweet chestnut trees in the wood were planted by the Romans, who introduced the tree to this country from southern Europe as a source of rot-resistant timber ideal for fence posts and the like. Coppicing creates a diverse woodland rich in wildlife, and the grassland and scrub nearby adds further variety.

An area of saltmarsh to the west of the railway line can be reached via a level crossing. The saltmarsh is used by wading birds such as redshank and greenshank.

Wivenhoe Marsh to the south is an area of former grazing marsh. From the sea wall path there are good views of the inner estuary of the Colne and over the ditches, dykes and ponds of the marsh. Unusual plants like strawberry clover and slender hare's-ear grow here, and it has a rich insect life, with many dragonflies and damselflies on the wing in summer and stag beetles blundering in from Wivenhoe Wood to the north. Whitethroats, reed warblers and sedge warblers nest in the dense vegetation.

Access via Rosabelle Avenue, a turning off The Avenue (B1028) north of Wivenhoe centre, or from the south via the sea wall path or public footpaths alongside the railway.

Wivenhoe station is a few minutes' walk from Wivenhoe Marsh and from the southern tip of Wivenhoe Wood. Regular buses run from Colchester to Wivenhoe.

Accessible at all times.

May/June for birdsong in the woods and scrub; July/August for insects along the woodland edge and in clearings, and around the marsh and foreshore.

A surfaced path runs from the car park at the end of Rosabelle Avenue to the picnic site. The footpath west of the railway is surfaced also.

available from Council offices or call 01206 853588.

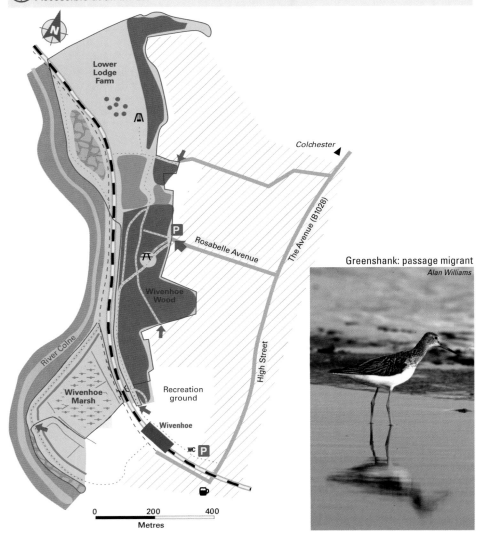

Greenshank: passage migrant
Alan Williams

Tendring

Tendring is named after a small village at its centre which earlier gave its name to Tendring Hundred. Also referred to as the Tendring Peninsula, it is bounded to the north by the River Stour and its estuary, to the south-west by the River Colne and its estuary, and to the south and east by the North Sea. In addition to the large estuaries, its key features are Hamford Water, a National Nature Reserve, and The Naze, the only significant stretch of cliffs on the Essex coast. Most of its important wildlife sites are on the coast or the estuaries, plus a few fine old woods and a former gravel pit inland.

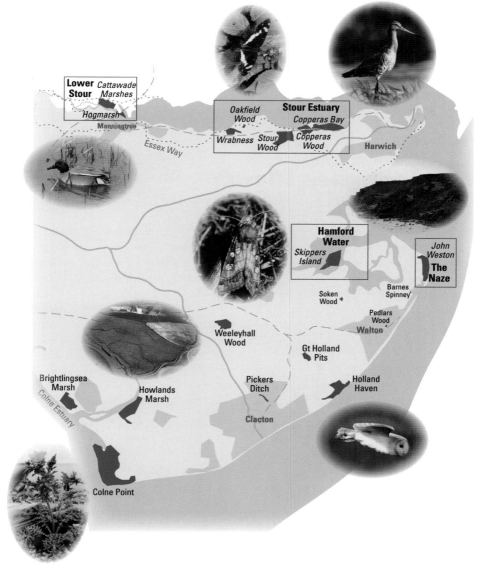

Lower Stour Cattawade Marshes

Hogmarsh

Manningtree

Essex Way

Oakfield Wood

Wrabness Stour Wood

Stour Estuary Copperas Bay

Copperas Wood

Harwich

Hamford Water

Skippers Island

John Weston

The Naze

Barnes Spinney

Soken Wood

Pedlars Wood

Walton

Weeleyhall Wood

Gt Holland Pits

Brightlingsea Marsh

Colne Estuary

Howlands Marsh

Pickers Ditch

Holland Haven

Clacton

Colne Point

Barnes Spinney

2ac/1ha   **OS Ex184**   **TM 258 277**

A small garden at Walton-on-the-Naze, left to Essex Wildlife Trust in 1984 by Mrs L. Barnes and named in memory of her husband, the Rt Hon. Alfred Barnes PC.

It contains fine displays both of cultivated plants, especially daffodils, fritillaries and primroses in spring, and of wild flowers, including tway-blade and good numbers of common spotted orchid.

On arriving in Walton, follow the main road north-east through High Street into Hall Lane, then on for about 800m. Turn sharp left into lane beyond Brenalwood nursing home.

Half-hourly buses from Walton church and from the bus station on the front.

Can normally be visited only on open days. These are announced and publicised locally, or call Essex Wildlife Trust on 01621 862960.

Unsuitable for dog-walking.

Brightlingsea Marsh

75ac/30ha   **OS Ex184**   **TM 076 164**   **NNR, SPA**

This area of grazing marsh right next to Brightlingsea is part of the Colne Estuary National Nature Reserve (NNR). Redshank and shoveler breed there in summer, while in winter it is used by brent geese and other wildfowl.

It has a huge density of ant hills, and these in turn attract green woodpeckers, for which ants are a favourite food. Its flowering plants include spiny rest-harrow and, on the ant hills, lady's bedstraw.

It is grazed by cattle or sheep in the traditional way. High water levels are maintained using overspill water from a gravel works nearby, to create good conditions for wading birds. The adjacent grazing marsh, outside the NNR, is managed in a similar way.

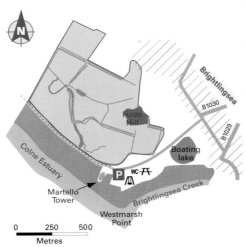

In Brightlingsea, follow the Promenade towards Westmarsh Point, parking near the Martello Tower.

Regular buses to Brightlingsea from Colchester and Clacton, or rail to Great Bentley and bus from there.

Good views at any time from the sea wall path.

May to July for breeding birds; winter for wildfowl.

Colne Point

683ac/273ha   **OS Ex184**   **TM 108 125**   **NNR, SSSI, SPA**

This large and important Essex Wildlife Trust reserve at the mouth of the Colne Estuary consists of a shingle ridge enclosing a considerable area of saltmarsh, through which Ray Creek flows. The shingle and sand is nearly all that remains of a much larger area between Walton-on-the-Naze and St Osyth that existed at the end of the 19th century but has now mostly been developed by the holiday industry.

For anyone wishing to explore the movement of shingle and the development of shingle structures, Colne Point is of great interest. It is the best developed spit on the Essex coast and includes various stages of stabilisation.

The reserve is rich in plants and animals, including many that are rare nationally or locally. The saltmarsh is a typical example of the habitat in Essex and supports golden samphire and small cord-grass (both nationally scarce) as well as sea wormwood, sea lavender and thrift. The shingle and sand ridge has many attractive plants which are now highly localised, such as sea holly, sea bindweed, sea spurge, yellow horned-poppy and sea kale. Nationally scarce species include sea heath, dune fescue, curved hard-grass, sea barley and rock sea-lavender. The stands of shrubby seablite are some of the best on the east coast.

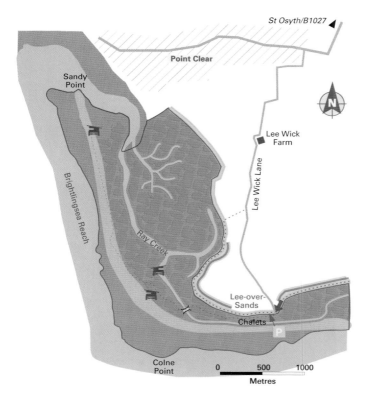

The exposed mudflats, shell banks and shingle pools provide a feeding ground for large numbers of waders that arrive in autumn and winter. Colne Point is on a major migration route for finches, chats, pipits, skylarks and hirundines and in autumn when the weather conditions are right birds constantly stream through the reserve. Birds of prey are seen frequently, particularly at migration times. The saltmarsh is used as a winter feeding ground by brent geese and various ducks, with grebes and divers offshore. In summer there is a small nesting colony of little terns, on the shingle with oystercatchers and ringed plovers. Other breeding birds include redshank, skylark, reed bunting and linnet.

The reserve is important as well for its invertebrates, with particularly good numbers of spiders, beetles and moths recorded. A variety of solitary bees and wasps find the sandy substrate ideal for nesting. Many of these invertebrates are rare, nationally or locally, and a number of Red Data Book species (the rarest of the rare) are present.

Access via the road running to Lee Wick Farm from St Osyth. A car parking space is provided just inside the reserve on the seaward side of the sea wall, but is liable to flood at very high tides. Please use the car park and do not drive along the track past the chalets which the Trust does not own. Please drive slowly and leave all gates as you find them.

Except for Essex Wildlife Trust members access is by day permit only, available from Trust HQ (01621 862960).

Migration periods for birds; summer for saltmarsh plants and insects.

Dogs not permitted.

During the breeding season (March to September) please walk below the last high tide mark as eggs and chicks are extremely difficult to see and are easily trampled.

At high tides various parts of the reserve can be flooded for some time, including around the car park and either end of the footbridge (the only access to the main part of the reserve), so consult a tide table before you visit. It is advisable to wear wellingtons or waterproof boots as it may be muddy, or even necessary to wade, at any time of year.

Colne Point vegetation
EWT library

Great Holland Pits

40ac/16ha   **OS Ex184**   *TM 204 190*

ESSEX
Wildlife Trust

Except that it does not border an estuary, this Essex Wildlife Trust reserve is in many respects a smaller version of Fingringhoe Wick. Gravel was worked here until about 1964 but the scars have virtually disappeared beneath vigorous growth. Habitats include heathy grassland, pasture, a remnant of old woodland, large and small pools, and wet depressions. From the high ground there are attractive views of Holland Brook meandering through water meadows.

It has a wide variety of flowering plants, including localised Essex species such as moschatel, yellow archangel, small-flowered buttercup, mousetail, carline thistle, several small clovers, true bulrush, and soft shield and hart's-tongue ferns.

There is a good variety of birdlife, with the nightingale among the summer visitors, and several aquatic species including kingfisher, coot and little grebe. Woodcock frequently use the reserve in winter.

As you would expect in such a varied site, there are many butterflies, moths and other invertebrates.

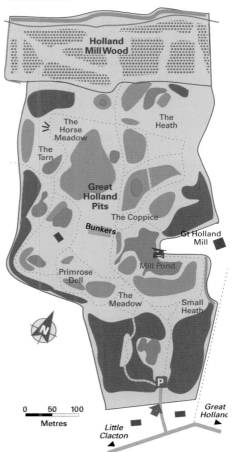

The reserve entrance is 800m west of the Lion's Den pub at Great Holland, north of the Little Clacton Road.

Buses stop at the Lion's Den on the route from Clacton to Walton.

Accessible at all times.

Spring and summer for flowers, birds and insects.

Holland Mill Wood

10ac/4ha   **OS Ex184**   *TM 202 195*

WOODLAND
TRUST

Holland Mill Wood, a recently planted Woodland Trust wood of about 10 acres, can be reached via Great Holland Pits.

Hamford Water

Most of the Walton Backwaters, a shallow tidal bay between Walton-on-the-Naze and Dovercourt, forms the Hamford Water National Nature Reserve, important principally (but not solely) because of its birdlife. Much of it is privately owned, but Skippers Island is an Essex Wildlife Trust nature reserve and it can also be viewed from sea wall footpaths starting from The Naze (see page 82) and from Dovercourt.

No fewer than 12 species of waterfowl winter in Hamford Water in nationally or internationally important numbers, including brent goose, teal, grey plover, black-tailed godwit and redshank. In summer it hosts one of the largest breeding colonies in Essex of little terns and a large breeding colony of black-headed gulls. In the less disturbed areas common seals breed.

The low dunes support distinctive flowering plants, including sea pea, sea holly and sea bindweed.

Hamford Water is also one of the few places in the UK where Fisher's estuarine moth occurs, along with its foodplant, hog's fennel.

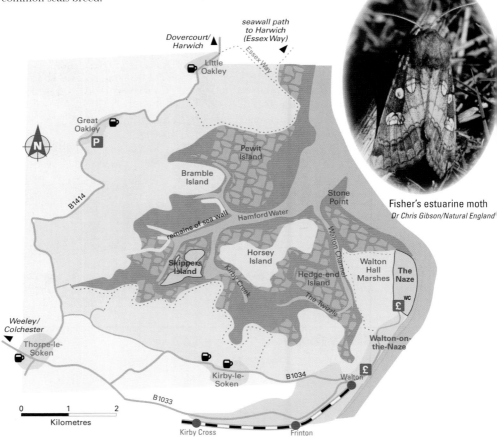

Fisher's estuarine moth
Dr Chris Gibson/Natural England

Skippers Island

233ac/93ha   *OS Ex184*   *TM 218 242*   *NNR, SSSI, SPA*

ESSEX
Wildlife Trust

Skippers Island is 1,500m long by 800m at its widest point, and surrounded by salt-marsh. It is about 500m from the mainland, linked by two causeways built in the 19th century for the passage of livestock but now reduced to muddy pathways. It was given to Essex Wildlife Trust by the late E.F. Williams.

The highest parts of the island, composed of London clay, are covered with extensive thorn thickets. Rides have been cut through them and are mown regularly, producing fine flower-rich swards of grass.

The lower land used to be enclosed from the sea as grazing marsh but now, following breaches in the sea wall, it has reverted to salt-marsh. About one-third of the island is rough pasture and it has several pools of fresh but often brackish water.

The island has large stands of hog's-fennel, foodplant of Fisher's estuarine moth, and also adderstongue fern, parsley water-dropwort, dyer's greenweed and lax-flowered sea-lavender.

Its breeding birds include shelduck, oyster-catcher and, in the thickets, several species of warbler and occasionally nightingales. Outside the breeding season there are good numbers of brent geese and many species of duck and wader. Birds of prey are often seen in winter, the most regular being the short-eared owl. Common seals occur frequently.

As well as Fisher's estuarine moth, it has large numbers of Essex skipper butterflies, feathered ranunculus and rosy wave moths, and Roesel's and short-winged conehead bush-crickets.

Access is via a private road to Birch Hall, Kirby-le-Soken. Cars can be parked next to the sea wall by the concrete shed.

No access to the reserve without prior application as the warden is required to notify the owners of the access road of visitors in advance. Please call Essex Wildlife Trust on 01621 862960 for details.

Unsuitable for dog walking.

Visitors need to be reasonably active as the saltmarsh and rough grassland can be tiring. Wellingtons or walking shoes are essential for crossing to and from the island at low tide via the causeway.

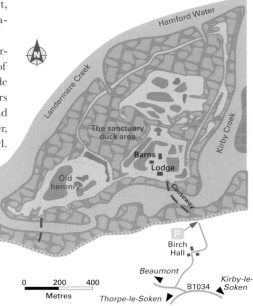

Holland Haven Country Park

Tendring
District Council

200ac/80ha   *OS Ex184*   *TM 220 175*   *SSSI (part), LNR*

This country park, managed by Tendring Council, consists of coastal grassland and marshland around the mouth of the Holland Brook, once the site of a small harbour called Holland Haven.

The coastal grassland is cut for hay and the inland marshes are grazed by cattle and overlooked by a bird hide. Water levels have been raised so that wildfowl and waders are attracted both to over-winter and to breed. Barn owls often hunt over the grassland at dusk.

It has a complex of dykes and a large brackish pond, all fringed by reeds and clubrush. All this makes for good aquatic insect life, including some rare beetles and damselflies.

Off the B1032 to Great Holland just north of Holland-on-Sea.

Bus services between Clacton and Walton run past the entrance.

Accessible at all times.

Winter for wildfowl and waders; summer for insects.

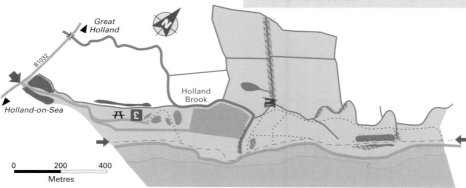

Barn owl: resident

EWT library

Howlands Marsh

186ac/74ha   OS Ex184   TM 115 169   SSSI, SPA

O ne of the best surviving coastal grazing marshes in Essex, consisting mainly of low-lying hummocky grassland, split up by dykes and fleets. The fleets and other natural depressions in the grassland are evidence of former creeks and saltmarsh before the seawall was built. A narrow fringe of salt-marsh outside the seawall widens into a large block where Flag and St Osyth creeks meet.

The grassland contains much reed, sedge, glaucous bulrush and sea clubrush, and a variety of other plants include spiny rest-harrow and, particularly on the many anthills, spring whitlow-grass. Uncommon plants such as slender hare's-ear, knotted parsley and sea barley grow on and near the seawall.

Among the plants in the dykes and fleets are great water-dock, lesser water-parsnip, tufted forget-me-not, marsh bedstraw and brackish water-crowfoot. In places on the saltmarsh are sea wormwood and some golden samphire, as well as the more usual saltmarsh plants.

Reed warblers, lapwings, skylarks and reed buntings breed here. In winter brent geese graze among hundreds of wildfowl along with small flocks of curlews. When the tide is low, large numbers of shelduck, dunlin and redshank feed on the exposed mud in the creeks. Little egrets and marsh harriers are frequent visitors.

The marshland also supports a great variety of invertebrates, including some rare species.

Reached via a public footpath which links a layby on the west side of the B1027, just south of Oaklands Holiday Village (600m from the reserve), with The Quay off Mill Street (900m away). Roadside parking is usually available.

Several bus services from Clacton-on-Sea and Colchester pass the starting points for the footpath.

Accessible at all times. The public path is often impassable for some time during high tides at and near The Quay.

September to March for wildfowl and waders on and around Flag Creek.

To prevent disturbance to wildlife and grazing stock, please keep to the public footpath and the paths to the hides and do not walk on the seawall.

Dogs must be kept on a lead near livestock and always under close control.

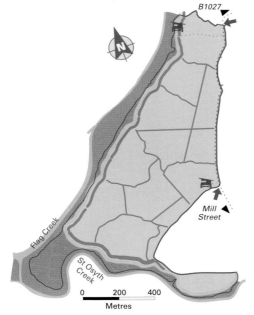

Lower Stour

Cattawade Marshes

109ac/44ha   *OS Ex184*   *TM 095 330*   *SSSI, SPA*

Acquired by the RSPB early in 2005, Cattawade Marshes is 44ha of lowland wet grassland with 2ha of reedbed, between the freshwater and tidal branches of the River Stour.

During the summer lapwing, redshank and several duck species breed, and in winter it has good numbers of wildfowl including teal and wigeon.

West of the A137 from Ipswich to Manningtree, south of Cattawade. Park along the Cattawade river barrage.

Manningtree railway station is about 15 minutes' walk.

No public access but good views can be had from the public footpath to Flatford on the south side of the river that leaves the A137 south of the White Bridge.

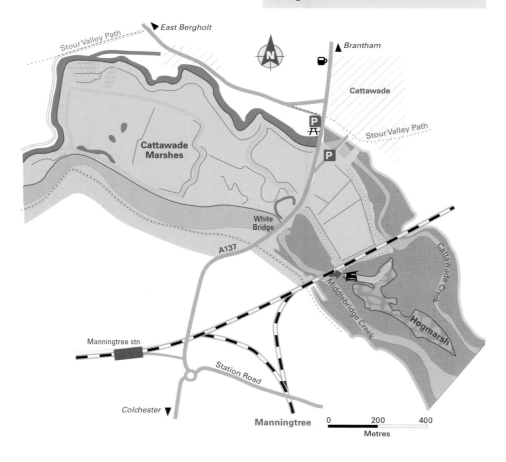

Hogmarsh

12ac/5ha   **OS Ex184**   **TM 103 325**   **SSSI, SPA**

ESSEX
Wildlife Trust

An area of saltmarsh jutting out into the tidal River Stour opposite Manningtree. It was donated to Essex Wildlife Trust by Lt.-Col. C.A. Brooks in 1973.

It has plants and animals typical of Essex saltmarsh. Mute swan, canada goose and oystercatcher nest and many other estuary bird species visit. Good views can be gained from the bird hide that overlooks it.

The saltmarsh is threatened by erosion and this is being fought by building faggot barriers and importing silt dredged from elsewhere in the river.

Park along the Cattawade river barrage on the A137 (Colchester–Ipswich) road, then walk south-east along the seawall and under the railway bridge.

Manningtree railway station is about 15 minutes' walk.

Hide accessible at all times (the reserve itself can only be entered at low tide).

Unsuitable for dog walking.

Very soft mud surrounds most of the reserve, so wellingtons are essential.

Pedlars Wood

7ac/3ha   **OS Ex184**   **TM 244 209**

This privately owned ancient wood between Frinton and Walton is in two parts either side of Central Avenue. It is well known for its bluebells which carpet much of the site. It hosts a large rookery and woodland birds such as woodpeckers.

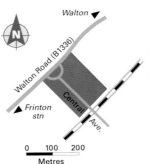

Walton

Walton Road (B1336)

Frinton stn

Central Ave.

0   100   200
Metres

On Walton Road (B1336) roughly midway between Frinton and Walton.

Frinton side accessible at all times. Walton side has an educational nature trail which is accessible by appointment only: call 01255 674735.

Teal pair (male on right): Britain's smallest ducks; resident

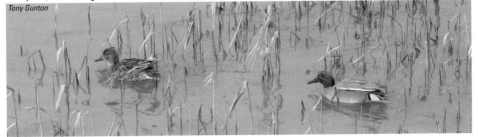

Tony Gunton

Pickers Ditch

7ac/3ha   *OS Ex184*   *TM 180 170*   *LNR*

A meadow in Clacton-on-Sea through which Pickers Ditch runs, declared a Local Nature Reserve in 1992. Hedges and copses have been planted to screen the site.

Runs south-east from Thorpe Road (B1442) in Great Clacton, the northern part of Clacton-on-Sea.

Accessible at all times.

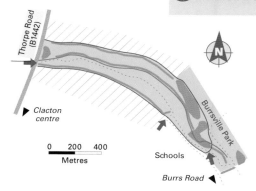

Saltmarsh plants

Shrubby seablite: the only saltmarsh shrub, up to 1m tall; evergreen; grows on the upper saltmarsh and on sand; insignificant green flowers July–October

Adrian Knowles

Golden samphire: a rare perennial growing on the upper saltmarsh and on coastal cliffs; flowers July–October

Chris Gibson/Natural England

Soken Wood

10ac/4ha   *OS Ex184*   *TM 220 223*

WOODLAND
TRUST

This wood is one of the Woodland Trust's 'Woods on your Doorstep' projects, bought in 1999. The dominant trees are oak, ash, and field maple with smaller numbers of willow, alder and downy birch. A mixture of shrubs have been planted around the fringes of the site including hazel, spindle, hawthorn and dogwood.

A special feature is a planting of 'prehistoric trees' known from the fossil record to have grown here. These include monkey puzzle, dawn redwood, tulip tree and oriental plane.

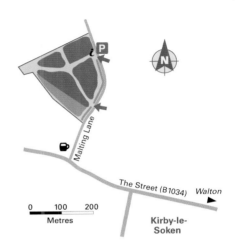

On Maltings Lane on the fringes of Kirby-le-Soken. Follow the B1034 from Walton and turn right after passing through the village centre.

Accessible at all times.

Sea purslane: grows on the banks of creeks and gullies in the saltmarsh; small yellow flowers from July to October

Laurie Forsyth

Glasswort, also known by its scientific name of *Salicornia* and as 'poor man's asparagus': one of the earliest plants to colonise new saltmarsh; turns red or yellow when it flowers in late summer

Tony Gunton

Stour Estuary

This section of the estuary of the River Stour to the west of Harwich has saltmarsh and intertidal mudflats adjoining ancient woodland and is the only place in Essex where you can see the one close alongside the other. The saltmarsh and mudflats of Copperas Bay are nationally important for wading birds such as black-tailed godwit, dunlin and redshank and, together with Stour Wood, form the RSPB's Stour Estuary reserve. Essex Wildlife Trust owns another ancient woodland alongside the bay, Copperas Wood, and to the west lies Wrabness nature reserve and Oakfield Wood, a 'green burial ground'.

Copperas Bay

717ac/287ha   *OS Ex184*   *TM 195 318*   *SSSI, SPA*

Copperas Bay has large areas of mudflats fringed by saltmarsh and reedbed, lying immediately west of the port facilities of Parkeston. It is reached by crossing the bridge over the railway and walking down the Essex Way to the public hide. This hide is best for birdwatching at low and half tide when many waders come to feed on the mudflats.

From the bridge another path runs along in a narrow strip of woodland between railway and estuary to two hides (reserved for RSPB members), which give good views of birds at their high-tide roost. It is unusual in Essex for a wood to run right down to the waterside as it does here and this makes it an enjoyable walk in its own right.

From the path there are occasional views through the screen of trees over Copperas Bay, which is used by a variety of birds in autumn and winter including brent geese, many ducks and a large flock of black-tailed godwits. The Stour estuary is the second most important UK wintering site for this bird after the Wash, with more than 2,000 present most winters. They are part of the population that breeds in Iceland.

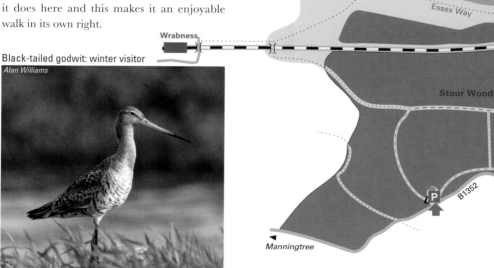

Black-tailed godwit: winter visitor
Alan Williams

Copperas Wood

34.3ac/14ha   *OS Ex184*   *TM 199 312*   *SSSI*

ESSEX
Wildlife Trust

This ancient wood, owned by Essex Wildlife Trust, consists mainly of coppiced sweet chestnut and hornbeam. It was severely damaged in the great storm of 1987 and sections of the wood have been left in their devastated state for wildlife value and for scientific study.

After the Trust bought the wood in 1980 coppicing was reintroduced, and this has produced carpets of bluebell, yellow arch-angel and red campion. Among other flowering plants are moschatel, climbing corydalis, and a few sweet woodruff and vervain. The wood is rich in ferns, and in particular soft shield-fern.

North of the B1352 from Ramsey to Manningtree, between the villages of Wrabness and Ramsey. Turn off the A120 Colchester to Harwich road on to the B1352. The main entrance to Stour Wood, with car park, is signposted from the road; Copperas Wood is 300m down a public footpath (the route of the Essex Way) beside a large white flat-roofed house, with parking for one or two cars on the verge. Copperas Bay and its bird hides can be reached via either.

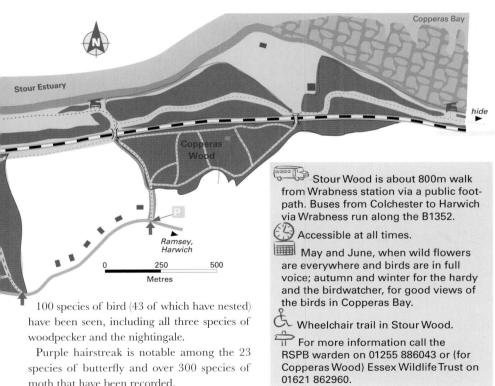

100 species of bird (43 of which have nested) have been seen, including all three species of woodpecker and the nightingale.

Purple hairstreak is notable among the 23 species of butterfly and over 300 species of moth that have been recorded.

Stour Wood is about 800m walk from Wrabness station via a public footpath. Buses from Colchester to Harwich via Wrabness run along the B1352.

Accessible at all times.

May and June, when wild flowers are everywhere and birds are in full voice; autumn and winter for the hardy and the birdwatcher, for good views of the birds in Copperas Bay.

Wheelchair trail in Stour Wood.

For more information call the RSPB warden on 01255 886043 or (for Copperas Wood) Essex Wildlife Trust on 01621 862960.

Stour Estuary (continued)

Stour Wood

135ac/54ha　　**OS Ex184**　　　**TM 192 311**　　**SSSI**

Stour Wood is one of the best ancient sweet chestnut woods in Essex. It was worked as coppice until the 1970s and coppicing has since been resumed by the RSPB, to whom the Woodland Trust has leased the wood. The sweet chestnut is being coppiced on a long (20-year) cycle. It has a mixture of trees apart from sweet chestnut, including a few surviving small-leaved lime and many field maple on the edge of the wood. Some unusual flowers characteristic of ancient woodland are sweet woodruff and early purple orchid.

It is full of birdsong in spring and early summer. Among the butterflies look out for white admiral, flying in July, a woodland butterfly that is common in woods further south and west but rare in East Anglia.

See previous page for map and visiting

Oakfield Wood

7ac/3ha　　**OS Ex184**　　　**TM 167 315**

Oakfield Wood is a 'green burial ground' overlooking the Stour Estuary at Wrabness, a natural alternative to traditional graveyard or crematorium burials. It was one of the first in the UK and has been visited by church and other organisers who have since set up sites throughout the country.

For each burial a native broadleaved tree is planted with a wooden plaque at its base, thus each burial contributes towards creating a new woodland on what used to be arable farmland. When the burial ground is full it will be managed as a nature reserve by Essex Wildlife Trust.

For more information about burials contact Peter Kincaid on 01255 503456.

White admiral: flies late June–mid-August

Tony Gunton

Yellowhammer (male): resident

David Harrison

Wrabness Nature Reserve

54ac/22ha   **OS Ex184**   ***TM 167 315***   *LNR*

ESSEX
Wildlife Trust

This area served as a mine depot until its demolition in 1963. Attempts to develop the site ran into public opposition and in 1992 it became a nature reserve under the care of the Wrabness Nature Reserve Charitable Trust. It is managed now by Essex Wildlife Trust.

It is mainly open grassland and scrub, with a pond, a bog, a wooded fringe and a bird hide overlooking the Stour Estuary. It attracts open country birds such as yellowhammers (increasingly scarce elsewhere) and whitethroats to nest, and has large numbers of grassland butterflies and other insects in summer.

Reached via Wheatsheaf Lane, which turns off the B1352 between Bradfield and Wrabness. A turning half-left just beyond the railway bridge leads to the Wrabness NR car park and the Oakfield Wood car park is on the left further on. From there a path takes you past the burial ground and joins the Essex Way footpath.

About a mile walk from Wrabness rail station via a public footpath. A bus service from Colchester to Harwich runs along the B1352.

Accessible at all times.

Good wheelchair access.

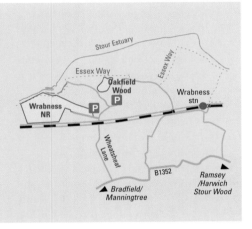

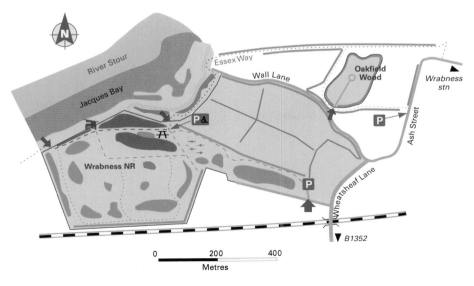

The Naze

137ac/55ha   OS Ex184   TM 264 235   SSSI (part)

Tendring
District Council

The Naze is from the Old English *naes*, meaning a nose. It is a headland roughly three miles long and one mile wide, stretching northwards from the town of Walton-on-the-Naze. Behind it is Hamford Water, which it shelters from the North Sea. At its southern end is a hill that is being eroded, with the result that 20-metre high cliffs rise directly from the beach – unique on the Essex coast.

The cliffs are important geologically because of a spectacular exposure of a sandy deposit called Red Crag, formed about 3 million years ago when the sea covered most of Essex and containing large numbers of fossils.

Red Crag also erodes easily. Two concrete pillboxes lying out on the beach show how quickly erosion is occuring: they were built on the clifftop during the second world war.

Originally the Naze was farmland, then a golf course, then was requisitioned at the beginning of World War II. In 1961 it was decided that the Naze should become a public regional open space, and Tendring Council owns it now.

In summer the cliffs provide secure sites for the nesting holes of sand martins. The large gorse bushes and elder scrub on top of the cliff provide cover for small birds such as linnets and goldfinches, as do the taller plants growing on the fallen cliff material at its foot. Waders, gulls and terns can be seen along the shore.

During migration periods it is a prime bird-watching site. Curlew sandpipers are regularly seen along the beach, with gannets and arctic skuas passing offshore. With east winds

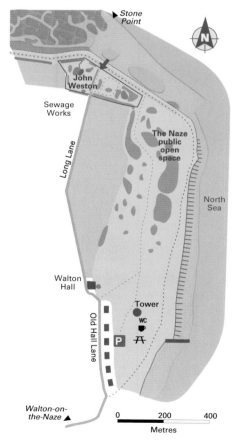

Head northwards along the coast road in Walton with the sea on your right. By the Eastcliffe Hotel take the left fork and follow Hall Lane and Naze Park Road for about a mile. This will bring you to the public car park on the cliff top.

Regular buses run from Clacton and Frinton via Walton station (train link to Colchester) and from the bus station on the front.

Accessible at all times.

April–June for early flowers and bird-song; autumn for migrating birds.

A waymarked nature trail about 2km long runs around the Naze open space, starting from the tower.

blowing, small birds such as firecrest and black redstart may be found sheltering in the bushes on the clifftop.

A mile-long shingle beach stretches forwards from the tip of the Naze, ending at Stone Point. This is an important nesting site for little terns and other shorebirds like oyster-catchers and ringed plovers. (It is cordoned off in the breeding season to prevent disturbance.)

John Weston

9ac/4ha   *OS Ex184*   *TM 266 245*   *SSSI*

ESSEX
Wildlife Trust

This Essex Wildlife Trust reserve lies within the Naze public open space. It consists of blackthorn and bramble thickets, rough grassland and four ponds or 'scrapes', three of them excavated since the reserve was established. It is named after the late John Weston, a leading Essex naturalist who was warden of the reserve until his death in 1984.

Its nesting birds include common and lesser whitethroat, joined recently by cetti's warbler. Water rail are seen and heard regularly. It is an important landfall for migrants, including many rarities, and also attracts a variety of winter visitors.

Notable among its flowering plants and grasses are parsley water-dropwort, slender thistle, pepper saxifrage, fenugreek and bush grass.

A circular path runs around the eastern section and is good for butterflies and other insects in summer.

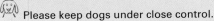

Accessed from the seawall via footpaths running from The Naze car park.

Acts mainly as a sanctuary although organised and casual visits are possible. For more information call Essex Wildlife Trust on 01621 862960.

Please keep dogs under close control.

Eroding cliffs at The Naze
Geoff Gibbs

Weeleyhall Wood

78ac/31ha   **OS Ex184**   *TM 156 212*   **SSSI**

Weeleyhall Wood is one of the finest surviving woods in Tendring, although it suffered severely in the 1987 storm. Standard oaks provide most of the timber but there are about eight acres of sweet chestnut coppice, a similar area of scots and corsican pine plantation, an area of hazel coppice, and alder glades with an important ground flora that includes moschatel. It is owned by Essex Wildlife Trust.

In spring the bluebells, which carpet almost half the wood, yellow archangel and climbing corydalis make a fine display. Several fern species are also to be found.

The wood has good numbers of woodland birds – including nightingales which have increased with the reintroduction of coppicing – and the commoner butterflies.

Reached from the B1441 (Colchester to Clacton). Park in front of Weeley Church. Access to the wood is down a private track just past the pond.

Several bus services to/from Clacton run along the B1441. Or train to Weeley and more than a mile walk each way.

Accessible at all times

May for early flowers and breeding birds.

Please keep dogs on a lead down the track across farmland and under strict control within the wood.

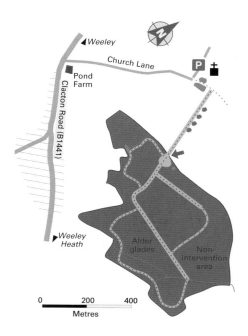

Nightingale: summer visitor
Alan Williams

Maldon itself sits at the base of the Blackwater Estuary, which has a cluster of important marshland sites further east, around the Salcott Channel. To the east stretches the farmland of the Dengie peninsula, fringed by Bradwell Shell Bank and a National Nature Reserve. The Dengie is sandwiched between the Blackwater Estuary and the Crouch Estuary to the south, which again has some important coastal marshland sites, plus a country park at Burnham.

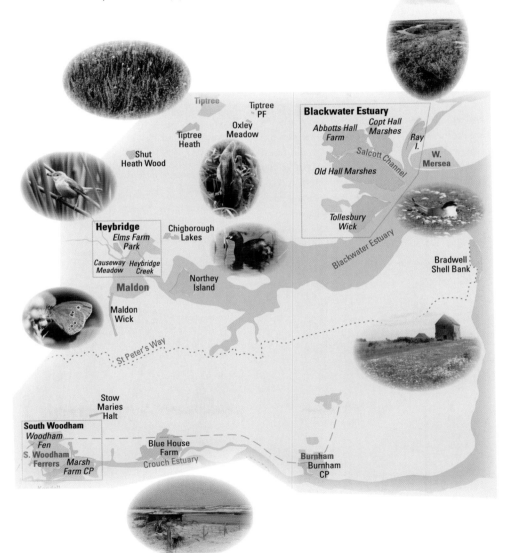

Tiptree

Tiptree PF

Oxley Meadow

Tiptree Heath

Shut Heath Wood

Blackwater Estuary

Abbotts Hall Farm

Copt Hall Marshes

Ray I.

Salcott Channel

W. Mersea

Old Hall Marshes

Tollesbury Wick

Blackwater Estuary

Heybridge
Elms Farm Park

Chigborough Lakes

Causeway Meadow

Heybridge Creek

Northey Island

Maldon

Maldon Wick

Bradwell Shell Bank

St Peter's Way

Stow Maries Halt

South Woodham
Woodham Fen

S. Woodham Ferrers

Marsh Farm CP

Blue House Farm

Crouch Estuary

Burnham

Burnham CP

Abbotts Hall Farm

700ac/280ha   *OS Ex184*   *TL 963 146*   *SSSI (part), SPA*

THE
wildlife
TRUSTS
ESSEX
Wildlife Trust

This coastal farm was bought by Essex Wildlife Trust in 2000 using a legacy from the late Joan Elliot, with support from Trust members, WWF, English Nature, the Environment Agency and the Heritage Lottery Fund. It is a demonstration site for sustainable coastal defence and also a working farm rich in wildlife.

Coastal realignment

The Blackwater estuary is among the largest estuaries in East Anglia. One of the main threats to this important wildlife area is 'coastal squeeze' due to sea-level rise. On the Essex coast sea level is rising by around 6mm per year due to the combined effects of global warming and the settling of the land mass in the south-east. The seawalls surrounding most of the Essex coast today were constructed more than 300 years ago to reclaim land from the sea. 'Coastal squeeze' is the result of the

Seven miles south of Colchester just off the B1026, south of Abberton Reservoir and west of the village of Great Wigborough. From Colchester take the B1026 towards Maldon and turn off left towards Peldon about 3km beyond the causeway across Abberton Reservoir, or follow the B1026 from Maldon and keep straight on where it turns sharp left about 4km beyond Tolleshunt d'Arcy. The entrance is about 1km down on the right.

Open to the public Monday–Friday only, 9am–5pm. Regular weekend walks are organised: call Essex Wildlife Trust on 01621 862960 to book. For up-to-date information check the Trust website at *www.essexwt.org.uk*.

Dogs not permitted on the farm. Dogs restricted to dog walk adjacent to main building

This is a working farm and sometimes paths will be closed for safety reasons.

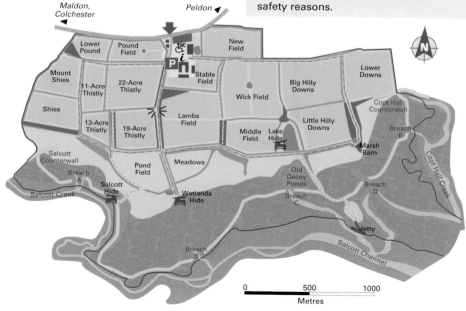

sea pinning the saltmarsh against the seawall and causing erosion. In the recent past 40% of Essex saltmarsh has been lost in this way.

The coastal realignment project at Abbotts Hall Farm was designed to recreate lost habitats by allowing salt water back on to the land reclaimed originally. Two new counter walls were constructed at either end of the site to protect neighbouring land but elsewhere the land rises gently, checking the incoming tide without additional sea defenses. This has allowed the creation of 200 acres of mudflat, saltmarsh and coastal grassland.

The seawall was breached in five places in October 2002 and very quickly saltmarsh plants moved in. Other signs of marine life include shore crabs, jellyfish, lugworms and shrimps, and a number of fish species.

New grassland has been created between the developing saltmarsh and the remaining arable fields, and sheep are now back grazing where in past times the Essex coastal grasslands supported large flocks, an important source of wool and meat.

Farming and wildlife

Over much of Essex, wildlife has been finding it more and more difficult to keep a foothold on the modern arable farm. Farmland birds such as skylark, grey partridge and corn bunting have all experienced massive declines. The Trust is aiming to improve the lot of wildlife on the farm while continuing to grow food economically.

For over 30 years the previous cropping regime was dominated by wheat. Now the Trust is growing a wide range of crops, including wild bird seed mixes. Further diversification into saline crops and other niche markets is planned.

Conditions for wildlife have been improved in other ways by planting and coppicing hedges, leaving uncultivated field margins, and creating beetle banks across the centre of fields to encourage predatory insects.

Already results for wildlife are looking good. The skylark population has increased along with many species of breeding bird, including yellowhammers, whitethroats, wagtails and owls. Large numbers of overwintering finches and thrushes feed on the food-rich field margins and in the hedgerows. Water voles breed on the stream and round the lake.

Visitor facilities

The site has a network of surfaced tracks with signposted nature trails, a large freshwater lake with nesting islands and a kingfisher bank, and several ponds.

Two bird hides give good views over the developing coastal habitats, and across the Salcott Channel to RSPB's Old Hall Marshes reserve opposite. Many waders and wildfowl feed on the marsh. Peregrine falcons and marsh harriers often fly through looking for prey, causing bird flocks to take flight in alarm. A third hide overlooks the maturing freshwater lake where you may see water rail, kingfisher and little egret.

Sea lavender on Abbotts Hall Farm saltmarsh
Chris Gomersall

Blue House Farm

601ac/240ha   OS Ex175-6   TQ 856 971   SSSI (part), SPA

Take the B1012 east from South Woodham Ferrers and after about 3 miles turn right to North Fambridge. Access is via a track on the left off Fambridge Road 400m south of Fambridge station.

An hourly train service runs to Fambridge via Wickford.

Accessible at all times.

Mid-October–March for brent geese and wintering wildfowl; April–June for breeding birds and for hares.

No dogs on the permissive footpath, please. Please keep dogs under strict control elsewhere.

Please take care to close gates behind you as this is a working farm as well as a nature reserve.

i at the reserve or from Essex Wildlife Trust visitor centres. For more information call the warden on 01621 740687.

Blue House Farm was bought by Essex Wildlife Trust in 1998 with support from the Heritage Lottery Fund and many other donors. Most of the farm was originally salt-marsh until seawalls were constructed to capture land from the sea. It was then used as grazing pasture, this practice continuing today. Some of the higher, drier fields were used for crops but have now reverted to grassland.

Its wildlife is internationally important, particularly overwintering birds and also coastal plants and insects. It is a working farm, managed by maintaining high water levels and balancing good livestock farming with good conservation practice.

The **flat fields** between the farmhouse and

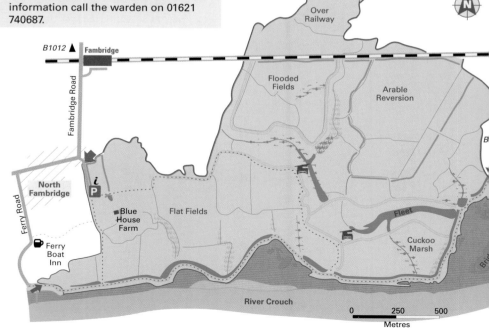

the seawall are used in winter as a feeding ground by brent geese. Often more than 2,000 geese are seen, grazing on the short turf. Throughout the year hares are abundant across the farm but are most easily seen on these fields where cover is scarce. Skylarks also thrive here, particularly in the hay fields where they nest.

The deep water in the **fleets** attracts diving birds including tufted duck and little grebe. Our smallest duck, the teal, and our largest, the shelduck, are both commonly seen here. At high tide wading birds move in from the mudflats beyond the sea wall.

Most of the pasture has never been ploughed and retains the features of the original salt-marsh, such as winding creeks and countless hollows and bumps often topped with the large anthills of the meadow ant. The **creeks and ditches** are important habitats for rare water beetles and other insects like the hairy dragonfly and scarce emerald damselfly. Those with thick vegetation support water voles and may in time again give shelter to otters, known to have lived here until at least 1963.

The **marshy fields** attract wading birds such as redshank, curlew and snipe to feed. Fifty acres near the railway are flooded every winter, attracting overwintering wildfowl and waders and particularly wigeon and teal. As water levels drop in spring, bare mud rich in insects is exposed. Lapwing and redshank chicks eat insects and this has brought breeding lapwing and redshank back on to the farm.

The **former arable** is now grazed and supports breeding yellow wagtails and corn buntings, plus the occasional grey partridge.

The saltmarsh and intertidal mud between seawall and river provide abundant food for wading birds such as oystercatcher and black-tailed godwit. In the river itself you will often see red-breasted merganser and cormorant and occasionally common seal, feeding on the rich marine life of the estuary.

Turf-roofed hide at Blue House Farm
Nick Robson

Bradwell Shell Bank

200ac/80ha   **OS Ex176**   *TM 035 081*   **SSSI, SPA, SAC**

This nature reserve on the Dengie peninsula consists of some 30 acres of shell bank, together with extensive saltmarsh. The shell bank is continuous between Tip Head and Gunner's Creek, but further south consists of a series of small cockle spits, many of which are separated by deep creeks and gullies. The adjoining saltmarsh in some places is several hundred metres wide.

The reserve is run jointly by Essex Wildlife Trust and the Essex Birdwatching Society. The latter also operates Bradwell Bird Observatory, situated in the grounds of Linnett's Cottage on the edge of the reserve.

Ringed plovers and oystercatchers breed on the shell banks, and the saltmarsh supports a wide variety of species including redshank, yellow wagtail, meadow pipit, reed bunting and linnet. In autumn and winter large flocks of up to 20,000 waders roost on the reserve at high tide. Snow bunting, shorelark and lapland bunting are occasional winter visitors.

A wide range of raptors frequent the area, among them hen harrier, merlin, peregrine and short-eared owl in winter; marsh harrier, sparrowhawk and hobby at other seasons.

The more stable parts of the shell banks are rich in flowers, including yellow horned-poppy, narrow-leaved birdsfoot trefoil, grass-leaved orache, sea rocket, sea holly, marram grass and occasional clumps of the locally rare sea kale. A wide range of specialised species can be found on the saltmarsh.

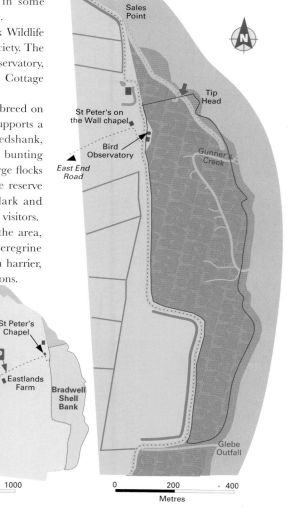

Head for Bradwell-on-Sea (a mile inland!) via Latchingdon or Southminster, following the B1010/B1018/B1021 from Chelmsford or Maldon. Turn right in Bradwell by the church and follow East End Road to its end and park at Eastlands Farm. The reserve is entered via the Saxon chapel of St Peter's on the Wall – a distance of about 800m from there. To reach the reserve, walk northwards along the seawall to Sales Point, then south-wards along the public beach to Tip Head Creek. This can be crossed quite easily at low tide and gives access to the first few hundred yards of the reserve, as far south as Gunners' Creek. *This creek is wide, with deep mud in parts, and no attempt should be made to cross it!*

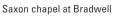 Accessible at all times. If you want to see waders, time your visit to coincide with high tide. At Bradwell this is just before Southend and about 90 minutes before London Bridge.

Access for the disabled can be arranged through the warden: call 01277 354034 or Essex Wildlife Trust on 01621 862960.

In order to protect breeding shore-birds, between April and August inclusive please keep to the seawall overlooking the reserve, or where no wall exists to the edge of the saltmarsh.

The mud and sandflats to the east of the reserve, extending some 3km from the shore, are part of the Dengie National Nature Reserve. These are internationally important for overwintering waders, and notably for grey plover, knot and bar-tailed godwit. Sales Point is a good spot from which to watch waders feeding, ideally when the tide is rising to cover the mudflats. As well as the waders just mentioned, you may see dunlin, redshank, oystercatcher and curlew.

As you continue along the seawall you may also find turnstone, sanderling and ringed plover. Flocks of brent geese could be on the fields, the mud or the sea. The small thicket between the Bird Observatory and Sales Point is used as a refuge by many migrating birds.

The barges sunk just offshore are there to protect the saltmarsh and seawall from erosion.

Saxon chapel at Bradwell
Tony Gunton

Flowers of the sea shore

Sea holly: powder-blue flowers June to September

Sea kale (in seed): white flowers May to August

Sea pea: flowers late May to end July

Yellow horned-poppy: flowers June to September

Jonathan Smith

Sea rocket: flowers June to September

Adrian Knowles

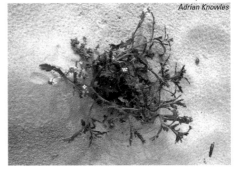

Burnham Country Park

40ac/16ha   **OS Ex176**   **TQ 942 961**

MALDON DISTRICT
COUNCIL

Maldon Council has landscaped and planted up this country park next to the Crouch Estuary at Burnham. It is largely open grassland with a few small copses and a small wetland area with open water, marsh and reedbed.

Skylarks nest in the rough grassland and the wild flowers, shrubs and young trees attract seed-eating birds such as linnets and goldfinches. Gulls and other birds visit from the estuary.

In summer, insect life is good with many butterflies over the grassland and dragonflies and damselflies over the wetland.

Entering Burnham-on-Crouch on the B1021, turn right just past the station into Foundry Lane or (for disabled parking) about 200m further on into Millfields.

Burnham station (from Liverpool Street via Romford and Wickford) is about 15 minutes' walk via Foundry Lane.

Accessible at all times.

Summer for birds and insects.

Easy access trail runs north–south.

Call Maldon Council's parks team on 01621 875823.

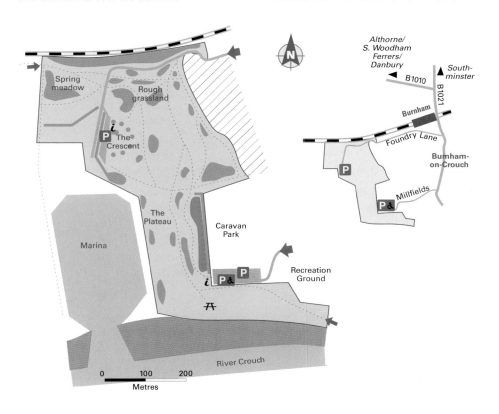

Chigborough Lakes

46ac/18ha   **OS Ex183**   **TL 877 086**

ESSEX
Wildlife Trust

This Essex Wildlife Trust reserve is one of a number of worked-out flooded gravel pits to the north of the Blackwater Estuary. It lies on a thin layer of sands and gravels on top of London Clay, hence the lakes are shallow. The western compartment was left unrestored after extraction resulting in a more varied topography than the restored eastern section. Because of this it has a wide variety of habitats, including willow carr, open water, small ponds, marshy areas, grazed grassland and blackthorn/hawthorn scrub.

Extraction has left some low-nutrient areas with interesting flowers, such as common spotted and bee orchids, heath speedwell, common stork's-bill and wild strawberry. Trees of note include a single wild service tree, a veteran oak pollard and two recently planted black poplar. It has eleven 'varieties' of willow, including almond and purple willow and several recently pollarded cricket-bat willows.

Over 120 species of bird have been recorded, and more than 40 of these have bred at some time, including great crested and little grebes, little egret, grey heron and kingfisher. The reserve has also seen recent increases in cetti's warbler and smew. Other birds of interest include hobby, bullfinch and barn owl.

Grass snakes can be seen and common lizards appreciate the log piles. Most of the common butterflies and dragonflies can be seen in summer. Harvest mice have been recorded also.

About a mile up the B1026 from Heybridge towards Tolleshunt d'Arcy, turn north into Chigborough road. Continue past the fishery entrance and Chigborough Farm buildings, until you see the entrance gate to Chigborough Quarry. The reserve entrance is about 50m beyond this, on the left.

Buses from Colchester to Maldon Leisure Centre run along the B1026.

Accessible at all times.

April–July for birds, flowers and butterflies; October–February for wintering wildfowl.

Please keep dogs on leads when there is livestock on the reserve.

Easy-access path leads north from car park to a seat overlooking Gadwall Lake.

from Essex Wildlife Trust visitor centres.

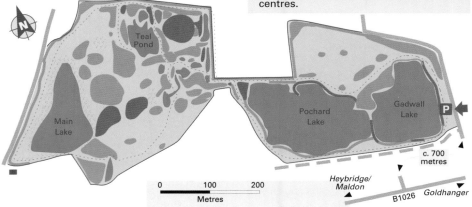

Copt Hall Marshes

400ac/160ha   *OS Ex184*   **TL 981 146**   *SSSI (part), SPA*

This working farm to the north of the Salcott Channel is owned by the National Trust. The Trust encourages its tenants to farm in a wildlife-friendly way, with conservation headlands and well-managed hedgerows.

Wildfowl such as brent geese overwinter on the grazing marsh and waders frequent the saltmarsh beyond the seawall. 'Red hills' on the grazing marsh, produced by the fires used to heat the salt pans, are evidence of salt extraction in the past.

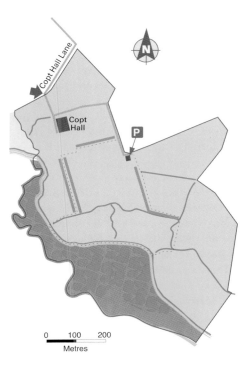

South of the minor road that joins the B1026 to the B1025 via Peldon, south of Abberton reservoir. Turn off on to Copt Hall Lane and follow signs to the car park at Lower Barn.

Accessible at all times.

Winter for wildlfowl.

A waymarked circular route runs across the grazing marsh and along the seawall. To reduce disturbance to birds, visitors are asked to use a shorter route in winter.

Great crested grebe: resident
David Harrison

Little grebe: resident
Alan Williams

Cudmore Grove Country Park

35ac/14ha *OS Ex184* *TM 055 147* *NNR, SSSI, SPA*

Essex County Council

Cudmore Grove country park takes its name from a small grove of elms growing on the cliff top. This was the only woodland on the island, but the original elms have died and even some of the replacement oaks have been lost as the sea has worn away the soft sands and gravels of the cliff, which contains fossils dating back 300 thousand years. It became a country park in 1974 and is managed by Essex County Council's Ranger Service.

With its flower-rich grassland and its views across the Colne estuary towards Brightlingsea and Colne Point, the country park is always worth a visit, but it and the Colne Estuary National Nature Reserve (NNR) alongside are really exceptional for birdlife in winter.

The damp pastures at the northern end are managed for brent geese, and also attract golden plover and snipe in winter. If you take

Bear left to East Mersea after crossing The Strood on to Mersea Island (B1025 from Colchester). The country park is beyond East Mersea village, off Bromans Lane.

Open from 8am until dusk, all the year round.

January/February for waders and wildfowl; autumn and spring migration times for unusual birds; July for salt-marsh colours. Plan your visit for round about high tide, when the birds will be closest – tide tables available from local shops.

Mainly flat with easy walking ground mostly accessible by wheelchair.

The Strood is sometimes covered by spring tides.

Information room open daily. Ranger telephone: 01206 383868.

Wintering waders

Curlew: Britain's largest wader, with a characteristic trilling call; breeds on moors and heaths

Alan Williams

Grey plover: form loose parties away from other waders; breed on Siberian tundra

Alan Williams

the seawall path beyond them you are likely to see birds all around you – waders feeding on the mudflats, songbirds finding cover in the saltmarsh, and sea ducks like goldeneye and red-breasted merganser on the estuary.

Areas of grass are left long throughout the year for small mammals, birds, lizards and insects, while other areas are cut each June as an organic hay crop. On summer days up to 15 types of butterfly can be seen feeding on meadows and hedgerows. The occasional common seal has also been seen visiting the Colne estuary.

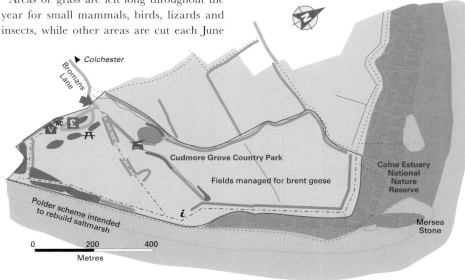

► Colchester

Bromans Lane

WC

Cudmore Grove Country Park

Fields managed for brent geese

Colne Estuary National Nature Reserve

Mersea Stone

Polder scheme intended to rebuild saltmarsh

0   200   400

Metres

Purple sandpiper: frequents rocky shorelines; breeds in Scandinavia

Alan Williams

Dunlin: a small, busy wader, forming large flocks; breeds on upland moors

Alan Williams

Heybridge

Causeway Meadow

15ac/6ha   *OS Ex183*   *TL 849 078*   *LNR*

MALDON DISTRICT
COUNCIL

Amarshy meadow with reedbeds and boardwalks, between the Chelmer estuary and the Chelmer & Blackwater Navigation. Look for breeding birds such as reed warblers from May onwards; later, in summer, look for dragonflies and other flying insects.

Access to Causeway Meadow and Elms Farm Park from Tesco car park via Chelmer & Blackwater Navigation towpath, or join the towpath via seawall footpath. Elms Farm Park also has a small car park on Heybridge Approach (B1018). Heybridge Creek can be reached via a public footpath off The Causeway near the Benbridge Hotel roundabout, or via Hall Road.

Free park-and-ride bus to Tesco store. Buses from Maldon to Witham, Tiptree and Tollesbury run along The Causeway.

Accessible at all times.

Contact Maldon District Council on 01621 854477.

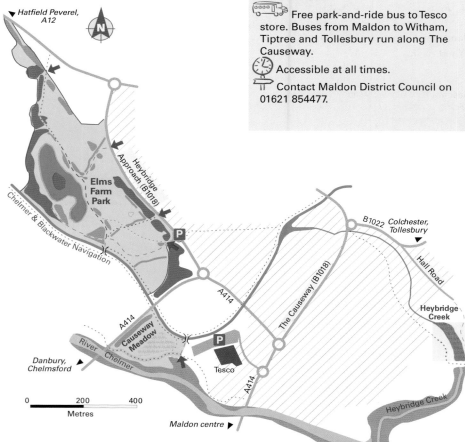

Elms Farm Park

MALDON DISTRICT COUNCIL

35ac/14ha   *OS Ex183*   *TL 847 080*

This country park on the edge of Heybridge was created in the mid-1990s as part of a large housing development. The Chelmer & Blackwater Navigation forms its south-western boundary.

It has open meadows, patches of dense vegetation and scrub, some mature woodland and a large lake with an island. Such variety means that there is usually some interesting wildlife around.

Heybridge Creek

MALDON DISTRICT COUNCIL

2ac/1ha   *OS Ex183*   *TL 859 076*   *LNR*

Heybridge Creek feeds the outflow from the Chelmer & Blackwater Navigation into the River Chelmer, and forms part of the flood relief scheme for the Heybridge area. Where it has been cut off by the seawall a large reedbed has developed. In spring and summer this is home to large numbers of breeding reed and sedge warblers and is used for food and shelter by many other birds.

Reed warbler: summer visitor
David Harrison

Maldon Wick

15ac/6ha   **OS Ex183/176**   **TL 842 057**

ESSEX
Wildlife Trust

This Essex Wildlife Trust nature reserve consists of one-and-a-half miles of the former Maldon–Woodham Ferrers railway line, most of it on embankment. The northern 250m of the embankment has been isolated by the Maldon southern link road. A meadow with a large pond was added to it later.

The reserve has earned a reputation for its butterflies, 28 different species having been recorded since it was established. They include purple, green and white-letter hairstreak, and large numbers of speckled wood and ringlet. Also, 17 species of dragonfly have been recorded in the meadow.

The central trackway is kept open and the Trust has created small clearings on the slopes, felled some trees and coppiced others. As a result flowering plants have increased dramatically. These include primrose, moschatel, sweet violet, field scabious and wild strawberry. It also has spindle and wild service trees.

It has many breeding birds, sometimes including nightingales.

On Limebrook Way (B1018) near the roundabout where it joins the A414 (Chelmsford–Maldon).

Close to the Maldon–Chelmsford bus route along the A414.

Accessible at all times.

May–July for flowers and butterflies.

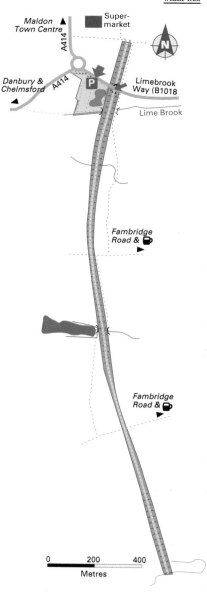

Northey Island

286ac/114ha   **OS Ex183**   **TL 872 058**   **SSSI, SPA**

Northey Island lies near the head of the Blackwater Estuary east of the port of Maldon, and is managed as a nature reserve by the National Trust. It is reached via a causeway (probably Roman in origin) that is covered for several hours every high tide.

Its large areas of undisturbed saltmarsh are important for overwintering wildfowl and the pasture is managed to be the right height when the brent geese arrive in the autumn. The geese commute on and off the island to bathe in Heybridge pits and in the tidal creeks and up to 5,000 can be present from January to March.

In summer, birds such as oystercatcher and shelduck nest.

Like Abbotts Hall Farm, the island has also been used as a testing ground for coastal realignment, by breaching parts of the seawall in order to recreate saltmarsh.

Reached from Mundon Road, Maldon, via South House Farm.

Access by permit only, available from the resident warden at a minimum of 24 hours notice either in writing to *The National Trust, Northey Cottage, Northey Island, Maldon, Essex* or by telephoning 01621 853142. A fee is payable for non-members of the National Trust.

Winter for large numbers of wildfowl; summer for insects and saltmarsh flowers.

No dogs allowed.

Speckled wood: flies April–September
Tony Gunton

Brent goose: winter visitor
Gerald Downey

Old Hall Marshes

1148ac/459ha   **OS Ex184**   *TL 959 124*   **NNR, SSSI, SPA**

Old Hall Marshes is a peninsula of grazing marsh at the head of the Blackwater Estuary, protected by 10km of seawall. Within the walls are large areas of ancient 'unimproved' grassland, reedbeds and open water and it has just about all the designations you can think of, including SSSI, NNR and SPA. It was bought by the RSPB in 1984 and is run as a working farm as well as a nature reserve. Grazing by cattle and sheep is managed to produce swards of different lengths to suit different bird species, and the water regime is managed to try to keep levels consistent summer and winter.

As a result the reserve attracts wildfowl and waders to breed and overwinter in internationally and nationally important numbers. Numbers of wintering brent geese, for example, average more than 4,500 and, of the 60 species of bird that breed there, numbers of garganey, shoveler, pochard, avocet and bearded tit are of national importance.

The reserve also supports scarce plant and insect species and has thriving populations of brown hare and water vole, both of which are in decline nationally.

Access by car is restricted to holders of permits only, obtainable by writing to the warden, 1 Old Hall Lane, Tolleshunt D'Arcy, Maldon, Essex CM9 8TP, but there is a public footpath running right round the reserve on the seawall and this can most easily be reached from Tollesbury. From Tollesbury the full circuit is over 10 miles, but a shortcut can be taken across the centre.

Bus services run to Tollesbury from Maldon, Colchester and Witham.

Accessible at all times via the public footpaths.

Winter for overwintering brent geese and other waterfowl on the fleets and on the estuary; spring and summer for breeding birds.

The sea wall path can be very muddy in winter.

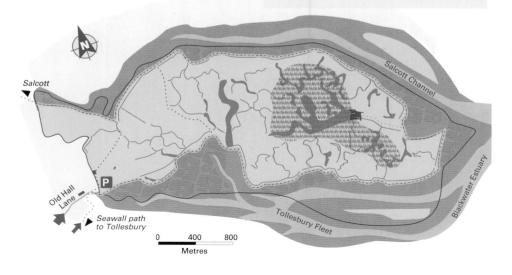

Oxley Meadow

8ac/3ha   **OS Ex184**   **TL 918 149**

ESSEX
Wildlife Trust

Despite its name, this Essex Wildlife Trust reserve consists of *two* flower-rich meadows, the larger one almost completely surrounded by wide luxuriant hedgerows with a number of mature oaks and other trees.

A large colony of green-winged orchids is scattered across the meadows, and adders-tongue fern is perhaps more numerous here than anywhere else in Essex.

The meadows support the commoner grassland butterflies, and the hedgerows provide nesting sites for a variety of birds, notably the lesser whitethroat.

Paternoster
Heath

Tiptree
Parish
Field

Park Lane

Tiptree

Barnhall Road

Mersea

Tolleshunt
Knights

0   50   100

Metres

From the A12 take the B1023 towards Tiptree, continuing through Tiptree village and down Factory Hill to a Y-junction, where you take the left fork (Brook Road, becoming Barnhall Road) towards Mersea. Turn down Park Lane (first turning on left after telephone box) and reserve entrance is second opening on left. Limited parking on the grassed area at the front of the reserve when conditions allow.

Regular Colchester to Maldon buses to Tiptree: the reserve is about 1 mile distant along footpaths.

Accessible at all times.

From late March up to the hay cut in mid-July; the orchids are usually in flower in April/May.

Please keep dogs on leads when there is livestock on the reserve.

Adderstongue fern
Owen Keen

Ray Island

100ac/40ha   OS Ex184   TM 011 154   SSSI, SPA

This large sandy mound rising out of the surrounding saltings is owned by the National Trust and managed by Essex Wildlife Trust. It has a shingly foreshore/beach area on its northern side, with a sizeable fresh-water pond nearby, and extensive areas of rough grassland. On higher ground, there are blackthorn thickets and some spectacular old hawthorns.

The island is grazed by Soay sheep, a primitive rare breed.

The southern edge of the island has some of the finest natural transition areas of salt-marsh–grassland–scrub to be found on the Essex coast. The wide range of saltmarsh plants includes lax-flowered sea lavender, golden samphire and sea rush.

Breeding birds include redshank (in some numbers), oystercatcher and shelduck. Large numbers of wildfowl and waders overwinter – flocks of more than 2,000 brent geese are not unusual. All the common finches can be seen throughout the year, but numbers increase dramatically in winter when large flocks feed on the seed heads of sea aster and other salt-marsh plants. Birds of prey are commonly seen, including long-eared and short-eared owl, hen harrier, merlin and barn owl.

A number of the commoner butterflies are abundant in normal summers and small mammals, particularly voles, are plentiful.

Soay sheep on Ray Island
David Nicholls

Bonners Saltings

63ac/26ha   **OS Ex184**   **TM 011 154**   **SSSI**

This saltmarsh between the Strood cause-way and Ray Island is private property, but the owners have kindly agreed to Trust members having access to study the natural history and to cross to Ray Island. Plant enthusiasts will find a large patch of dittander by the Strood causeway.

To the west of the Strood – the causeway that carries the B1025 from Colchester across to Mersea Island. Footpath access for Trust members only across Bonner's Saltings. General public access using your own boat, leaving Mersea moorings at high tide and heading up Ray Channel.

Regular bus services (half-hourly on weekdays, hourly on Sundays) run between Colchester and West Mersea and will drop off and pick up at Strood Villa.

General public access to the reserve as part of the management agreement with the National Trust.

From late September through to May for birds; July for acres of flowering sea lavender.

Unsuitable for dog walking.

Check the state and times of the tide before crossing Bonner's Saltings as the pathway is often flooded to a depth of several feet – do not attempt to cross in the two hours preceding high water. The pathway is approximately one mile long and visitors have to negotiate a number of single-plank bridges without hand-rails. Care must be taken as these can be very slippery. Wellington boots and weatherproof clothing are essential.

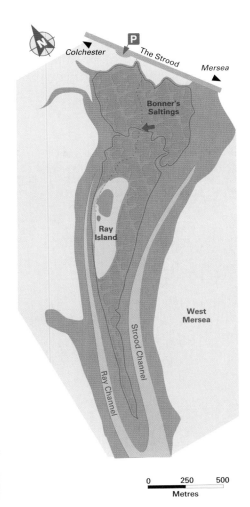

Shut Heath Wood

50ac/20ha   **OS Ex183**   **TL 853 133**

ESSEX
Wildlife Trust

This Essex Wildlife Trust reserve, just below the crest of the Great Totham Ridge, includes 23 acres of ancient woodland forming part of the Chantry Wood complex. The remaining 27 acres are arable land managed by a tenant farmer.

The wood comprises large oak standards with sections of sweet chestnut and hornbeam coppice, and ash, elder and hazel understorey. The eastern edge is wet, with an open glade and thick scrub areas, while the southern edge consists of secondary woodland of silver birch and hawthorn that has colonised the adjacent field edges. The Trust has resumed coppicing and created some open areas to rejuvenate the wood.

In spring, bugle, cuckoo flower, wood sorrel, bluebells, wood anemone, primrose and dog violet flower, followed in summer by yellow pimpernel, red bartsia, greater birdsfoot trefoil and wood sage.

Dragonflies and damselflies may be seen in the glade and, in July, glow-worms. Large amounts of standing dead wood in the site make it excellent for invertebrates, including many wood ants.

Recently coppiced area at Shut Heath Wood
Susie Torino

Leave the B1022 at Roundbush Corner, Great Totham, taking Mountains Road. After about 1200m take the first turning on the right (Tiptree Road), and the entrance is about 400m down on the left with double gates at the entrance. Take care when leaving as visibility is restricted.

Bus to Great Totham from Maldon or Colchester and get off at Great Totham post office. The reserve is 800m north.

Accessible at all times.

March and April for spring flowers.

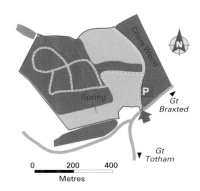

South Woodham Ferrers

On the Crouch Estuary, right next to South Woodham Ferrers new town, is a large area of coastal marshland that has been set aside as Marsh Farm Country Park. A mile or so north of the country park via a walk along the seawall is Woodham Fen, an Essex Wildlife Trust nature reserve. Part of the country park also is managed as a nature reserve.

The area has something to suit most tastes – a long-established grazing marsh that is rich in wildlife; farm animals to interest children; and some relics of the eventful history of the Essex coast. Finally, Woodham Fen is one of the few places where you can still see the natural transition from saltmarsh to dry grassland. Elsewhere, seawalls force an abrupt change from one to the other.

Marsh Farm Country Park

350ac/140ha   **OS Ex175**   **TQ 810 961**   **SSSI, SPA**   Essex County Council

This country park is centred on Marsh Farm, which is operated by Essex County Council on a semi-commercial basis. Both the farm itself, which raises cattle, sheep and other animals, and the surrounding grazing marsh are open to the public, with a small charge for entry to the farm. A number of themed walks have been laid out.

The grazing marsh has a long history going back to when the first seawall was built in the 18th century. The land was purchased originally to build the new town, but it was decided that land below the 5-metre contour was not suitable for building because of the risk of flooding, and for that reason it became a country park. Part of the seawall surrounding Marsh Farm was in fact breached during

the 'Great Flood' of 1953 and the remains are still visible from the new wall built further back.

At the eastern end of the park is a nature reserve consisting of rough grassland, salt-marsh and a scrape – a shallow water lagoon. Hares are often about in the grassland and reed buntings nest along the dykes. The scrape attracts many wildfowl in winter and at migration periods, and especially wigeon and teal.

Shelduck, dunlin and redshank feed in Clementsgreen Creek when the mud is exposed. In winter brent geese graze the fields west of the entrance and you may see flocks of snow buntings along the seawall. The wetland area extending north is good for dragonflies in summer.

South Woodham Woodham Fen

20ac/8ha   **OS Ex175/6**   **TQ 798 975**   **SSSI, SPA**

This Essex Wildlife Trust reserve lies between and near the tidal limits of two small creeks running south into the River Crouch. It was common land given in the 12th century by the Lords of the Manor to the poor of the community to graze animals. The southern part is saltmarsh and the northern rough grassland with a transitional zone between the two – of special interest because this natural transition is now very unusual in Essex. It has a wide range of saltmarsh plants, including sea wormwood, and the grassland is full of wild flowers, including unusual ones such as slender birdsfoot trefoil, grass vetchling, wild carrot and crested hair-grass.

It also attracts many unusual birds, such as reed bunting, yellow wagtail and meadow pipit, and a variety of small waders occur on passage. Teal, common and jack snipe, and rock pipit are to be found in winter, when kingfishers hunt along the creeks for eels. Barn owls and other birds of prey

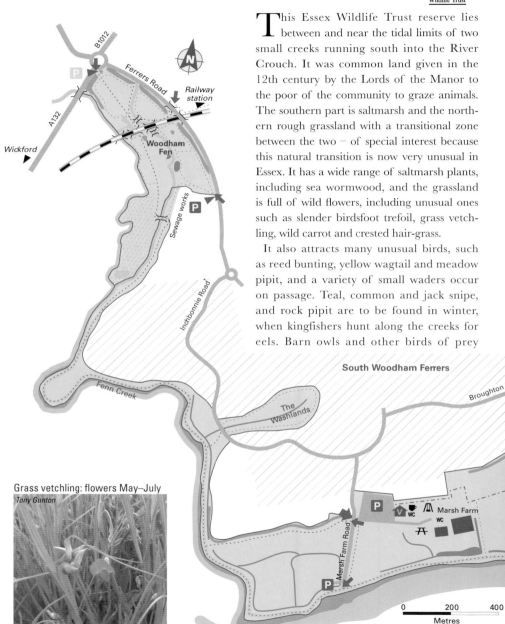

Grass vetchling: flowers May–July

Tony Gunton

hunt over the grassland for the many field voles.

Bush-crickets and saltmarsh moths are notable among the insects. Essex skipper and a number of the other common butterflies are abundant, as are common lizards and slow worms.

The reserve lies within a much larger area of common land owned by South Woodham Ferrers Town Council. This area is managed on advice from the Trust and in all includes about 85 acres of grassland, scrub, ditches and ponds.

Woodham Fen can be entered from the A132 (Basildon/Wickford–Woodham) at the Shaw Farm roundabout, 4½ miles from Wickford, where it meets the B1012. To reach Marsh Farm turn right down Ferrers Road and follow Inchbonnie Road round to Marsh Farm Road.

The railway station at South Woodham Ferrers is about five minutes' walk from Woodham Fen via a footpath, and two miles from Marsh Farm via the creekside path. Bus services run to and from Chelmsford, Wickford and Basildon.

Accessible at all times via footpaths. Marsh Farm visitor centre open daily March–October, otherwise weekends only; 10am–5.30pm weekends, bank holidays and in summer, otherwise 10am–4.30pm. Accessible at all times . Visitor centre car park open 9am–6pm; riverside car park 8am–dusk.

Midsummer onwards for wild flowers and butterflies; migration periods and winter for birds.

Paths can be very muddy in winter.

Woodham Fen ℹ️ available from Woodham Town Council office in Reeves Way or Town Information Office in Baron Road Parade.

Marsh Farm ℹ️ Website www.marsh-farmcountrypark.co.uk. Information line 01245 324191, otherwise 01245 321552.

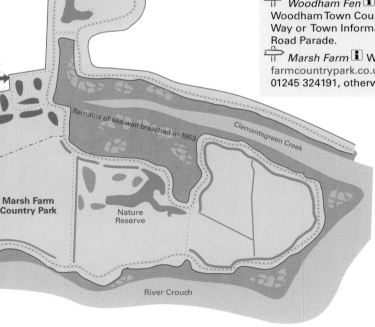

Remains of sea wall breached in 1953

Clementsgreen Creek

Marsh Farm Country Park

Nature Reserve

River Crouch

Stow Maries Halt

5.5ac/2ha   *OS Ex175*   *TQ 835 991*

ESSEX
Wildlife Trust

This Essex Wildlife Trust nature reserve consists of the former Stow Maries Halt on the disused Maldon to South Woodham Ferrers railway line, along with an adjoining four-acre meadow acquired later.

The remains of the platform are still visible by the reserve entrance and four species of fern – wall-rue, maidenhair spleenwort, black spleenwort and hartstongue – grow in the mortar of the bridge here. This part of the reserve grades from cutting to shallow embankment and consists largely of hawthorn and blackthorn scrub with occasional privet and a scattering of young oak and ash.

Scrub has been cleared from the lower part and a pond has been excavated in marshy ground in the north-west corner. In late spring there are many common spotted orchids and a number of adderstongue ferns, followed in summer by common fleabane (in profusion), wild carrot and St John's worts.

The reserve has a good selection of butterflies, including purple and white-letter hairstreaks, and dragonflies. Glow-worms reliably put on a show in July every year, scattered throughout the reserve.

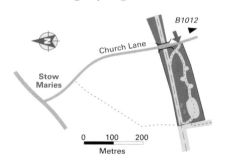

B1012
Church Lane
Stow
Maries

0   100   200
Metres

Reached via Church Lane, which connects the lower Burnham road between South Woodham Ferrers and North Fambridge with the road through Stow Maries village. Cars can be parked on the wide grass verge of the bridge over the dismantled railway.

Accessible at all times.

Late spring for orchids; summer for wild flowers and insects (glow-worms in July).

Please keep your dog on a lead when sheep are grazing the reserve.

Glow-worm (male): active in July

Tiptree Heath

60ac/24ha   **OS Ex184**   **TL 883 147**   **SSSI**

ESSEX
Wildlife Trust

Tiptree Heath is a small fragment of a huge heathland that used to stretch from Maldon to Messing, covering thousands of acres. It is the finest and largest area of heath in Essex, and the only place where you will find all three heather species growing together.

The heath had been nibbled away by enclosure for centuries before it received what seemed like a death blow during World War II, when the common land laws were suspended and it was ploughed up for agriculture. But it produced only poor crops, and in 1955 was sown with grass seed and left to look after itself. The result was that some of it turned into light woodland and scrub, but on large areas the heathland plants reappeared.

In 1973 the present heath was designated a Site of Special Scientific Interest (SSSI). It is privately owned, and managed by Essex Wildlife Trust with the support of the Friends of Tiptree Heath.

Ling heather, which is tall and vigorous enough to survive in gorse, covers large areas, and there are areas of bell heather and a small amount of cross-leaved heath that prefers the wetter parts. In late summer, harebells can be seen with their dainty blue bell-shaped flowers. The heath also has a number of other unusual wild plants, including heath dog-violet, allseed and chaffweed.

Its birdlife includes many willow warblers, nightingales, turtle doves and the occasional woodcock.

Heathland is very difficult to recreate once scrub and trees have taken over. Radical measures have had to be taken to restore Tiptree Heath, including bulldozing down to the mineral soil. Routinely, areas are flailed on rotation, so you can see ling heather at all stages of growth. These destructive conservation methods are still not enough to keep back the continually invading scrub and it is planned to graze a few cattle inside fenced areas during summer months as a more sustainable tool.

The heath straddles the B1022 (Colchester–Maldon) 800m on the Maldon side of Tiptree.

A regular bus service between Maldon and Colchester runs along the B1022 past the heath.

Accessible at all times.

April to see acres of gorse in flower; July–September for late flowers, including the heather, and grassland butterflies.

Call the Community Warden on 07842 110051.

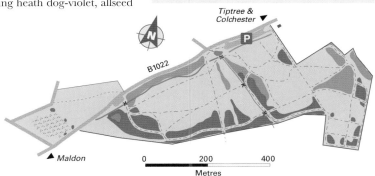

Heathland plants

All three kinds of heather together on Tiptree Heath

Fred Boot

Gorse: grows up to 2m. tall; flowers all year round

Laurie Forsyth

Tormentil: a creeping plant; flowers July–October

Tony Gunton

Bell heather: dry heath; flowers July–September

Tony Gunton

Cross-leaved heath: wet heath; flowers July–September

Tony Gunton

Tiptree Parish Field

Tiptree Parish Council

6ac/2.4ha   **OS Ex 184**   **TL 913 159**   *LNR*

Tiptree Parish Field is an area of wet grassland that has probably never been ploughed. It is rich in flowers including a number of heathland species. A stream runs across the bottom (southern) edge of the field, where a pond has been dug out attached to the stream.

About 500m down Park Lane, an unmade road leaving Newbridge Road between a factory and a house opposite the end of Grove Road, about 1km from the junction with the B1023 (Kelvedon–Tolleshunt). Newbridge Road leaves the B1023 opposite the jam factory.

Accessible at all times.

Call the warden on 01621 815016.

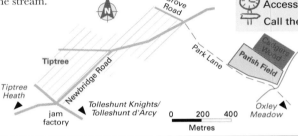

Tollesbury Wick

599ac/240ha   **OS Ex176**   **TL 970 104**   *SSSI, SPA*

This is a rare example of an Essex fresh water grazing marsh, worked for decades by traditional methods sympathetic to wildlife. Owned by Essex Wildlife Trust, it is grazed by the Trust's own rare breed sheep and cattle. The main pillars of management are water level control and getting the right level of grazing to create good conditions for wildlife.

Wildlife is abundant in its 600 acres of rough pasture, borrowdykes, seawalls, wet flushes, pools and saltmarsh. Large areas of rough pasture suit small mammals such as field vole and pygmy shrew. In winter, they in turn attract hunting hen harriers and short-eared owls.

Dry grassland on the slopes of the seawalls supports a wide variety of insects, including butterflies, bush crickets and grasshoppers. In spring spiny rest-harrow, grass vetchling, slender hare's-ear and many other wild flowers can be found in ungrazed areas.

Borrowdykes trace the inland edge of the sinuous seawall for its entire length. Common reed, sea clubrush and fennel pondweed are typical plants of these brackish areas where reed warbler and reed bunting nest in spring, and heron and little grebe search for food. Wet flushes, dykes and small pools in the pasture support aquatic plants such as water crowfoot, and breeding populations of dragonflies and other aquatic species.

Golden plover, lapwing, brent geese and wigeon feed or roost on the winter-wet grassland.

Outside the seawall, creeks, saltmarsh and exposed mud support typical communities of invertebrates, coastal birds and saltmarsh flowers. The shingle spits have yellow horned-poppy, and also a small breeding colony of little terns.

Little tern: summer visitor

Follow the B1023 to Tollesbury via Tiptree, leaving the A12 at Kelvedon, then follow Woodrolfe Road towards the marina and car park at Woodrolfe Green.

Bus services run to Tollesbury from Maldon, Colchester and Witham.

Accessible at all times along the footpath on top of the seawall.

Suitable for motorised wheelchair access up to Blockhouse Bay. Remaining stiles are to be replaced in 2008/9.

May for birdsong; July for saltmarsh colours and for insects; winter for wildfowl and waders.

Sheep ticks can be a problem in April–June: keep out of the long grass or wear light-coloured (so the ticks can easily be seen) long trousers for protection.

from Essex Wildlife Trust visitor centres. For more information, call the warden on 01621 868628.

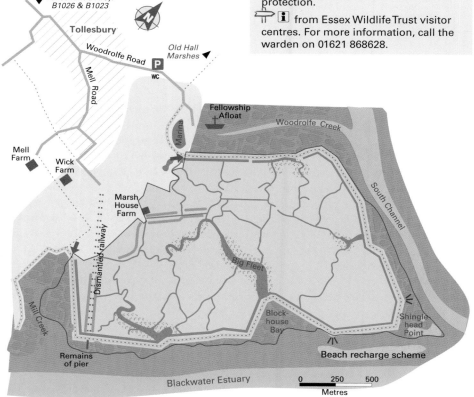

can be found many wild flowers, including unusual plants such as heath milkwort and goldenrod.

Poors Piece sits in the angle to the west of Little Baddow Heath. It contains many oak pollards, suggesting that it was once used as wood pasture. In its southern corner is a marsh full of wetland plants, and notably hemp agrimony, hop sedge and lady fern.

The southernmost tip is Scrubs Wood, consisting mainly of hornbeam and chestnut coppice with oak standards, plus some wild service trees. It is fairly flat except for the gently sloping bank on its southern boundary which has a fine display of wood anemones. Other flowering plants include tormentil and broad-leaved helleborine.

Spring Wood, added most recently, is nine acres of secondary woodland towards the south-west corner.

Dormice, once common but now much reduced in numbers, are found in many parts of the reserve. The birdlife includes nuthatch, all three species of woodpecker, migrant warblers and, intermittently, nightingale. There are good numbers of butterflies including brimstone, ringlet and small copper.

Lily of the valley is a special feature of Danbury Ridge, and other unusual wild flowers here include yellow archangel, greater butterfly orchid and sanicle.

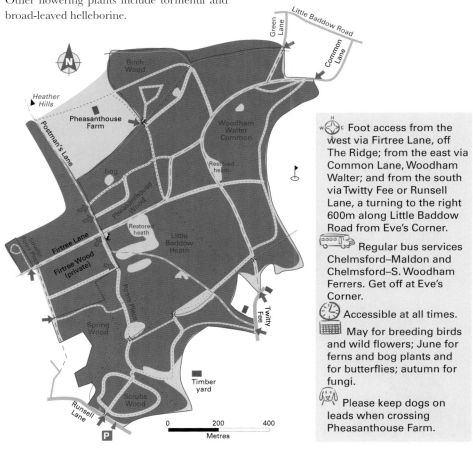

Foot access from the west via Firtree Lane, off The Ridge; from the east via Common Lane, Woodham Walter; and from the south via Twitty Fee or Runsell Lane, a turning to the right 600m along Little Baddow Road from Eve's Corner.

Regular bus services Chelmsford–Maldon and Chelmsford–S. Woodham Ferrers. Get off at Eve's Corner.

Accessible at all times.

May for breeding birds and wild flowers; June for ferns and bog plants and for butterflies; autumn for fungi.

Please keep dogs on leads when crossing Pheasanthouse Farm.

Danbury Country Park

41ac/16ha   **OS Ex183**   **TL 771 048**

Essex County Council

What is now Danbury Country Park was once a deer park belonging to the estate of Danbury Manor, dating back to the Norman conquest of 1066. It was re-landscaped in Elizabethan times, and some massive oaks in the park today are believed to date from then, along with exotics such as cedars and redwoods and a fine collection of rhododendrons and azaleas.

The eastern part of the park is dense woodland, extending also along the southern boundary. This is dominated by hornbeam and oak, including the massive ancient trees mentioned above, which provide good accommodation for owls and bats. Seven species have been recorded, including daubenton's bats which can be seen feeding low over the lakes on warm summer evenings.

There are three ornamental lakes, excavated around 1290, one of them used for angling. North of them, next to Danbury Palace, is an ornamental garden bounded by yew hedges. A wildflower meadow to the west is full of St John's wort, field scabious and wild carrot, and doubles as a mini-arboretum.

North of the park is a large meadow. Most of this is close-mown grassland but sections are left wild to naturalise.

The mix of woodland, open grassland and ornamental garden attracts a good selection of birds, with many ducks and other water birds on the lakes.

Entrances on Woodhill road (the Sandon road) west of Danbury Common.

Accessible at all times via public footpath. Car parks open 8am to dusk.

Spring and summer for birds; warm summer evenings for bats.

Easy and moderate trails, toilets and picnic benches designed for wheelchair users. Battery operated buggies phone first (01245 222350) to ensure gates are opened.

Guided walks available on request. School groups welcome by arrangement. Call the Rangers on 01245 222350.

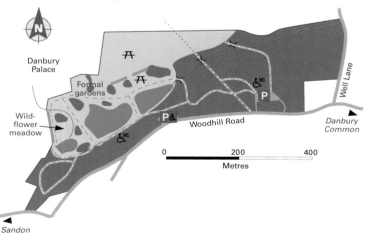

Meadow flowers

Red clover: flowers June–October

Birdsfoot trefoil: flowers May–September

Devilsbit scabious: flowers July–October

Wild carrot: flowers June–August

Greater knapweed: flowers June–August

Common fleabane: flowers July–September

Danbury Heather Hills

16ac/6ha   **OS Ex183**   **TL 780 077**

ESSEX
Wildlife Trust

This reserve, licensed to Essex Wildlife Trust by Little Baddow Council, is divided in two by a very steep stream valley, on either side of which are slopes once covered in heather. The heather had become overgrown and retreated to the summit and edges, but the Trust is clearing overgrown areas, including parts of the stream valley, to restore it.

Its many native trees and shrubs include a row of elms and stands of mature beech, scots pine and european larch. Flowers include moschatel, climbing corydalis and heath bedstraw. Several species of fern grow along the stream along with a variety of wetland plants.

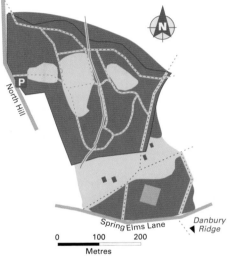

0   100   200
Metres

On the east side of North Hill, Little Baddow. The main entrance is off North Hill, using a trackway known as York Street. Parking at St Andrews Rooms on North Hill.

Regular bus services Chelmsford–Maldon or Chelmsford–S. Woodham Ferrers, getting off at Eve's Corner, or bus to Little Baddow.

Accessible at all times

Spring for early flowers; August for heather.

Take great care when descending the steep scarp to the valley floor.

Lingwood Common

57ac/23ha   **OS Ex183**   **TL 780 858**   **SSSI**

Lingwood Common is another former heath that has 'tumbled down' to woodland. Like Danbury Common it is under the care of the National Trust, and the Trust has opened up several clearings along the bridleway that runs from one end to the other, and some of the heathland plants have returned. The woodland is mainly oak with birches to the west, and aspen and willow down the stream valleys.

Just stroll round it, or use it as a link between Danbury Common to the south and Blake's Wood and Danbury Ridge further north.

From Eve's Corner walk west along Main Road (A414) for 200m, and turn down a steep footpath on the right just before the road turns sharp left. The footpath leads through farmland and woodland on to the common.

Buses to Eve's Corner.

Accessible at all times.

High summer

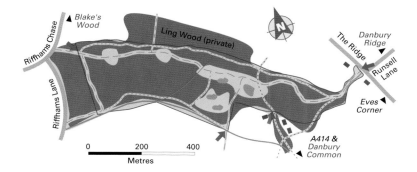

Waterhall Meadows

5.7ac/2ha   *OS Ex183*   *TL 759 072*

ESSEX
Wildlife Trust

A ncient unimproved flood meadows on the west bank of Sandon Brook, with a small spinney and an area of blackthorn thickets. Formerly flooded regularly, they rarely flood today.

Cowslip and meadow saxifrage flower in the meadows in spring, lady's bedstraw is conspicuous in mid-summer, and devilsbit scabious and pepper saxifrage appear later. At the far corner of the meadow is a small pond in which grow amphibious bistort, great water dock and fine-leaved water dropwort. Goldilocks buttercup flowers nearby in spring

and a little further on hemp agrimony and spindle grow together by the brookside.

Among the 84 bird species recorded are eight species of warbler, at least six of which nest regularly. The kingfisher is a regular visitor and has bred in the reserve.

The reserve is rich in insect life. Its dragon-flies and damselflies are particularly notable: 17 species have been recorded including the unusual white-legged damselfly, present in large numbers.

In Little Baddow. Turn off the A414 into Hammonds Road at the roundabout signposted Boreham, and after 1 mile turn right into Hurrells Lane. Entrance is by a stile on the right before a ford through Sandon Brook. There is limited parking by the entrance and across the ford on the left.

Accessible at all times

Spring and summer for flowers; summer for dragonflies along the brook.

Please keep dogs on a lead when there is livestock on the reserve.

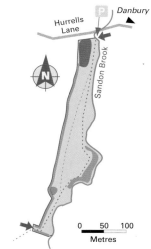

Galleywood Common

60ac/24ha   **OS Ex183**   *TL 704 025*   **LNR**

This fine piece of common land two miles south of Chelmsford is a typical common in its irregular shape, including several enclaves containing buildings, and in the many pits and depressions caused, no doubt, by commoners digging out gravel in the past.

It packs a great variety of habitats into a relatively small space. These include lowland heath with ponds, mire, marsh, grassland, bracken-covered areas and woodland. Rare or uncommon plants include star sedge, lesser skullcap and heath spotted orchid.

Leave the A12 at its junction with the B1007 and turn north towards Galleywood and Chelmsford.

Buses from Chelmsford to Basildon, Billericay and Wickford run down the B1007 past the common.

Accessible at all times.

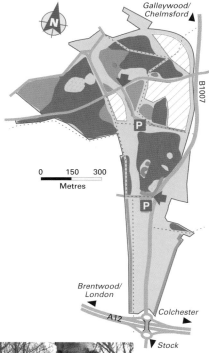

Galleywood Common

Nick Robinson

Hanningfield Reservoir

100ac/40ha   OS Ex175   TQ 725 971   SSSI

ESSEX
Wildlife Trust

This mixture of ancient and secondary woodland at the south-eastern end of Hanningfield Reservoir has been managed by Essex Wildlife Trust since 1992, on lease from Essex & Suffolk Water. The reservoir itself is a Site of Special Scientific Interest (SSSI) for its important populations of wildfowl, and is among the top places in Essex to watch birds.

The spectacle of thousands of swifts, swallows and martins feeding over the water during peak fly hatches is one of the delights for the summer visitor, although most people will probably associate the reservoir with large numbers of waterfowl. Gadwall, tufted duck and pochard are three of the important breeding species and year-round coot numbers are nationally important.

Some 30 acres of the woodland, Well Wood and Hawk's Wood, are ancient in origin. Ditch and bank boundaries dating back centuries mark the extent of the old coppice and some of the original hornbeam trees survive. There is a great diversity of wildlife, with many species indicative of ancient woodland. The show of spring flowers, in particular bluebells, yellow archangel and stitchworts, is not to be missed. In summer, many dragonflies and damselflies can be seen around the ponds.

From the visitor centre waymarked trails lead through the woodland to four birdwatching hides. Much of the reservoir can be scanned from the hides, with especially good views over an island that is popular with wildfowl and a raft provided for terns to nest.

Coot: resident
Tony Gunton

Gadwall (male): winter visitor
Alan Williams

Pochard (male): resident
Alan Williams

Turn off the B1007 (Billericay–Chelmsford) on to Downham Road and turn left on to Hawkswood Road. The Visitor Centre entrance is just beyond the causeway, opposite Crowsheath Lane.

Wickford–Chelmsford bus to Downham village and walk 800m down Crowsheath Lane.

Visitor Centre open daily 9am–5pm except Christmas Day and Boxing Day, serving refreshments and offering a wide range of optical equipment and gifts.

April–July for breeding birds in woodland and on water and for wild flowers; winter and migration periods for wildfowl.

Disabled parking and toilets at the centre; disabled pathway runs from there to a bird hide equipped for disabled users.

Sorry, no dogs except guide dogs allowed on site.

For information about events and activities call the Centre on 01268 711001.

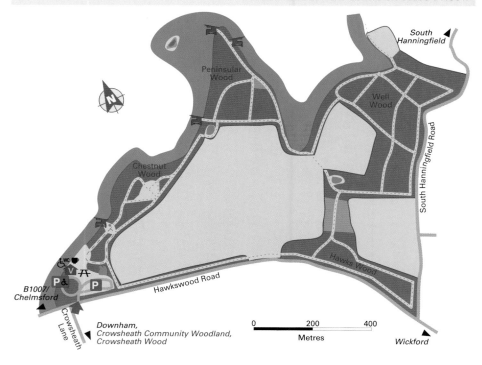

Hutton Country Park

100ac/40ha   *OS Ex175*   *TQ 633 959*   *LNR*

*Brentwood
Borough
Council*

This area of former grazing land opposite the Hutton industrial estate in Brentwood was acquired by Brentwood Council in 1997 to form a new country park. It is mainly open grassland with some thick hedges and scattered patches of woodland and scrub. It has several ponds and some marshy areas with tall aquatic vegetation. It is bisected by a railway line and the northern section runs up to the River Wid.

It is a good place for both birds and insects. Kingfishers, barn owls and green woodpeckers can be seen, and in summer a good selection of dragonflies and butterflies.

The woodland in the south-eastern corner is ancient and carpeted with bluebells in spring. Part of this is private and access is by permission of the owner.

Entrance on Wash Road opposite the Hutton industrial estate. Enter Wash Road from the south off the A129 Brentwood – Billericay, or from the north via Lower Road which turns off the B1002 just north of the A12/A1023 junction. Also accessible from Goodwood Avenue and Sunray Avenue on the adjoining estate.

Buses from the centre of Brentwood run along Wash Road up to the industrial estate.

Accessible at all times.

Call Brentwood Countryside Management Service on 01277 312649 or 01277 312651.

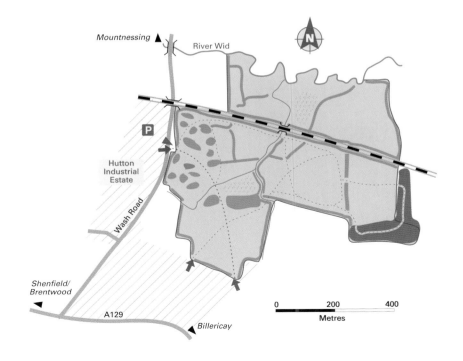

Hylands Park

578ac/234ha **OS Ex183** **TL 683 043**

Many people will associate Hylands Park with major events such as the annual V-Festival, but in fact it is an historic park offering a great deal for anyone interested in wildlife. Landscaped parkland, designed by Humphry Repton in the 18th century, surrounds Hylands House and its formal garden. Later the estate was extended from its original 213 acres to nearly 600 today. It was acquired by Chelmsford Council in 1966 for what today seems the trifling sum of £150,000.

As you would expect of a long-established wood-pasture, it has some fine ancient trees, and also some patches of ancient wood-land. The largest of these, South Wood, is former coppice rich in flowers, including large numbers of early purple orchids. Add to this some flower-rich grassland, a number of ponds – with a thriving population of great crested newts – and a stretch of the River Wid. A herd of fallow deer graze within the park but are not enclosed within it.

A circular walk around the fringes takes you through the best wildlife habitats and there is also a network of surfaced paths.

Additional attractions include Hylands House with its formal garden, an arboretum and the Stables Centre, which has a café and gift shop.

Chelmsford

Harlow

A414

River Wid

Serpentine Lake

London Road (A414)

P &

WC

Arboretum

WC
Formal garden
P
WC
Stables Centre

Hylands House

South Wood

A12/Brentwood

0   250   500
Metres

Access from the A414 about a mile west of the St Mary's Church roundabout, at the southern end of Chelmsford's inner ring road.

Brentwood—Chelmsford bus 351: from Chelmsford nearest bus stop is next to the St Mary's Church roundabout; from Brentwood on London Road direct-ly outside the entrance gates. There is a signed cycle route from Writtle village.

Entrance gates open at 7.30am and close at dusk. Stables Centre open daily and Hylands House open Sunday and Monday, both excluding Christmas Day and Boxing Day. Sometimes access may be restricted because of events: call Chelmsford Council on 01245 605500 for this or other information.

Worth a visit at any time of the year, but especially late April to May for early purple orchids in South Wood.

Laindon Common

30ac/12ha   **OS Ex175**   **TQ 670 927**

Asmall common just south of Billericay, set aside originally as grazing land. Now that grazing has ceased it has largely been colonised by trees, mainly oak and birch. As is typical of commons it is irregular in shape and criss-crossed by footpaths.

It is managed now by the Laindon Common Conservators, supported by Basildon Council.

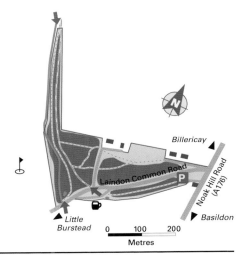

South of Billericay on the A176 to Basildon, just beyond its junction with the B1007.

Regular bus services along the A176.

Accessible at all times.

Merrymeades Country Park

84ac/34ha   **OS Ex175**   **TQ 600 948**

Brentwood Borough Council

Acountry park close to the centre of Brentwood, formerly part of the grounds of Anglia Polytechnic University. It is mainly grassland, cut twice a year, with patches of scrub, a small area of woodland, a pond and a stream. Cuckoo flower, heath bedstraw, pignut and devilsbit scabious grow in the meadows, which support good numbers of grassland butterflies in summer. The mature hedgerows have some large oaks, with occasional hornbeam, field maple and hawthorn, and provide shelter and nest sites for many birds.

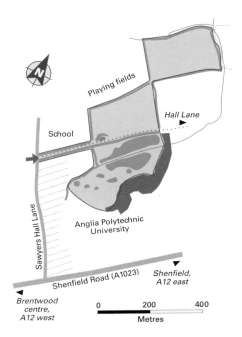

Access via a public footpath leaving Sawyers Hall Lane or from the same footpath off Hall Lane. Sawyers Hall Lane leaves Shenfield Road east of Wilson's Corner in the centre of Brentwood.

Frequent buses along Shenfield Road.

Accessible at all times.

Mid-Chelmer valley

The Chelmer valley north of Chelmsford has two Essex Wildlife Trust nature reserves within easy walking distance of one another.

Little Waltham Meadows

22ac/9ha **OS Ex183** **TL 713 119**

ESSEX
Wildlife Trust

A chain of old flood and dry meadows on the east bank of the River Chelmer south of Little Waltham, including a patch of alder carr woodland. It was acquired by Essex Wildlife Trust in 1996 with the help of a local appeal and a grant from the Heritage Lottery Fund.

A range of grassland plants can be found in the meadows, including meadow saxifrage, bee orchid and yellow oat-grass. The interconnecting network of old hedgerows contain many ancient pollard or coppice stools of elm, common and midland hawthorn, hazel, willow, alder and oak.

Tawny owl, sparrowhawk and kestrel all use the hedgerows and wood or hunt over the meadows. Kestrels regularly nest both here and in Newland Grove downstream.

The meandering River Chelmer has a good range of plants, including water lilies, brooklime and flag iris, and supports water voles. Emperor dragonfly, common darter, ruddy darter and black-tailed skimmer occur in the

400m west of the A130 Essex Regiment Way, just south of Little Waltham. Access is via Back Lane, Little Waltham, parking on the wide verge at the end of the bridleway. The reserve can also by reached from Broomfield from the other end of that bridleway to Croxton's Mill.

 Bus services from Chelmsford run to Little Waltham via Broomfield to the west and via Essex Regiment Way to the east.

Accessible at all times.

Please keep dogs on a lead when there is livestock on the reserve.

summer. Kingfishers and, on warm summer evenings, bats hunt for food along the river.

The alder spinney provides a fine show of marsh marigolds in spring, followed by yellow iris, fool's watercress and flote grass in summer.

Kestrel: resident
Alan Williams

Kingfisher: resident
Gerald Downey

Newland Grove

8ac/3ha   **OS Ex183**   **TL 716 108**

Newland Grove consists of rough grassland alongside the River Chelmer, with thorn thickets and a small wood.

Such a mixture of habitats makes for a variety of plants – over 230 species have been recorded. Cowslips and hairy violet are among the spring flowers, and in midsummer the area sloping down to the river in particular is a riot of colour, with common St John's wort, knapweed, musk mallow and many other species. Twayblade, wood spurge and pale wood violet can be found in the wood.

The reserve is also rich in butterflies – 23 species have been recorded.

Among the birds, good numbers of warblers of several species nest in the thickets and wood, while mallard, kingfisher and sedge warbler are often seen by the river.

Adjoins the A130 north of Chelmsford about 1,200m from the North Springfield housing estate. Entry is from the west side of a roundabout on the A130 east of Broomfield, opposite the turning to the Channels Golf Club and Windsurfing Centre. Parking for 2–3 cars at the entrance.

Accessible at all times

Midsummer for wild flowers and butterflies.

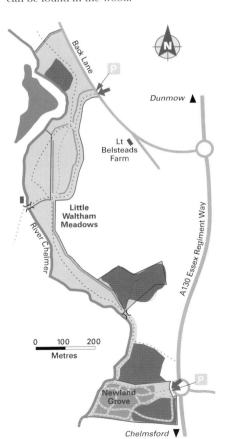

River Chelmer
Janet Spencer

Mill Meadows

90ac/36ha　　**OS Ex175**　　**TQ 678 943**　　**SSSI (part), LNR**

This large area of old meadows not far from the centre of Billericay was acquired by Basildon Council in 1991 and is now a Local Nature Reserve. The meadows lie in rolling countryside cut by streams and ditches with occasional marshy areas. Scrub and young woodland has encroached in places but grazing by cattle is keeping much of the area open.

Stoats and foxes and many birds frequent the meadows, but it is the plant life that makes them special. There is a succession of colour from bluebells and cuckoo flower in spring, then common spotted orchids and betony, through to devilsbit scabious in late summer. It also has some plants that are scarce locally among them harebell, ragged robin and sneezewort. Such a range of nectar sources also attracts a wealth of butterflies and other insects.

A group of local volunteers helps Basildon's Countryside Service team to manage the site.

Alan Sadgrove

Common spotted orchid: flowers mid-May–early August

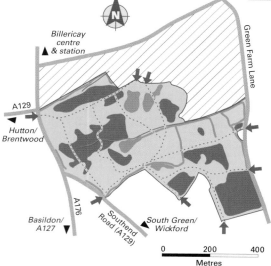

Stretches between Southend Road (A129) and Greens Farm Lane just south of Billericay Centre. Limited parking close by: use car parks in Billericay.

About 600m from Billericay station. A number of bus services run along the A129.

Accessible at all times.

Late spring to late summer for wild flowers and insects.

Norsey Wood

165ac/66ha   **OS Ex175**   **TQ 691 955**   **SSSI, LNR**

Norsey Wood, just east of Billericay, has had an eventful history: Iron Age and Roman remains have been found there and it is believed to have been used as a last refuge by the rebels who took part in the Peasants' Revolt of 1381, led by Wat Tyler, before they were destroyed by the forces of the Crown.

It consists of 165 acres of mixed coppice woodland, at least part of it continuously wooded since Roman times. It is criss-crossed by ancient woodbanks and ditches, marking former boundaries of ownership. Like a number of woods in southern Essex it lies on gravelly deposits on top of London Clay, so the vegetation varies greatly from a well-drained plateau down to the damper and heavier soils in the southern valleys.

There is mainly sweet chestnut coppice on the higher and better-drained soils, with occasional colonies of heather. Not far from the visitor centre are some massive stools of coppiced hornbeam, which must be at least 500 years old.

Descending into the marshy valleys you find different trees and plants from the higher gravelly parts. Alder, ash and willow coppice grow here with areas of pendulous sedge, buckler fern and sphagnum moss (from which peat bogs are formed).

It has one of the greatest concentrations of bluebells in the world and large numbers of hard fern. Water violets grow in the ponds.

Norsey Road turns off the B1007 just north of Billericay centre.

About 10 minutes' walk from Billericay rail station.

Site and car park open at all times; Visitor Centre weekends only.

April–May for bluebells and song-birds; October for fungi.

Call the Information Centre on 01277 624553.

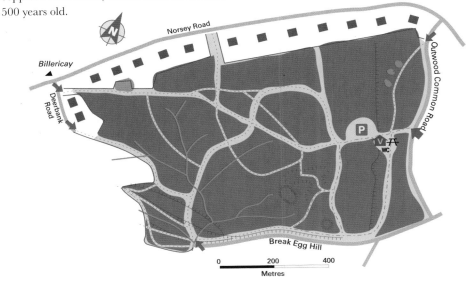

Queens Park Country Park

60ac/24ha   *OS Ex175*   *TQ 672 966*

Former amenity parkland, now managed by Basildon Council primarily for wildlife.

It features a large meadow that is cut for hay once a year and as a result is developing a diversity of wild flowers. Green woodpeckers are often seen there feeding on ants.

The islands of trees, the mature hedgerows and the young woodland offer feeding and nesting opportunities for small birds, while the rough grass and scrub is good for small mammals, which in turn attract kestrels and owls looking for food.

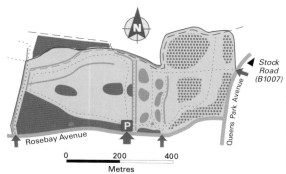

◄ Stock
Road
(B1007)

Queens Park Avenue

Rosebay Avenue

P

0   200   400

Metres

On the northern fringe of Billericay turn off Stock Road (B1007) on to Queens Park Avenue.

Hourly bus service Billericay–Basildon runs past the park.

Accessible at all times. Car park closes at 9pm.

St Faith's Country Park

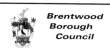

**Brentwood
Borough
Council**

40ac/16ha   *OS Ex175*   *TQ 586 938*

Formerly the grounds of St Faith's Hospital, this country park consists of undulating open grassland surrounded by mature hedgerows, with a small wood, streams and a pond. From its highest points it provides views across to South Weald.

The grassland is cut twice a year and supports many wild plants, including cuckoo flower, burnet saxifrage and coltsfoot. Kestrels

can often be seen hunting for small mammals in the rough grass. Slow worms and grass snakes use the habitat piles created by local volunteers.

North of London Road (A1023) Brentwood, a short distance west of the High Street. Entrances from London Road, Weald Road, Honeypot Lane and Sir Francis Way.

Accessible at all times.

Surfaced path suitable for wheelchairs crosses the site.

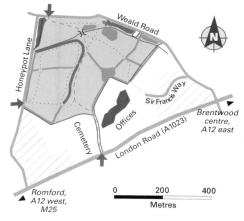

Weald Road

Honeypot Lane

Sir Francis Way

Cemetery

Offices

London Road (A1023)

Brentwood centre, A12 east

Romford, A12 west, M25

0   200   400

Metres

Swan Wood

32ac/13ha   *OS Ex175*   *TQ 688 993*

WOODLAND
TRUST

This ancient woodland has a mix of broadleaved trees, including sweet chestnut and hornbeam coppice. Remnants of its mediæval wood banks can still be seen. An attractive stream runs through the wood, with alder trees along its banks. It is a bluebell wood, and yellow archangel, wood sorrel and wood anemone can also be found.

It has a good range of woodland birds, including hawfinches.

The traditional practice of coppicing has been reintroduced for the hornbeam and sweet chestnut. Sycamore invading the wood is being felled.

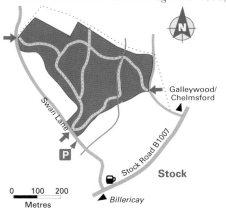

From Chelmsford or from the A12 take the B1007 south towards Billericay. In Stock turn right by The Cock PH into Swan Lane. Swan Wood is on the right after 400m. Park in the layby on the left.

Buses from Chelmsford to Billericay pass through Stock.

Accessible at all times.

Cuckoo flower, also known as lady's smock: flowers April–June

Tony Gunton

Coltsfoot: flowers February–April

Pat Allen

The Mores

38.8ac/16ha   *OS Ex175*   *TQ 565 967*

WOODLAND TRUST

This attractive mixed woodland near Brentwood is long established and includes some ancient mature oaks and hornbeam coppice. The eastern section was once part of Weald Common, since taken over by pioneer trees such as birch and holly. To maintain its diversity the Woodland Trust is encouraging the natural regeneration of native trees such as oak, hornbeam and rowan.

A stream runs through the wood and floods in winter, creating several marshy patches with alder trees and some interesting flowers.

Many birds breed here. Siskins and sometimes redpolls feed in the alders in winter.

Turn off the A128 north of Brentwood on to a minor road to Bentley. Turn right after the church in Bentley and the entrance is 300m further on, on the left. Park by St Paul's church, off Snakes Hill.

Buses from Brentwood to Stondon Massey and Ongar run along the A128.

Accessible at all times.

Spring for early flowers and songbirds; autumn for fungi.

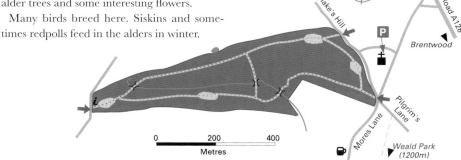

Ancient tree at Thorndon Park

Tony Gunton

Thorndon

Few areas offer such variety as Thorndon Park and its surroundings. Ancient woodland and historic deer parks lie close alongside recently planted woodland and a landscape of small pastures, while nearby is the high forest of Hartswood and former common land.

Thorndon Country Park

529ac/214ha   **OS Ex175**   *TQ 605 915*   *SSSI (part)*

Thorndon Country Park is in two parts, the northern section on a gravel ridge and the southern part on clay soil lower down. The two parts are now linked by Old Thorndon Pastures, which is farmland that has been restored to a traditional farming landscape with small hedged fields, grazed by cattle.

It has ancient woodland and parkland, ponds, a marsh and meadow. Ancient trees are an outstanding feature. Giant oak and hornbeam pollards with towering canopies remind us that this was once a deer park. Parts of it used to be heathland, now a scarce habitat in Essex, and to restore it parts of the park, both north and south, are being grazed on rotation by goats and sheep.

The park attracts a large number of woodland birds and sees more than its fair share of passage migrants and winter visitors. For example, large flocks of siskins and redpolls often gather in the birches, and bramblings can be seen near to the centre feeding on beech mast.

It also hosts an unusually wide variety of butterflies, including the uncommon purple and white-letter hairstreaks.

The park is managed by Essex County Council's Ranger Service. Conifer plantations are being returned to grassland or broadleaved woodland as mature trees are harvested. The storms of 1987 and 1990 have lent a powerful hand here – where windblown conifers have been cleared a new woodland of native trees is regenerating naturally, while in other areas new native trees have been planted.

The Countryside Centre in Thorndon Park North is managed by Essex Wildlife Trust in a joint venture with Essex County Council. It was built just after the 1987 hurricane and some of the storm-fallen timber was used in its construction. It is the Trust's most popular centre with over 100,000 visitors per year, and provides refreshments, a gift shop, displays and interpretation.

The Old Park

135ac/54ha   **OS Ex175**   *TQ 620 906*

Hatch Farm (still privately owned) was built as a 'model farm' in 1777 to raise deer and cattle. A large section of the farm lying between the two halves of Thorndon Country Park has been acquired by the Woodland Trust as one of its Plant-a-Wood sites. Oak, ash, sweet chestnut and hornbeam have been planted and 84 acres have been sown with grass and wildflower seed, to recreate a parkland atmosphere.

Thorndon (continued)

Brentwood
Borough
Council

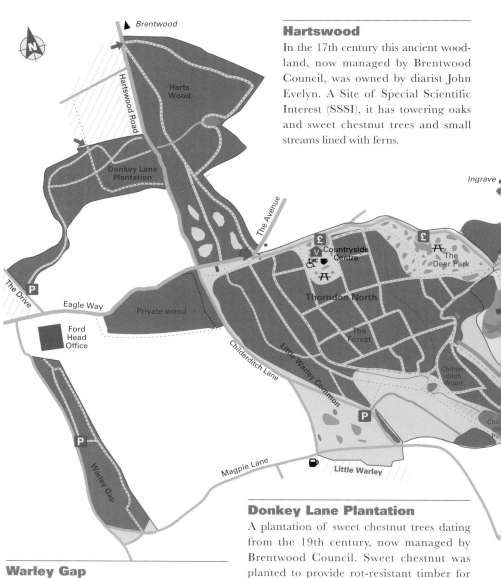

Hartswood

In the 17th century this ancient woodland, now managed by Brentwood Council, was owned by diarist John Evelyn. A Site of Special Scientific Interest (SSSI), it has towering oaks and sweet chestnut trees and small streams lined with ferns.

Donkey Lane Plantation

A plantation of sweet chestnut trees dating from the 19th century, now managed by Brentwood Council. Sweet chestnut was planted to provide rot-resistant timber for fencing and the like. The council resumed coppicing in the 1980s, creating a dense woodland with open glades.

Warley Gap

A strip of former common now covered with trees, including some fine beeches, descending steeply from behind the Ford offices.

Little Warley Common

Little Warley Common was used by local commoners to graze their cattle up to the end of the 19th century. After grazing stopped it filled with trees and is now mainly woodland – principally oak and birch which are 'pioneer' species quick to colonise new territory. Some more open areas remain both at the northern end where it meets Hartswood and at the southern end near Little Warley, where it is open common that is cut every year.

Like Hartswood, Little Warley Common is managed by Brentwood Council. Both are good places to head for on busy summer weekends if you want to avoid the crowds in Thorndon Country Park.

South of Brentwood, just west of the A128, which runs from Ongar through Brentwood to join the A127. The main entrance to Thorndon North is off The Avenue, which links the A128 and the B186 (Brentwood–South Ockendon). The entrance to Thorndon South is off the A128 just north of Halfway House.

Brentwood railway station is about 2km (via Hartswood and Little Warley Common) from Thorndon North. Buses from Brentwood Town Centre run to Eagle Way, Warley.

Open all year from 8am to dusk. The Countryside Centre in Thorndon North is open every day except Christmas Day and Boxing Day, from 10am to 5pm.

May for spring flowers and birdsong in the woods; October for fungi.

The Countryside Centre has wheelchair access and a disabled persons' toilet. A battery-powered scooter can be provided on request.

For more information about the park or about events and activities call the Rangers on 01277 211250 or the Countryside Centre on 01277 232944.

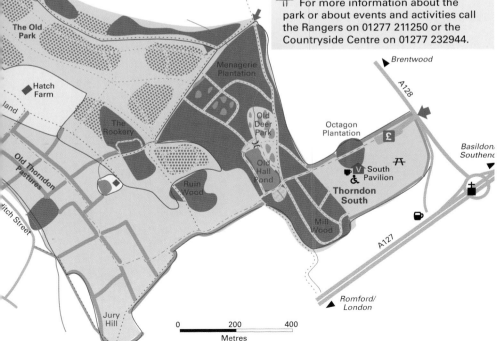

Thrift Wood

48ac/19ha   *OS Ex183*   *TL 790 017*   *SSSI*

This ancient wood, owned and managed by Essex Wildlife Trust, consists of hornbeam coppice with many oak standards, some birch, ash and coppiced sweet chestnut, and a number of wild service trees.

It is one of the principal Essex sites of the common cow-wheat, food plant of the heath fritillary butterfly. After becoming extinct in Essex, this butterfly was re-established in the reserve in 1984. It also has lots of slender St John's wort, heath wood-rush and pale and pill sedges.

There is a sizable pool with a raised bog, thought to have been formed many years ago from clay-digging for brickmaking. Here can be found greater spearwort, hop sedge and other aquatic plants, three species of sphagnum moss and the hair-moss *Polytrichum commune*.

Birds include woodpeckers and a good population of woodland warblers. The wood teems with wood ants and has a wide range of other insects.

Coppicing has been reintroduced, resulting in a marked increase in both resident and summer migrant birds and also in plantlife. The pond with its raised bog is cleared annually of rank vegetation.

The entrance is on the B1418 road 400m south of the Brewer's Arms PH in Bicknacre. There is parking for a few cars at the main gate, with overflow parking on the verge opposite.

Buses run every half-hour between Chelmsford and South Woodham Ferrers, stopping at the main gate.

Accessible at all times.

May for spring flowers and birdsong; late May on for heath fritillary and other butterflies.

Do not attempt to cross the pool's raised bog as conditions are dangerous.

Common cow-wheat: flowers May–September
Dr Chris Gibson/Natural England

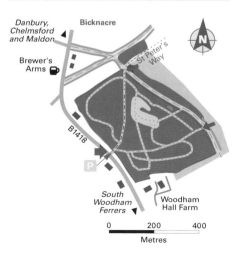

Warley Country Park

52ac/21ha   *OS Ex175*   *TQ 585 927*

**Brentwood
Borough
Council**

This new country park has been developed on the open land adjoining the former Warley Hospital near Brentwood, sloping steeply down to the railway. Much of it has been colonised by woodland and scrub, and additional native trees have been planted. It also has a stream and a reedy pond.

With such a mix of habitats, a good variety of breeding birds can be seen in spring and many insects are on the wing in summer.

Access from Vaughn Williams Way (via Mascalls Lane) and Crescent Road (via London Road, A1023).

Regular bus services along London Road.

Accessible at all times.

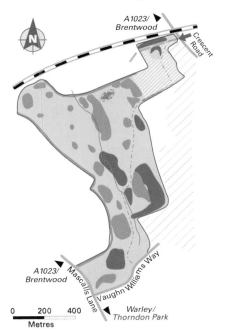

Warley Place

25ac/10ha   *OS Ex175*   *TQ 583 906*

**ESSEX
Wildlife Trust**

Warley Place is the site of a house and once-famous gardens said to have been laid out by the diarist John Evelyn in the 17th century. The house was demolished in the 1930s and the last occupant was Miss Ellen Willmott, who died in 1934. She remodelled the gardens and introduced into them a vast assortment of new plants from all over the world. It is now a nature reserve managed by Essex Wildlife Trust.

The garden had fallen into neglect but has now been restored by an enthusiastic team of volunteers, although not in its original form. Parts of the built remains can still be seen and a number of the surviving plants. Daffodils, snowdrops, winter aconites, anemones, cranesbills and ferns grow in profusion again, mingling with native species. Among a variety of trees, some exotic, is a line of huge sweet chestnuts.

The reserve attracts a wide variety of birds, including the nuthatch, and has a good selection of invertebrates, including stag beetles.

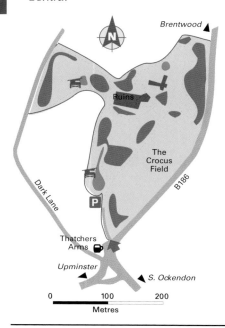

On the B186 (Brentwood–S. Ockendon) just south of Brentwood. Entrance next to the Thatchers Arms PH.

Infrequent buses from Brentwood to Romford and Grays run past the entrance: ask for Thatchers Arms.

On weekends from end February to early April the gates are manned by volunteers and several thousand visitors come to see the daffodils and other spring flowers. Otherwise access for Essex Wildlife Trust members and holders of day permits only: call Essex Wildlife Trust on 01621 862960.

No dogs allowed except guide dogs.

Weald Country Park

424ac/170ha   **OS Ex175**   **TQ 570 939**

Essex County Council

Weald Country Park, which lies just north-west of Brentwood, is an attractive mix of semi-formal parkland with large areas of woodland and the remnants of the 'tree pasture' of a deer park. Its south-eastern quarter, called The Park, is scattered with massive oak and hornbeam pollards, some of which are probably more than 500 years old. It was bought by Essex County Council in 1953.

The woodland to the north positively shimmers with bluebells in spring, particularly where conifers have recently been removed. Golden saxifage, an unusual ancient woodland plant, grows in Foxdown Wood, which escaped conifer planting.

Such a variety of habitats attracts a wide variety of birds. Great crested grebes and moorhens breed on the lakes. Nuthatches and

From M25 junction 28 with the A12 take the A1023 towards Brentwood and turn left on to Wigley Bush Lane. This meets Weald Road in South Weald village, from which there are several entrances.

Regular bus services from Brentwood to Pilgrims Hatch. Occasional services to South Weald village.

Accessible at all times. Car parks open from dawn to dusk. Visitor centre open daily except Mondays 10am–5pm from April–October, otherwise weekends only 10am–4pm.

April–May for bluebells and birdsong; July for butterflies, dragonflies and wild flowers in the damper parts.

Battery-powered scooters can be provided on request.

For more information call the Rangers on 01277 261343.

woodpeckers are often seen in and around the woods. Flocks of seed-eating birds such as goldfinches and siskins can sometimes be seen feeding on the ground or in the lakeside alders. Little owls can be seen hunting in the early evening.

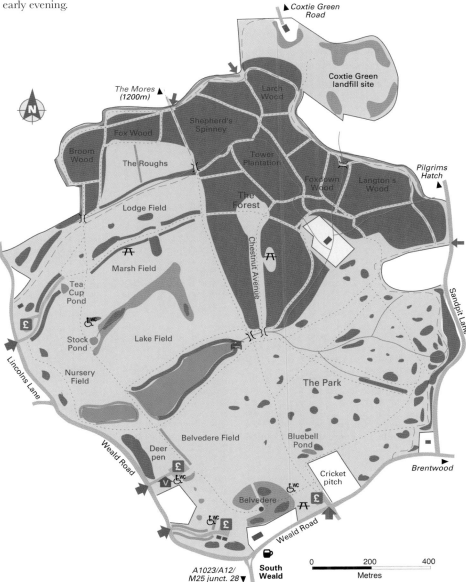

Writtle Forest

500ac/200ha   OS Ex183   TL 638 012

Sizeable parts of what was once Writtle Forest survive in private ownership but are still accessible via public footpaths and bridleways. These woods have all the diversity and also much of the wildness that you might have found in mediæval woods – areas dense with bracken and bramble and others where the woodland floor is dark and bare; little streams and bogs; occasional glades. The trees are mainly sweet chestnut coppice, with oak and hornbeam in the damper parts, and maple, spindle and dogwood on the fringes.

Unlike Hatfield Forest, Writtle Forest had the woods in the middle and the 'plains' – open areas used for grazing – around the outside. Mill Green Common is a surviving part of the plains. It has been heavily invaded by birch and other trees, but still has some heather in the open parts, which are alive with insects in summer.

Maple Tree Lane is a broad ancient green lane, bounded for much of its length by massive ditches and banks topped with huge coppice stools of hornbeam and massive oaks. Short sections have been surfaced, but for most of the way the tracks followed by horses (and with more difficulty, people) meander round patches of bramble and scrub and occasional pools and boggy areas.

North of Ingatestone and west of Chelmsford. Leave the A12 at Ingatestone and take the minor road from the centre of Ingatestone to Fryerning. Turn right and follow Mill Green Road to Mill Green, or turn left and follow Blackmore Road to reach Fryerning Wood and Maple Tree Lane.

Accessible at all times.

May–June for early flowers and birdsong; July–August for flowers and butterflies.

Many of the paths are heavily used by horses and can be boggy and wet even in the summer.

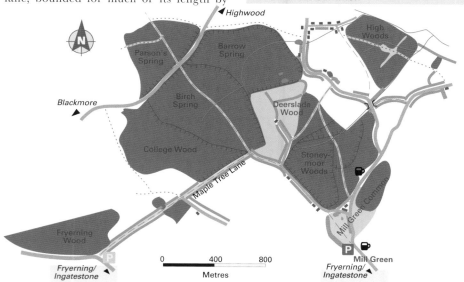

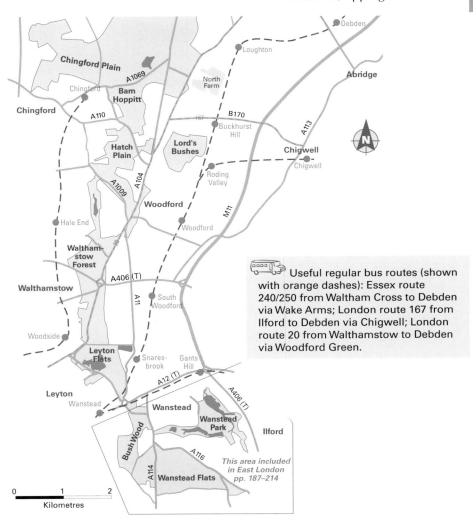

Useful regular bus routes (shown with orange dashes): Essex route 240/250 from Waltham Cross to Debden via Wake Arms; London route 167 from Ilford to Debden via Chigwell; London route 20 from Walthamstow to Debden via Woodford Green.

This area included in East London pp. 187–214

Hatch Plain

Woodford Golf Course occupies most of the southern part, surrounded by some attractive grassland with petty whin and heath bedstraw, plus some patches of scrub and many anthills.

Much of the rest is hornbeam woodland, with the River Ching flowing into it from the north. Wood anemones, goldilocks and violets grow on its banks along with some gnarled old hornbeam pollards.

Epping Forest Green Lanes

88ac/35ha   *OS Ex174*   *TL 440 060/TL 396 030*

These Green Lanes are now completely separated from the rest of the Forest, running in an arc starting near Fishers Green in the River Lee Country Park and finishing north of Epping.

They consist of pleasant green lanes interspersed with grassy areas, small woods and occasional ponds. Surrounded as they are by intensive farmland their wildlife value is high. Yellowhammers and linnets, for example, are still seen along them regularly in summer but have almost disappeared elsewhere.

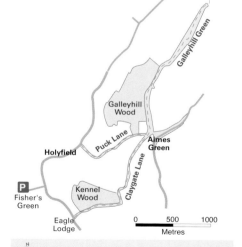

Linnet (male):resident
Alan Williams

Park at Fishers Green (see River Lee Country Park p. 172) and walk from there.

Harlow–Waltham Abbey bus to Eagle Lodge or Holyfield. Harlow–Epping bus to Epping Green.

Accessible at all times.

Recently pollarded hornbeams at Gernon Bushes

Great Monk Wood

Epping Forest **Lower Forest**

478ac/191ha   **OS Ex174**   **TL 475 035**   **SSSI**

CITY
OF
LONDON

The Lower Forest north of Epping is predominantly wood-pasture of oak and hornbeam, much of it dense with holly and scrub. Two broad Green Lanes, bordered by a number of repollarded hornbeams, divide it into four. One of these – Stump Road, once the main road from London to Cambridge – runs alongside Cripsey Brook which has many flowers on its margins, including primroses, dog's mercury, sanicle and angelica. It runs into Wintry Wood Common which is also flower-rich.

Epping Plain at its south-west corner was once open grassland that has been heavily invaded by oak. It has several large ponds with unusual aquatic plants such as water violet and a wide range of dragonflies.

Between High Rd (B1393) and Epping Road (B181) north-east of Epping. There is a parking area on The Woodyard south of the B181.

Buses between Epping and Harlow run along the B1393.

Accessible at all times.

Spring and summer for woodland flowers and insects.

Gernon Bushes

79ac/32ha   **OS Ex174**   **TL 478 030**   **SSSI**

THE
wildlife
TRUSTS
ESSEX
Wildlife Trust

This is the last remnant of the old Coopersale Common that once linked Epping Lower Forest (now cut off by the disused Central Line tube) along the hill ridge to Ongar Park. It has many ancient hornbeam pollards plus some more recent woodland and a network of ponds originally dug for gravel extraction, and descends steeply from the plateau of the ridge across pebbly clay drift and claygate beds to London clay lower down.

In the north of the reserve the gravel workings have developed into sphagnum bogs. In the south two springs rise on the edge of the plateau and their streams descend steep-sided valleys through a series of bogs with large patches of the rare marsh fern. Other notable plants include lady fern, bogbean (in one of its very few Essex sites), marsh valerian, marsh marigold and ragged robin.

It has a good variety of resident and summer migrant birds.

Turn off the B181 towards Coopersale village and turn left on to Garnon Mead 200 yards after passing under the railway bridge.

A bus service runs to Coopersale from Harlow via Epping.

Accessible at all times

Spring for songbirds; summer for marsh and bog plants.

Bogbean: flowers April–June

Tony Gunton

Thornwood Flood Meadow

2.7ac/1ha   **OS Ex174**   **TL 471 045**   *LNR*

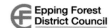

**Epping Forest
District Council**

This wet meadow was acquired by Epping Forest District Council in 1998. Scrapes (shallow lakes) have been created for wading birds. Flowers include ragged robin, oxeye daisy and knapweed.

Access via a public footpath from North Weald High Road.

Buses between Epping and Harlow run along the B1393.

Accessible at all times.

June for wild flowers.

Thornwood
Common

Thornwood
Flood Meadow

Wintry
Wood
Common

N

Woodside

North
Weald

Wintry Wood

Stump Road

Lower
Forest

High Road B1393

Epping Road B181

Disused railway

Epping
Plain

P

Coopersale

P

Gemon
Bushes

Essex Way

Ongar

Epping

Essex Way

Epping

M11

0   200   400

Metres

Epping Forest **Heart of the Forest**

2224ac/900ha   *OS Ex174*   *TL 412 981*   *SSSI*

The heart of Epping Forest, with its massive ancient trees, lies to the west of the Epping Forest Conservation Centre at High Beach. To see many of the best of the Forest's habitats, follow Three Forests Way – signposted Loughton – from the High Beach car park and turn left at Debden Slade on to Green Ride. Follow Green Ride all the way to Long Running, then return via St Thomas' Quarters and Verderer's Ride.

Loughton Camp

Loughton Camp is a circular earth bank believed to date from the late Iron Age. It is set in a woodland of tall beech pollards, with occasional clumps of heather. Below it is Debden Slade, a grassy glade beside a stream with pollard oaks and hornbeams. Many streams run through this area, some with boggy flushes full of ferns, sedges and wetland flowers.

Honey Lane Quarters

Honey Lane Quarters slopes down steeply to the west with good views over the Lea Valley. It is wood-pasture, with beech at the top and hornbeam lower down. A broad ride leads down to the grassy plain and stream at its foot.

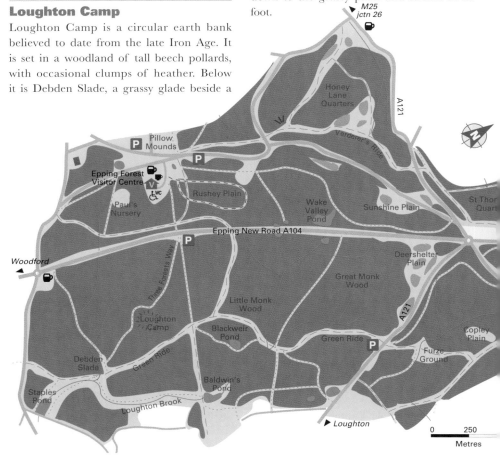

Wake Valley

The Wake Valley is a mosaic of beechwood and heathland with a number of ponds. These have good dragonfly populations, and especially Wake Valley Pond, in which the downy emerald breeds. The marsh to the the north has a good range of wetland plants including ragged robin, lesser spearwort, marsh violet and marsh fern.

St Thomas' Quarters

This is mostly beech wood-pasture, with some very large beech pollards. It has a number of streams with boggy flushes and two fine valley bogs east of Lodge Road. Visitor pressure is relatively low so it serves as a refuge for fallow deer.

Furze Ground & Copley Plain

These are restored heathland, surrounded by ancient pollards and some 'coppards', that is trees that have first been coppiced then the multiple stems have been pollarded.

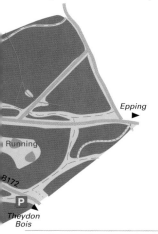

Gt & Lt Monk Woods

Here you will find many very old beech and oak pollards, a good number of which have died, creating small clearings in which dense stands of young trees spring up. A number of streams cut deeply into the gravelly slopes.

Leave the M25 at junction 26 and head east along the A121 towards Loughton. This brings you to the Wake Arms roundabout where the A121 meets Epping New Road and the road to Theydon Bois (B172). The Wake Road turns off the A121 on the right just before the roundabout and leads to the Conservation Centre.

A long walk from Loughton or Theydon Bois stations on the Central Line, and bus services run from Debden station on the same line.

Forest accessible at all times. Visitor centre open every day except Christmas Day, 11am–6pm summer, 10am–3pm winter.

Worth a visit at any time of year.

Please keep dogs under control at all times and especially near horses. Please keep dogs on leads near livestock.

Call Forest Visitor Centre on 020 8508 0028. (The Conservation Centre is run by the Field Studies Council: for school visits phone 020 8508 7714.)

Long Running

Long Running has probably the best areas of restored heathland in the Forest. One section is being grazed by cattle and others have been cleared of invading birch and the original vegetation of cross-leaved heath and ling has reappeared. In the open areas there is a good chance of seeing tree pipits, a once-common bird that has become very scarce in Essex in the last 20 years, and they also support many reptiles.

Loughton Brook

Loughton Brook meanders in a deep valley cut through beech and hornbeam wood-pasture, bordered by ferns, sedges, flag iris and heather. Kingfishers and grey wagtails nest along its banks. It leaves the Forest at Staples Pond which has marsh marigolds and a good range of dragonflies.

Epping Forest around Chingford

741ac/300ha   **OS Ex174**   **TQ 397 948**   **SSSI**

CITY
OF
LONDON

It is estimated that about one-sixth of Epping Forest was originally open country, and kept so by grazing by deer and cattle. As grazing declined during the 1970s and 1980s, so scrub and then trees moved in, and as a result wildlife was lost that requires open, grazed habitats. In 2002 a small grazing herd of English Longhorns, a rare breed, was reintroduced to this part of Epping Forest, north of Chingford, and the Conservators hope to extend grazing in future.

This area still has attractive, rolling open country and is particularly good for birds, because of the variety of habitats, ranging from mature woodland via scrub to open grassland, much of it damp. Try a tour from Queen Elizabeth's Hunting Lodge via Connaught Water, Fairmead Bottom, Whitehouse Plain and Woodman's Glade to Yardley Hill, returning via Chingford Plain.

Queen Elizabeth's Hunting Lodge is on the A1069 next to the Royal Forest Hotel. Leave the M25 at junction 26 and head east along the A121. At the Wake Arms roundabout head south down the A104 then turn right on to the A1069.

Chingford station (Liverpool St line) is a short walk from Queen Elizabeth's Hunting Lodge.

Accessible at all times.

May to early June for breeding birds. Come in the very early morning and avoid sunny weekends if you want to miss the crowds.

Please keep dogs under control at all times and especially near horses. Please keep dogs on leads near livestock.

Many paths are very boggy in winter, and some all year round.

Yardley Hill

Once open farmland, Yardley Hill is now virtually covered with oak and thorn scrub. It has patches of chalky soil where plants such as clematis and sweet violet grow. From the top there are good views across the Lea Valley reservoirs into north London. At its foot is Yate's Meadow, which is full of wild flowers in summer and where skylarks and meadow pipits breed.

Chingford Plain

Chingford Plain was under arable cultivation until 1878. Part of it forms Chingford golf course and some of it has returned to scrubland, which attracts many birds. In early winter large numbers of fieldfares and redwings, visiting from Scandinavia, often gather on the golf course.

Barn Hoppitt
Jeremy Dagley

The Plains

Almshouse Plain, Whitehouse Plain and Fairmead Bottom are interconnected areas of grassland, some of it damp. They are dotted with large patches of scrub and crossed by flower-lined ditches and are good territory for insects and small mammals. There is a scattering of ponds, the best of which is Fairmead Pond, where grass snakes are common.

Connaught Water

Connaught Water is a large shallow lake with wooded islands, made in 1880. The grass around it is cropped short by canada geese, and mallard and moorhen breed on its wooded islands. In the winter the Forest's considerable population of mandarin ducks roost there.

Barn Hoppitt & Whitehall Plain

Barn Hoppitt and Whitehall Plain were part of the Forest's 'plains': open areas used for grazing cattle. Barn Hoppitt is the best example of oak wood-pasture in the Forest, with well-spaced ancient oak pollards over sparse grassland with many anthills and a mosaic of scrub patches.

The River Ching meanders through from north to south and its corridor supports unusual shrubs such as spindle, buckthorn and purple osier.

Once open grassland, Whitehall Plain has been invaded by thorn scrub which has driven out most of its flowering plants, but these are returning now that it is being cut for hay.

Queen Elizabeth's Hunting Lodge

Queen Elizabeth's Hunting Lodge is a three-storey timber-framed building, completed in 1543 by Henry VIII. Its purpose was to provide the monarch and court with a good view of the hunt, and hence its upper windows were originally open. It now houses the Epping Forest museum.

Epping Forest Lord's Bushes

133ac/53ha   *OS Ex174*   *TQ 413 935*   *SSSI (part)*

CITY OF LONDON

Lord's Bushes has many veteran oak and hornbeam pollards and many beech trees as well, some of the largest of which are showing signs of old age. Among a variety of other tree species, along the eastern boundary is a grove of wild service trees, an indicator of ancient woodland.

Wide pathways cross the wood, fringed by gorse, sheep's sorrel, pendulous sedge and fine grasses.

Knighton Wood to the south-west was owned and landscaped by E. N. Buxton, once a Forest Verderer, and returned to the Forest after his death in 1930. It has a mixture of trees – predominantly oak, hornbeam and beech with a scattering of exotics such as red oaks and copper beech – and an attractive lake with islands.

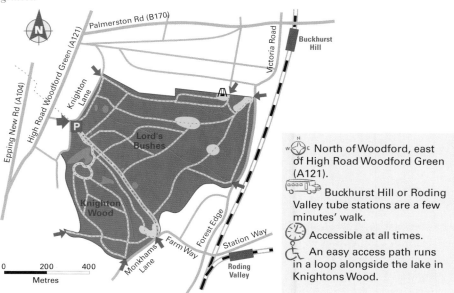

North of Woodford, east of High Road Woodford Green (A121).

Buckhurst Hill or Roding Valley tube stations are a few minutes' walk.

Accessible at all times.

An easy access path runs in a loop alongside the lake in Knightons Wood.

Highams Park

88ac/35ha   *OS Ex174*   *TQ 393 922*

CITY OF LONDON

Higham's Park is pollard woodland of oak and hornbeam that was landscaped by Humphrey Repton in the 1790s. The River Ching flows into it from the north to feed one of the largest lakes in the Forest, which supports many species of dragonfly. It has carpets of bluebells in spring, along with red campion, wood anemone and periwinkle.

The woodland to the south has some large oaks, hornbeam coppice and some planted conifers. The small ponds in the open grassland in the south-east corner are rich in wildlife, including great crested newts.

Walthamstow Forest

128ac/51ha   **OS Ex174**   *TQ 391 910*   *SSSI (part)*

CITY
OF
LONDON

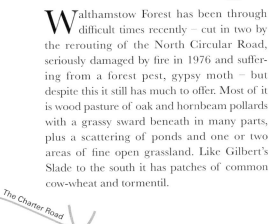

Walthamstow Forest has been through difficult times recently – cut in two by the rerouting of the North Circular Road, seriously damaged by fire in 1976 and suffering from a forest pest, gypsy moth – but despite this it still has much to offer. Most of it is wood pasture of oak and hornbeam pollards with a grassy sward beneath in many parts, plus a scattering of ponds and one or two areas of fine open grassland. Like Gilbert's Slade to the south it has patches of common cow-wheat and tormentil.

North of the junction between the A406 North Circular and A104 Woodford New Road, stretching to Chingford Hatch in the north. No parking areas in the Forest.

Highams Park station is a short walk away. Buses from Walthamstow to Loughton via Woodford Green run along Woodford New Road.

Accessible at all times.

Red campion: flowers March–October

Tony Gunton

Epping Forest Gilbert's Slade & Leyton Flats

316ac/126ha   **OS Ex174**   **TQ 395 891**   **SSSI**

CITY OF LONDON

Gilbert's Slade, to the east of Woodford New Road, is open woodland with many fine old gnarled oak and hornbeam pollards

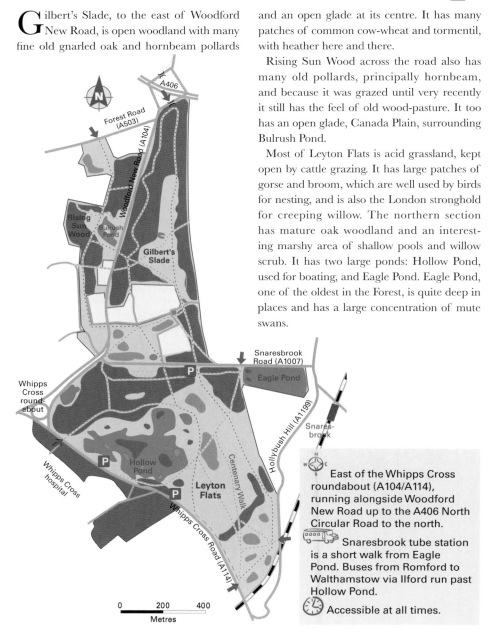

and an open glade at its centre. It has many patches of common cow-wheat and tormentil, with heather here and there.

Rising Sun Wood across the road also has many old pollards, principally hornbeam, and because it was grazed until very recently it still has the feel of old wood-pasture. It too has an open glade, Canada Plain, surrounding Bulrush Pond.

Most of Leyton Flats is acid grassland, kept open by cattle grazing. It has large patches of gorse and broom, which are well used by birds for nesting, and is also the London stronghold for creeping willow. The northern section has mature oak woodland and an interesting marshy area of shallow pools and willow scrub. It has two large ponds: Hollow Pond, used for boating, and Eagle Pond. Eagle Pond, one of the oldest in the Forest, is quite deep in places and has a large concentration of mute swans.

East of the Whipps Cross roundabout (A104/A114), running alongside Woodford New Road up to the A406 North Circular Road to the north.

Snaresbrook tube station is a short walk from Eagle Pond. Buses from Romford to Walthamstow via Ilford run past Hollow Pond.

Accessible at all times.

Harlow & Latton Commons

124ac/50ha　　*OS Ex174*　　*TL 480 080*

Two large areas of common land on the south-eastern fringe of Harlow, either side of the A414 and linked by a pedestrian underpass. It is mainly open grassland, parts of which are grazed by horses and parts cut for hay, so it has a diversity of wild flowers. There are patches of woodland on Harlow Common, one just east of the A414 and another surrounding the lake. The southern fringe of Latton Common is wooded also, mainly oak.

There is a network of footpaths, including the Forest Way long-distance path that runs all the way through from west to east.

Access from Harlow Common or from Latton Common Road, reached from the A414 northbound by turning right (then via Potter Street) or left (then via Trotters Road) respectively at the roundabout where the A414 meets Southern Way (A1169), i.e. the first roundabout north of M11 junction 7.

Frequent service except Sundays by bus route M15 from Harlow Town stn to Potter Street. Route 500 from Romford and 501 from Brentwood runs hourly via Potter Street except Sundays.

Accessible at all times.

Summer for wild flowers and for dragonflies around the lake and ponds.

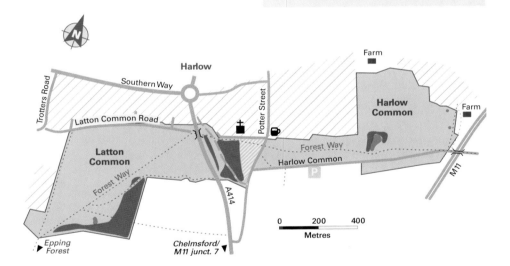

Harlow Marshes Hunsdon Mead

68ac/27ha   *OS Ex174*   *TL 421 114*   *SSSI*

This area of common land between the River Stort and the Stort Navigation is one of the finest surviving areas of unimproved grassland in eastern England. The Hertfordshire & Middlesex and Essex Wildlife Trusts acquired it jointly in 1981.

It provides a superb display of flowering plants. In April and May it is yellow with cowslips and marsh marigolds. As May gives way to June colours change continually, as plants such as yellow rattle, ragged robin, cuckoo flower, meadowsweet, bugle and many others flower in profusion. There are small colonies of green-winged orchid and adders-tongue fern. Quaking grass and several uncommon sedge species are also present.

In summer you can expect to see all the typical grassland butterflies, plus many mayflies and dragonflies.

During the winter, when the Mead floods, large flocks of lapwing and golden plover come to feed along with other winter migrants.

Follow the Stort Navigation towpath from Roydon in the direction of Harlow – a walk of about one mile. The easiest parking is at Roydon station.

Roydon station (Liverpool St–Cambridge).

Accessible at all times.

From mid-April until the end of June for flowers, and later in the summer for dragonflies and other insects.

Between March and July please do not walk across or into the Mead itself until the hay is cut: trampling damages the plants and reduces the value of the grass as hay for the farmer. During this period please keep to the towpath or walk in single file along the permissive path beside the River Stort.

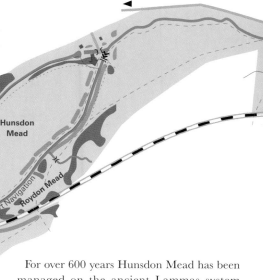

For over 600 years Hunsdon Mead has been managed on the ancient Lammas system under which it is grazed by cattle or sheep in late summer after a July hay cut. It is this which accounts for its abundance of wildlife.

Harlow Marshes

33ac/13.3ha   **OS Ex174**   **TL 453 115**   **LNR**

Harlow Council owns several sections of former flood meadow along the River Stort north of Harlow which together form the Harlow Marshes LNR.

Parndon Moat Marsh is a former moated manor house and mill dating from the 12th century and to the east beyond Harlow Town Park is Maymeads Marsh, which is damp grassland with a large pond surrounded by reeds and marshland. Southern marsh orchids and other wildflowers grow in Maymeads Marsh and its pond, with nesting islands, attracts many wetland birds including the occasional rarity, such as jack snipe.

They are linked by the towpath footpath and crossed by other footpaths and a Green Lane.

Access via Burnt Mill Lane which turns off the A414 a short distance north of the roundabout where it meets the A1019 from Harlow town centre and the A1169. Walk through Harlow Town Park or west along the towpath.

Harlow Town station is right next to the car park at the end of Burnt Mill Lane.

Accessible at all times.

May and June for breeding birds and meadow flowers; July and August for dragonflies and other insects.

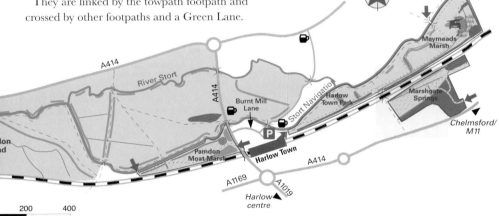

South of the railway and accessible via a footbridge (and a lengthy walk!) is Marshgate Springs, which is marshland fed by natural springs with mature woodland, mainly oak and hornbeam.

Continuing west along the towpath you reach Parndon Mead, which is common land.

The combination of rough grassland with plenty of water makes for good insect and bird life. In summer, grassland butterflies mingle with dragonflies on the waterways, including the banded demoiselle, while moorhens and ducks look after their young families on the river and the occasional common tern flits gracefully past looking for prey.

Hawkenbury Meadow

4ac/1.5ha   **OS Ex174**   **TL 434 088**   **LNR**

A strip of flower-rich grassland alongside Parndon Brook in Great Parndon, Harlow, bounded by mature woodland. It has yellow rattle, common spotted orchid, wild carrot and grass vetchling. There are plenty of butterflies in summer, including the brown argus.

Accessed from Paycock Road in the west of Harlow, near to the junction with Katherine's Way (A1169).

Accessible at all times.

June and July for wild flowers and butterflies.

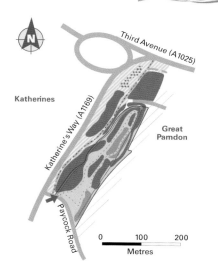

Hawksmere Springs

4.2ac/2ha   **OS Ex175**   **TQ 508 993**

This small Essex Wildlife Trust reserve is mostly ancient unimproved pasture, part of it marshy, with a tiny remnant of ancient damp woodland and a boundary stream.

The reserve is extremely rich in flowers. In the meadows grow cowslip, betony, agrimony, sneezewort, fleabane and a profusion of knapweed and meadowsweet. Yellow rattle and ragged robin can also be found. In spring, bluebells and ramsons (wild garlic) carpet the small wood.

Willow warblers and other warblers join the resident birds in summer and butterflies and other insects are numerous.

The meadows are grazed by sheep to keep them in optimum condition for wild flowers.

Betony
Ken King

Access is by footpath from Tawney Lane, from about 400m east of Little Tawney Hall where there is a small 'Hawksmere Springs' sign on the roadside. Go down the embankment slope and along the grass headland with the stream on your left until you come to a bridge, leading to the reserve entrance on the other side of the stream.

Accessible at all times.

May and June for birdsong; July and August for butterflies, when the meadows are in full bloom.

Unsuitable for wheelchairs or those with walking difficulties.

Please keep your dog on a lead on the access path and when sheep are grazing on the reserve.

Take care when parking where indicated on the verge because it is narrow and steep.

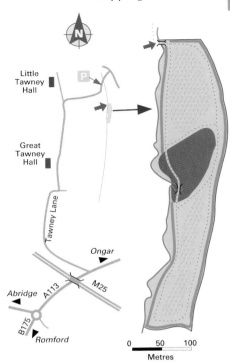

Home Mead

4ac/1.8ha   **OS Ex174**   **TQ 439 978**   **LNR**

Epping Forest District Council

A mosaic of secondary woodland, scrub and grassland just north of Loughton. It has a small area of heather, suggesting that it might once have been part of a larger heathland. Bugle grows in the woods and tormentil and ragged robin feature in the grassland.

Access from England's Lane, Loughton, opposite Loughton Golf Course. Street parking.

Accessible at all times.

A surfaced circular path runs around the reserve.

Larks Wood

43ac/17ha   *OS Ex174*   *TQ 382 925*

Waltham Forest

Waltham Forest Council owns and manages this ancient, former coppice woodland. It covers two adjacent hills and has many hornbeam and mature oaks, plus wild cherry and rowan and a good number of wild service trees. Bluebells and wood anemones flower near the woodland edge in spring.

Between Chingford and Walthamstow. Access to Larks Wood from Inks Green, New Road and Larkshall Road and to Ainslie Wood from Royston Avenue, Woodside Gardens or Ropers Road.

Highams Park station is about 600m away. Buses run along New Road.

Accessible at all times.

Spring for bluebells and other early flowers.

Ainslie Wood

5ac/2ha   *OS Ex174*   *TQ 377 921*

Waltham Forest

This fragment of ancient woodland was once part of Epping Forest. The canopy is dominated by ancient oaks and it also has many wild service trees. Parts of the wood have carpets of bluebells in spring, along with wood anemones and lesser celandine. It has a good selection of woodland birds, including treecreepers.

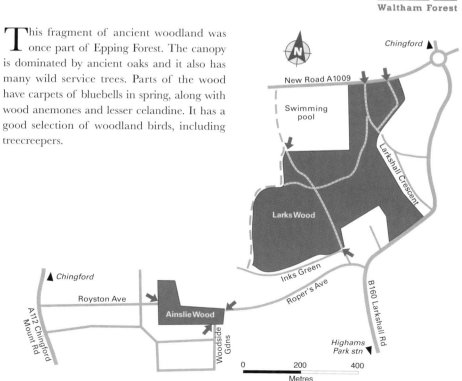

Lee Valley Regional Park

4000ac/1600ha   OS Ex174   TL 377 033   SSSI (part), SPA

The Lee Valley Regional Park extends some 25 miles down the valley of the River Lea (or Lee?), from Ware in the north deep into London as far as the Thames in the south, straddling the borders of Hertfordshire and Essex.

The gravel beds of the valley were left behind by retreating ice at the end of the last Ice Age 10,000 years ago. There has been massive extraction since the 1920s and this has created a huge complex of lakes and marshes in the northern part of the park, while in the south there are a number of large water supply reservoirs. Together these provide an area of open water to rival even the Norfolk Broads.

It is a spectacular place to watch birds, both on the open waters of the gravel pits and reservoirs, on the many channels and streams, and in the surrounding marshes and meadows. But you do not need to be especially interested in birds to enjoy wandering around in this tremendous (in both senses) wetland.

The largest areas of accessible open space are around Waltham Abbey. The River Lee Country Park is an area of unbroken countryside stretching north from Waltham Abbey to Broxbourne, including the dragonfly sanctuary at Cornmill Meadows (pictured below). Just south of Waltham Abbey lies Gunpowder Park, a new country park mainly on reclaimed land once used for testing munitions.

Further south between Walthamstow and Hackney is a small complex of sites including Walthamstow Marsh and two little jewels of nature reserves on former water company filter beds.

There are a number of other good wildlife sites within the Regional Park. For birdwatchers, the most interesting of these are the Thames Water Authority's reservoirs at Chingford and Walthamstow, for which permits can be obtained from Thames Water. There are also nature reserves just across the border in Hertfordshire, notably at Rye House Marsh and Amwell Nature Reserve.

LVRPA

Lee Valley River Lee Country Park

Lee
Valley
Park

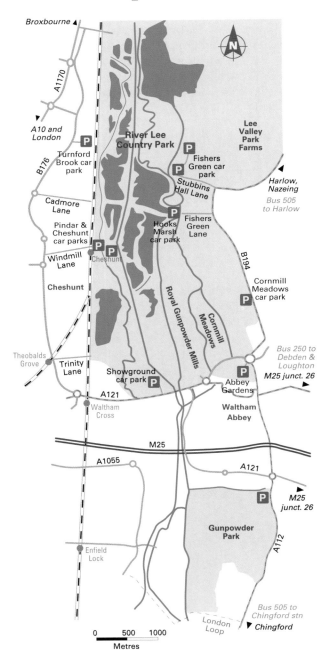

Several car parks serve the country park on the Essex side. All can be reached by leaving the M25 at junction 26 and following the signs to the Lee Valley Park. The Showground car park is just north of the A121 between Waltham Cross and Waltham Abbey. Cornmill Meadows, Hooks Marsh and Fishers Green car parks are all signposted from the B194 to Nazeing.

Train to Cheshunt station from Liverpool St for River Lee Country Park or to Waltham Cross for Cornmill Meadows (bikes welcome). Many bus services serve the area: routes 505 and 250 should be most useful for access from Essex – see map.

Accessible at all times.

Winter and migration periods for birds; late spring through the summer for wetland wildlife.

Many paths are shared-use paths, intended for pedestrians and cyclists: most of these are also suitable for wheelchair users.

Leaflets available from the information service: tel. (01992) 702200, email info@leevalleypark.org.uk or web www.leevalleypark.org.uk.

Holyfield Lake

Holyfield Lake is the largest of the gravel pits in the Lee Valley and has many wooded islands where birds breed and shelter while sailing is in progress on the lake. Goldeneye, goosander and smew visit in winter; yellow wagtail and sedge warbler join residents like great crested grebe and kingfisher in summer, when terns, swallows, martins and swifts feed over the lake.

Cormorants roost on the wooded islands. The tangle of wet alder and willow woodland on the margins and islands also suits breeding warblers and nightingales. Grasshopper warblers, finches and green woodpeckers may be seen or heard in the marshy scrub and woodland in the centre of the island.

The Grand Weir Hide gives different views of Holyfield Lake. The path to it passes the Goosefield where golden plovers, lapwing and canada geese may be seen in winter. Here there are several shallow pools which attract waders in summer and in migration periods.

Cheshunt Gravel Pits

The lakes of Turnford and Cheshunt Gravel Pits and North Metropolitan Pit are the oldest in the valley. With their varying depths of water and many spits and islands they have developed a very varied wetland vegetation, showing all the stages between reedbed, carr and wet woodland. Near Cheshunt Lock orchids (flowering May–July) grow on fly ash dumped from local power stations a couple of decades ago. A few hundred yards further you come to wild flower meadows near Aqueduct Lock, where cowslips flower in spring.

The reedbeds of Seventy Acres Lake are now well established following their creation in 2002. The lake is a wintering site for gadwall, shoveler, coot and, most importantly, bittern. The bittern is one of Britain's rarest birds, once down to only 20 males but now increasing. In winter the resident birds are joined by

visitors from Europe and up to seven birds have previously wintered in the Lee Valley, attracted by the reedbeds and a good food supply. A special Bittern Information Point has been set up overlooking Seventy Acres Lake. This is reached via Fishers Green car park and is open every day.

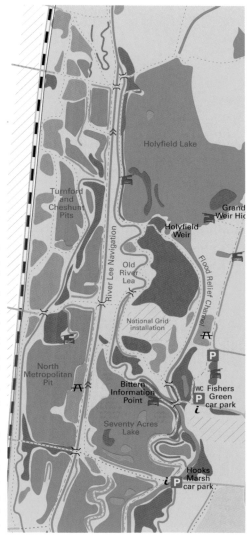

LVRPA
Bowyers Water

Seventy-acres Lake
LVRPA

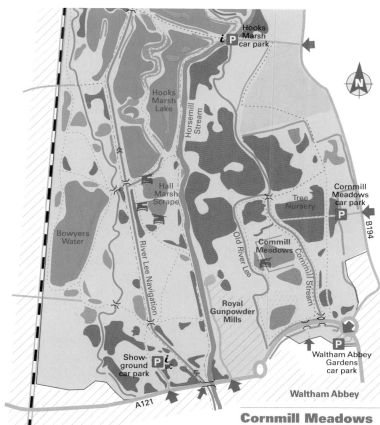

Hooks Marsh car park *i* P

Hooks Marsh Lake

Horsemill Stream

N

Hall Marsh Scrape

Tree Nursery

Cornmill Meadows car park P

B194

Bowyers Water

River Lee Navigation

Old River Lea

Cornmill Meadows

Cornmill Stream

Royal Gunpowder Mills

Show-ground car park P *i* wc

Waltham Abbey Gardens car park P

Waltham Abbey

A121

0   250   500
Metres

Hall Marsh Scrape

Hall Marsh Scrape (scrape meaning an area of shallow water) was created on land backfilled with refuse after gravel extraction. Shallow pools had formed there and were attracting ducks and waders. Shallow water like this is an increasingly rare habitat, so the pools were enlarged and sluice gates were installed to control the water level. Now redshank, little ringed plover and lapwing breed regularly, and teal, shoveler, wigeon and snipe visit in winter.

Cornmill Meadows

The man-made Cornmill Stream used to power the corn mills of Waltham Abbey. Most of the Lee Valley waterways have been canalised, but the Cornmill Stream and the Old River Lea meander in natural channels. Consequently they have a much wider range of waterside plants including some scarce ones like flowering rush (bright pink, July–August). It is also rich in aquatic insect life – more than half of all Britain's dragonfly and damselfly species have been seen here including the banded demoiselle (the best place to see them is the fast-moving water near the weir where the Cornmill Stream leaves the River Lea) and the hairy dragonfly.

Comfrey, branched bur-reed and purple loosestrife grow alongside the Old River Lea.

Lee Valley Gunpowder Park

222ac/90ha   **OS Ex174**   **TQ 382 992**

This country park opened in 2004, much of it created on reclaimed land previously used for testing munitions, and linking into the former grazing meadows of Sewardstone Marsh.

Much of the current wildlife interest is found in the former Sewardstone Marsh, now known as Osier Marsh. This consists of wet woodland that regenerated naturally on pulverised fuel ash dumped into holes created by the extraction of sand and gravel. It contains a variety of willow species and over the years a tangle of dense woodland has formed. It lies wet in the winter and attracts snipe and woodcock, wintering thrushes and large mixed tit flocks. With lots of dead wood and several shallow ponds it is good for invertebrates and amphibians also.

On the reclaimed land to the north, meadows have been created with areas of wild flowers and clumps of trees, and 80 acres are managed as arable farmland, with wildlife features such as permanent grass margins and conservation headlands. Seed-rich crops are sown here to provide winter food for declining farmland birds such as linnets and yellowhammers.

The site is bounded to the west by the Cattlegate Flood Relief Channel and to the north by Black Ditch, formerly used to transport goods into and out of the ordnance factory. These are densely vegetated and populated by water voles and by breeding birds such as sedge and reed warblers, and reed buntings,.

This is already a fine site with lots of wildlife interest and can only get better as the newly created habitats mature.

The main entrance is on the Sewardstone Road (A112), south of the roundabout junction with the A121, south of Waltham Abbey. There are several 24-hour pedestrian and cycle route access points.

The nearest train stations are Enfield Lock or Waltham Cross, both 20–30 minutes' walk away. Bus route 505 from Chingford station to Harlow runs along Sewardstone Road past the main entrance.

Accessible at all times.

Winter for birds; late spring through the summer for wetland wildlife.

The main pathways are wheelchair accessible.

Web www.gunpowderpark.org

Common dragonflies

Migrant hawker (female): breeds in gravel pits and reservoirs; flies August–October

Tony Gunton

Southern hawker (female): breeds in lakes and woodland ponds; flies July–September

Tony Gunton

Ruddy darters mating: breeds in shallow, well-vegetated ponds and ditches; flies July–October

Tony Gunton

Broad-bodied chaser (female); breeds in ponds and ditches, even if mildly polluted; flies May–July

Pat Allen

Black-tailed skimmer (female – male is blue): breeds in sparsely vegetated water bodies; flies May–July

Pat Allen

Lee Valley Walthamstow Marsh

95ac/38ha   **OS Ex174**   **TQ 354 871**   **SSSI**

One of the last surviving marshlands in London, declared a Site of Special Scientific Interest in 1985. Formerly grazed as common land under the Lammas system (under which the grass was left uncut until late summer), it was being cut for hay until cattle were reintroduced in 2003. These regimes encourage wild flowers and over 160 species have been recorded here. One particular beneficiary of the grazing is creeping marshwort, which favours the grazed edges of ditches.

Reed and sedge warblers nest in the reed beds, while snipe and stonechat visit in winter.

On Lea Bridge Road between Walthamstow and Hackney. Park at the WaterWorks Visitor Centre or the Lee Valley Ice Centre on Lea Bridge Road (A104) and follow footpaths from there to reach the other sites.

Clapton railway station is about 10 minutes' walk from the Lee Valley Walk alongside the river, via Southwold Road. Regular bus services into London from Walthamstow and Leyton run along Lea Bridge Road.

WaterWorks open from 8am to dusk, others accessible at all times.

Summer for wild flowers, dragonflies and other insects.

Middlesex Filter Beds

10ac/4ha   *OS Ex174*   *TQ 359 865*

Until they were closed in 1969 these filter beds were used to clean water taken from the River Lea for supply all over northeast London. After that nature took over and created, in a relatively small area, a mosaic of different habitats, including open water, reed bed, scrub, wet woodland and, last but not least, old brickwork that provides many crevices for toads, frogs, lizards and other animals.

Reed buntings, coot and moorhen nest in the reeds and the reedmace, and the area hosts a wide range of dragonflies.

WaterWorks Nature Reserve

25ac/10ha   *OS Ex174*   *TQ 362 868*

The Essex Filter Beds were built over 150 years ago to purify London's drinking water at the height of the cholera epidemic, and closed in the late 1970s. Nature has reclaimed much of it and now, renamed the WaterWorks Nature Reserve, it is managed for wildlife. The visitor centre has interactive displays helping to interpret the history of the site and the wildlife now to be found on it. It also has a six-station bird hide, built over the central well-head.

It supports a wide range of plants and hosts of amphibians and dragonflies. Birdlife includes little grebe, kingfisher and reed bunting, with teal and gadwall visiting in winter.

WaterWorks Nature Reserve
LVRPA

Linder's Field

10ac/3.85ha   **OS Ex174**   **TQ 415 945**   **LNR**

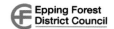
Epping Forest District Council

O nce the garden of local businessman Charles Linder, half of this LNR in Buckhurst Hill is ancient woodland and the other half a wildflower meadow. Bluebells, wood anemones and wild service trees indicate the great age of the woodland. Amphibians breed in the several small ponds.

Epping Forest Countrycare and its team of volunteers are preventing trees and scrub from invading the meadow and cutting the grass to encourage wildflowers to spread.

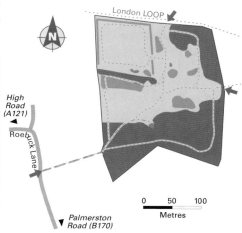

Access from Roebuck Lane, Buckhurst Hill, which runs north from Palmerston Road (B170) towards High Road (A121). On-street parking.

Central Line tube to Buckhurst Hill.

Accessible in daylight hours.

Surfaced pathway from the main entrance to a viewing platform by one of the ponds.

Nazeing Triangle

1ac/.6ha   **OS Ex174**   **TL 414 065**   **LNR**

Epping Forest District Council

A small wetland in Nazeing, enclosed by a triangle of roads. It has three ponds populated by great crested newts, and a reedbed.

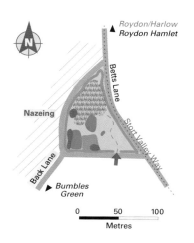

Nazeing lies between Waltham Abbey and Harlow and can be reached via a minor road joining the B194 with the B181 via Bumble's Green. Street parking.

Accessible in daylight hours.

Good for dragonflies in summer.

Surfaced path for wheelchair use.

North Weald Church Lane Flood Meadow

8ac/3.25ha   *OS Ex174*   *TL 494 047*   *LNR*   Epping Forest District Council

Three flood storage areas designed to protect North Weald from flooding have been turned into attractive wildlife sites by Epping Forest District Council.

Church Lane flood meadow is a large bowl that can hold 35 million litres of water. The former arable fields were seeded with hay cut from two SSSI wet meadows – Hunsdon Mead and Roding Valley Meadows. Today it contains ragged robin, bugle and marsh cinquefoil, and in late summer is covered with the pale blue flowers of devilsbit scabious. Around a stream-fed pond in the middle grow purple loosestrife, lady's smock and common spotted orchids.

Access via public footpaths running south from Vicarage Lane near where it joins Church Road. Vicarage Lane is a turning on the left off the A414 about 500m west of the roundabout where it meets the B181 at Tyler's Green.

Accessible at all times.

July to September for wild flowers and flying insects.

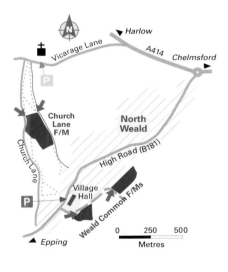

Weald Common Flood Meadows

Epping Forest District Council

7ac/2.9ha   *OS Ex174/183*   *TL 499 039*   *LNR*

These two flood meadows on Weald Common were acquired in 1996. New hedgerows have been planted and the grassland is cut annually for hay. As a result the meadows are covered in cowslips in spring, giving way to ragged robin in early summer.

Off High Road, North Weald (B181). Reached via Weald Common open space. Park by village hall.

Accessible at all times.

June for wild flowers.

Parndon Woods & Common

129ac/52.3ha   **OS Ex174**   **TL 444 072**   **LNR, SSSI (part)**

Parndon Wood, an ancient woodland on Harlow's southern ridge, was bought by Harlow Council in 1968 to become a Local Nature Reserve. It consists mainly of hornbeam coppice with oak standards. Coppicing lapsed after World War II but has now been resumed and this has encouraged woodland plants and animals. The wood is visited by deer and fencing has to be used to prevent them from damaging the newly coppiced trees.

In 2004 the reserve was extended to include Parndon Common and two more ancient woods to the west. Parndon Common is cut annually for hay and before the hay cut provides a good show of yellow rattle, common spotted orchids and cowslips. It has occasional mature oaks.

Hospital and Risden's Woods are mainly coppiced hornbeam and oak, like Parndon Wood, plus some large ash in the wetter southern part. Coppicing has been resumed here also.

Bats are a special feature and six species have been recorded in the reserve. Pipistrelles, the smallest British bats, are the commonest, and it also has daubenton's and brown long-eared bats.

Access via Parndon Wood Road, on the southern fringe of Harlow. Turn off the A414 on to the A1169 and follow signs to Parndon Wood Crematorium. Go past the crematorium entrance and use the parking on the right. The entrance to Parndon Wood is through the green gates next on the right. The rest of the reserve can be reached via the public footpath near the crematorium entrance.

All except Parndon Wood accessible at all times. Parndon Wood is open on weekends and Bank Holidays throughout the year, and on Tuesday evenings 7pm–9pm April to September inclusive. Education and group visits by arrangement with the warden (01279 430005).

One hide in Parndon Wood accessible by wheelchairs via a boardwalk.

Dogs are not allowed into Parndon Wood.

Migratory insects unable (so far) to survive the British winter

Clouded yellow (female) on red clover: breed around the Mediterranean in winter then fly north, arriving here in greatly varying numbers from June on

Red admiral, laying eggs on nettle: breed around the Mediterranean and spread rapidly north across Europe, arriving here from early spring on

Painted lady: breed in north Africa then follow prevailing winds northwards across Europe. The first may arrive in April but the main rush is in June

Humming-bird hawkmoth at rest (bottom) and as usually seen, drinking nectar: may arrive as early as April but especially in August and September

Roding Valley Meadows

158ac/63ha *OS Ex174* *TQ 430 943* *LNR, SSSI (part)*

ESSEX
Wildlife Trust

This Essex Wildlife Trust nature reserve comprises the largest surviving area of traditionally managed river-valley habitat in Essex. It consists of flower-rich unimproved hay meadows, both wet and dry, bounded by thick hedgerows, together with a small amount of scrub, secondary woodland and tree plantation. It follows the River Roding for some 1.5 miles between Chigwell Lane and Roding Lane, Buckhurst Hill, as it meanders across this ancient landscape.

The meadows are rich in flowers, including pepper saxifrage, southern marsh orchid, ragged robin, marsh marigold and devilsbit scabious. The impressive green lane that runs from near the river to the M11 motorway by Grange Farm forms part of the old route from Epping Forest to Romford market, and has many woodland flowers.

In spring and summer, sedge warbler, skylark, reed bunting and whitethroat can be found about the river and meadows. Late summer sees flocks of finches and other seed-eating birds on the seed heads of thistle and teasel. Grey heron, little grebe, snipe, green and common sandpiper are regular winter visitors.

Many insects inhabit the meadows and hedgerows, both unusual and common. Most summers produce drifts of meadow brown butterflies with their lazy, dipping flight.

The meadows are managed in the traditional way by taking a hay cut in summer, followed by cattle grazing. A total length of almost ten miles of hedgerow is managed by laying and coppicing.

Longhorn cattle graze Roding Valley Meadows
Patrick Bailly

River Roding with purple loosestrife
Patrick Bailly

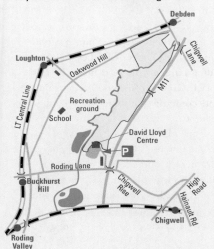

Accessible from the Roding Valley recreation ground via a number of entrances on the Loughton side of the river. The car park is next to the David Lloyd Tennis Centre off Roding Lane.

🚌 Buckhurst Hill, Loughton and Debden tube stations are all within a few minutes' walk of the reserve. Many bus services run to Debden and Loughton stations.

🕐 Accessible at all times.

▦ For meadow flowers, any time from late spring up to the mid-July hay cut.

♿ One-mile linear surfaced track for wheelchairs; all kissing gates adapted to accommodate wheelchairs and scooters.

🐕 Please keep dogs on leads when there is livestock on the reserve.

🚻 ℹ from Essex Wildlife Trust visitor centres or Epping Forest DC (01992 564222). For help call the warden on 020 8508 1593.

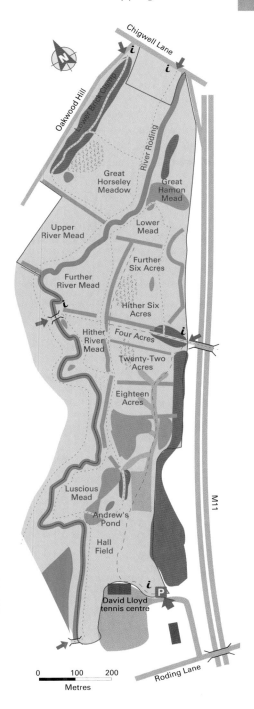

Roughtalleys Wood

8ac/3.4ha   *OS Ex174*   *TL 489 036*   *LNR*

Epping Forest District Council

A mixture of ancient and recently planted woodland on an old World War II air base near North Weald. The ancient woodland, alongside the disused railway, is hornbeam coppice with oak standards. Cowslips and orchids grow in the open grassland within the planted woodland.

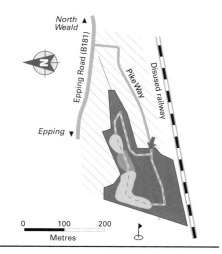

Access from Pike Way, North Weald, a turning on the left off the B181 as you leave North Weald heading for Epping. On-street parking.

Accessible at all times.

700m circular surfaced pathway.

Theydon Bois

94ac/38ha   *OS Ex174*   *TQ 458 980*

WOODLAND
TRUST

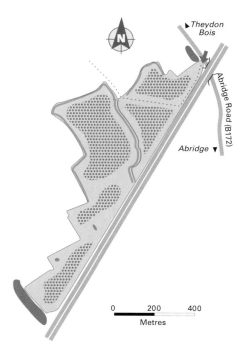

The Woodland Trust acquired this farmland near Theydon Bois in 2006 and started planting trees in autumn 2007. Eventually 50,000 native broadleaved trees will be planted to create a new woodland on the fringes of Epping Forest itself.

Access off Abridge Road east of Theydon Bois village, south of the road just before it passes under the M11. Local parking difficult.

Accessible at all times.

East London's key geographical features are the gravel ridges across the north of Redbridge and Havering; the river valleys of the Lea, Beam and Ingrebourne, running southwards into the Thames; and the Thames Estuary itself.

The gravel ridge across the north has a string of ancient parklands and the largest remaining ancient woodland in the area, Hainault Forest.

There are a few sites deep in the metropolis, the largest of which are Claybury Park in Redbridge and Wanstead Park at the southern end of Epping Forest. Otherwise most are in the Metropolitan Green Belt and in the Dagenham Corridor, a wedge of open land almost splitting the metropolis into two, with the Beam Valley at its southern end. Here you will find ancient woods and historic parks alongside new woodlands planted by the Woodland Trust and the Forestry Commission, most within the Thames Chase Community Forest.

In the south-east lie the Ingrebourne Marshes, holding much of London's remaining floodplain grassland and its largest continuous reedbed.

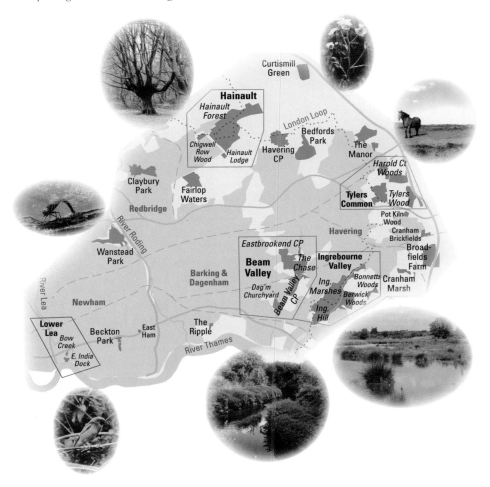

Beam Valley

The Beam Valley divides the London boroughs of Barking & Dagenham and Havering, and forms part of the Dagenham Corridor, a valuable green corridor that extends all the way through eastern London from rural Essex to the Thames. This is designated as Green Belt and much of it is now publicly accessible and managed for wildlife.

The Chase Nature Reserve

120ac/49ha   **OS Ex175**   **TQ 515 860**   **LNR**

This nature reserve with two large lakes occupies land shaped by gravel extraction. When extraction finished in the late 1960s some of the pits escaped infilling and formed a valuable wetland habitat of ponds, lakes and marshes. The area was turned over to horse pasture which retained its open nature until it became a nature reserve in the mid-1980s. Most of it is owned by Barking & Dagenham Council and the remainder by Havering, and it is managed by London Wildlife Trust – the largest reserve under the Trust's care.

The Chase is of interest principally for its birds, with over 190 species recorded. Kingfishers, skylark, little ringed plover and lapwing all breed here. Teal and shoveler visit in winter, and it attracts the occasional rarity such as spotted crake.

For those not especially interested in birds, it is a haven of quiet within easy reach of much of urban east London.

Eastbrookend Country Park

The London Borough of
Barking & Dagenham

188ac/76.1ha   **OS Ex175**   **TQ 510 860**

Eastbrookend is an extensive country park created on land between Dagenham and Hornchurch damaged by gravel extraction, next to The Chase nature reserve. It opened in 1995.

Fels Fields to the north of Dagenham Road has large grassland areas frequented by skylarks and meadow pipits.

Eastbrook Grove to the south houses the visitor centre, built with the support of the Heritage Lottery Fund and designed to showcase environmental features such as low energy use. It has several large water bodies and the eastern section, adjoining The Chase nature reserve, has a heath-like character.

Signposted off Dagenham Road which runs south from Rush Green Road (A124 Upminster–Hornchurch–Dagenham).

District line tube to Dagenham Heathway and then bus 174 to Rush Green; or 15-minute walk from Dagenham East station via the footpath alongside the chemical plant.

Accessible at all times. Car parks open dawn till dusk.

May for breeding birds, with gorse and hawthorn in flower; September to March for birds on passage and wintering in the reserve.

To avoid disturbing the birds, please do not go inside the fence around The Slack and keep dogs under strict control.

Call the Eastbrookend rangers on 020 8595 4155.

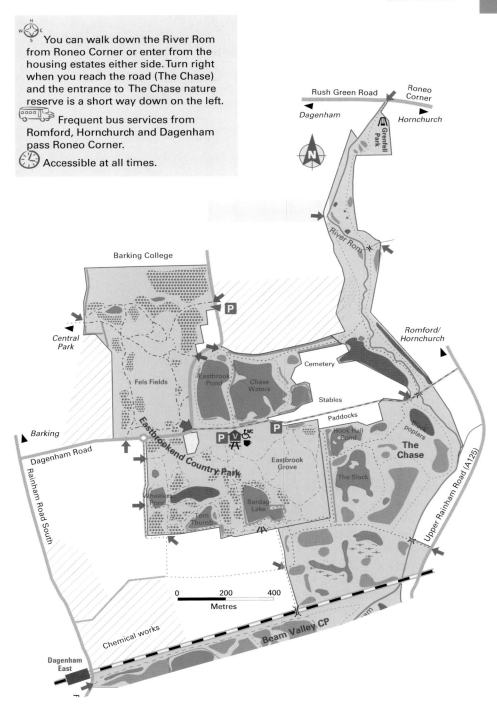

You can walk down the River Rom from Roneo Corner or enter from the housing estates either side. Turn right when you reach the road (The Chase) and the entrance to The Chase nature reserve is a short way down on the left.

Frequent bus services from Romford, Hornchurch and Dagenham pass Roneo Corner.

Accessible at all times.

Rush Green Road

Roneo Corner

Dagenham

Hornchurch

Grenfell Park

River Rom

Barking College

Central Park

Romford/ Hornchurch

Cemetery

Fels Fields

Eastbrook Pond

Chase Waters

Stables

Paddocks

Hook Hall Pond

Black poplars

Barking

Dagenham Road

Eastbrookend Country Park

Eastbrook Grove

The Chase

The Slack

Rainham Road South

Wheelers Pond

Tom Thumb

Bardag Lake

Upper Rainham Road (A125)

0   200   400
Metres

Chemical works

Beam Valley CP

Dagenham East

Beam Valley Country Park

183ac/74ha   *OS Ex175*   *TQ 512 850*

This new country park in Dagenham runs alongside the River Beam, from Dagenham Village and the railway in the north almost all the way to New Road in the south, opposite the Ford plant.

The area has been partly worked for gravel, leaving a wide diversity of habitats, with wet and dry grassland, tall herbs and scrub, and one small area of willow woodland, a scarce habitat in London.

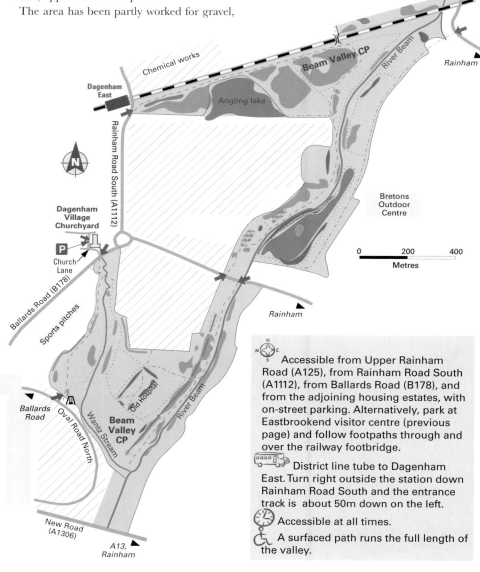

Accessible from Upper Rainham Road (A125), from Rainham Road South (A1112), from Ballards Road (B178), and from the adjoining housing estates, with on-street parking. Alternatively, park at Eastbrookend visitor centre (previous page) and follow footpaths through and over the railway footbridge.

District line tube to Dagenham East. Turn right outside the station down Rainham Road South and the entrance track is about 50m down on the left.

Accessible at all times.

A surfaced path runs the full length of the valley.

Along the river kingfishers are seen regularly, and reed warblers and reed buntings breed. Skylarks breed in the drier grassland. The valley is also worth a visit in migration periods, because migrating birds follow the Dagenham Corridor – of which the Beam Valley forms a part – through London.

Dense wetland vegetation grows alongside the river in places, especially in the north-ern section and along the Wantz Stream in the south, and snipe sometimes find refuge here in winter. A series of ponds have been created and these are used for breeding by great crested newts and other amphibians.

Remnants of World War II defences can still be seen and one pillbox has been converted into a bat cave, providing a secure space for roosting.

Dagenham Village Churchyard

The London Borough of
Barking & **Dagenham**

2ac/.8ha   **OS Ex175**   *TQ 500 844*   **LNR**

Reached via Church Lane off Ballards Road (B178), Dagenham.

Dagenham East station is a few minutes' walk. Buses run along Church Lane.

Accessible at all times.

This churchyard is a tranquil refuge in a busy residential area of East London. Kestrels sometimes nest in the mature trees and small birds in the church tower.

The Chase nature reserve
Alan Cooper

Beckton Park

74ac/30ha   **OS Ex162**   *TQ 419 814*

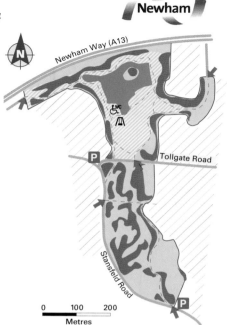

An urban park landscaped by Newham Council in the early 1980s. They have created a good range of habitats, including a lake, areas of scrub and woodland, and a wildflower meadow. The lake supports common breeding waterfowl, including mute swan. The broad belts of native trees and shrubs provide valuable habitat for birds.

In Beckton just north of London City Airport. Access from Tollgate Road, which links Manor Way (A13) with Woolwich Manor (A117), or from Stansfeld Road.

A few minutes' walk from Royal Albert DLR station via Stansfeld Road.

Open dawn to dusk.

Bedfords Park

90ac/36ha   **OS Ex175**   *TQ 518 924*

Bedfords Park was enclosed in the 15th century and the manor house and gardens were laid out around it later. The 90-acre park was acquired by the local council in 1933, but the house fell into disrepair and was demolished in 1959. It is now managed by Havering Council as an urban park.

The upper section has all the scenic grandeur of landscaped parkland, with its exotic trees, its deer enclosure and its close-mown slopes. The lower section is managed for wildlife, with hay meadows and some mature woodland and scrub. The area of marsh to the east of the north–south bridleway is fed by springs seeping out at the top of the slope. Beyond it is a large meadow which is one of the finest flower-rich grasslands in Essex. Here

you will find cuckoo flower, pignut and ragged robin flowering in spring, and later sneezewort and pepper saxifrage.

Birdlife is varied with many warbler species arriving in summer to breed, particularly in the scrub and woodland in the south of the park. A wide variety of dragon- and damselflies can be seen around the lake and ponds in summer.

The visitor centre, run by Essex Wildlife Trust, commands superb views over much of east London and into Kent. It incorporates many sustainable features by reusing parts of the earlier building, incorporating high insulation and using modern roof design such as the suspended stonecrop roof.

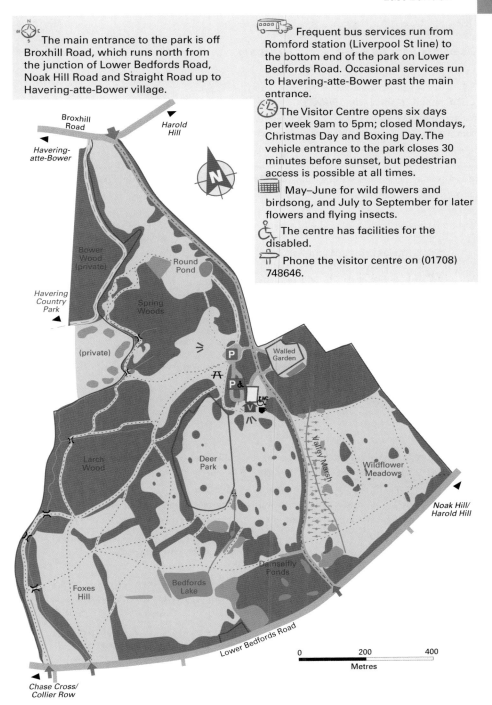

The main entrance to the park is off Broxhill Road, which runs north from the junction of Lower Bedfords Road, Noak Hill Road and Straight Road up to Havering-atte-Bower village.

Frequent bus services run from Romford station (Liverpool St line) to the bottom end of the park on Lower Bedfords Road. Occasional services run to Havering-atte-Bower past the main entrance.

The Visitor Centre opens six days per week 9am to 5pm; closed Mondays, Christmas Day and Boxing Day. The vehicle entrance to the park closes 30 minutes before sunset, but pedestrian access is possible at all times.

May–June for wild flowers and birdsong, and July to September for later flowers and flying insects.

The centre has facilities for the disabled.

Phone the visitor centre on (01708) 748646.

Broadfields Farm

140ac/56ha   **OS Ex175**   *TQ 583 862*

Forestry Commission

This former arable farm is now the Thames Chase Forest Centre, head-quarters of the Thames Chase Community Forest team. It is managed by the Forestry Commission. New woodlands have been planted over much of the site, and its broad rides and occasional glades have been sown with a grass and wildflower mix. Just north of the farm buildings is a new orchard of traditional Essex varieties of apple. There are two ponds, one with a hide and one a dipping platform, and a network of paths, most of them fully accessible.

Such a large site should develop a great deal of wildlife interest as it matures. Already skylarks nest in the open grassland, and birds such as green woodpecker, yellowhammer and whitethroat exploit the young woodland.

The visitor centre, next to the farm buildings which include a traditional Essex barn dating from the 17th century, has displays, a cafe and gift shop.

The main entrance is off Pike Lane, a narrow lane running south from St Mary's Lane (B187) about a mile east of Upminster centre.

Upminster station is about 20 minutes' walk.

Site open 8.30am to dusk. Forest Centre open 10am–5pm (4pm in winter) Tuesday to Sunday, plus Bank Holiday Mondays.

Call the Forest Centre on (01708) 641880.

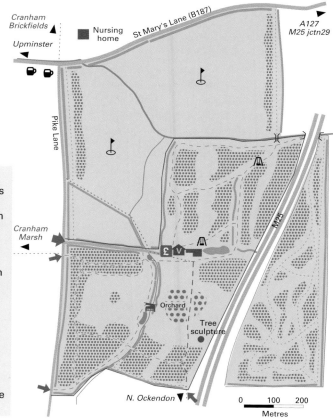

Claybury Park

177ac/71.5ha   *OS Ex174*   *TQ 435 911*   *SSSI (part)*

London Borough of
Redbridge

Claybury Park occupies the south-facing slopes of a ridge east of Woodford Bridge. It consists of parkland associated with Claybury Hall, ancient woodland formerly in the grounds of Claybury Hospital, plus other land owned by the London Borough of Redbridge that has secondary woodland, an old orchard once part of Hospital Farm, patches of scrub, a few ponds and open rides. With such a variety of habitats, many long-established, it is rich in wildlife including some unusual species.

From high up on the slope there are spectacular views over East London, Docklands and the Kent hills – even better, no doubt, from the buildings such as Claybury Hall that dominate the northern skyline.

The western part of the ancient woodland, Claybury Wood, contains many ancient hornbeam coppice stools and pollard oaks and is carpeted with bluebells, wood anemones and ramsons garlic in spring. It also has many wild service trees, butchers broom and broad-leaved helleborine orchids. Hospital Hill Wood to the east is dominated by oak and, probably because of a lack of management in the past, is less interesting botanically. Typical woodland birds are found here, including tawny owl, nuthatch, treecreeper, sparrowhawk and

Just east of Woodford Bridge. Take Fulwell Avenue west from the Fulwell Cross roundabout (A123), or leave the M11/North Circular Road (A406) at their junction and follow Southend Road (A1400) east, turning left into Roding Lane North. On-street parking.

Fairlop tube station (Central line) is on Forest Road about 100m east of Fulwell Cross. Turn right outside the station. Or train to Ilford then bus 169.

Daylight hours only.

Something of interest at all times of the year, but especially May for songbirds and July/August for grassland butterflies and other insects.

A good network of surfaced paths.

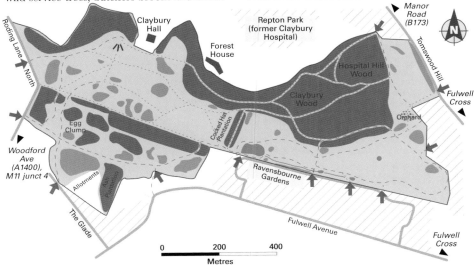

woodpeckers. Migrant warblers such as black-cap visit in summer.

The parkland design was influenced by Humphrey Repton, a landscape designer of the late 18th and early 19th century who lived in Romford, not far away, and also designed Wanstead Park, a couple of miles to the south-west. Several historic landscape features have survived, including Cocked Hat Plantation (a linear woodland of oak, birch and hornbeam),

Ash Plantation (dense elm scrub with mature oak and grey poplar – no ash!) and Egg Clump (oak, ash and hawthorn).

Claybury Park's soils are varied and this makes for variety in its grassland plants also. These support a variety of the commoner grassland butterflies, including small heath. Birds using the grassland, scrub and young woodland include kestrel, skylark, whitethroat, meadow pipit, reed bunting and goldfinch.

Cranham Brickfields

44ac/18ha   *OS Ex175*   *TQ 582 874*   *LNR*

This former brickfield has large areas of unmanaged grassland and scrub full of the commoner wild flowers such as birdsfoot-trefoil and knapweed, and a much rarer plant, pepper saxifrage. A speciality here is dyer's greenweed, whose yellow flowers appear in June. Many rushes and sedges grow in the wetter patches.

Franks Wood, an ancient hornbeam coppice woodland, can be reached via Cranham Brickfields. Bluebells flower in spring and honeysuckle later in the year.

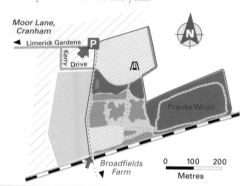

Accessed from Cranham Village via Moor Lane and Limerick Gardens, or via the footpath from St Mary's Lane (B187).

Bus 248 frequent service from Upminster station to Cranham village.

Accessible at all times.

Cranham Marsh

32ac/13ha   *OS Ex175*   *TQ 567 856*   *LNR*

Cranham Marsh is all that remains of a marshland habitat that once covered many square miles of southern Essex, but which has now mostly been converted to arable farming. It contains a variety of habitats including marsh, sedge fen (one of the best surviving in Essex) and ancient woodland.

The three small woods consist mainly of hazel coppice, with some very large oak and

ash trees, patches of wild cherry and a grove of alder. Dogwood, guelder rose, spindle and midland hawthorn are also found here, indicating that it is very old woodland.

The grassland across the south of the reserve is bisected by old reed-filled drainage ditches. It contains a large concentration of betony and, in the wetter patches, southern marsh orchids, marsh marigold and ragged robin. It also has three large patches of the rare yellow loosestrife.

The reserve attracts marshland birds such as sedge warbler and reed bunting, with green and great spotted woodpeckers and tawny owl in the woods. Kestrel and sparrowhawk nest in the large trees regularly, and sometimes hobby.

Grass snakes are often seen in the grassland and there is abundant insect life. Twenty-three butterfly species have been recorded, including small copper, wall brown and speckled wood.

Because of changes in land use around the marsh it is not as wet as it used to be. To make the most of the available water, dams have been built along the main stream. For the grassland and marsh a combination of cutting and grazing by sheep is used to create a mosaic of varying habitats. Parts of the woods are being coppiced on a 12-year cycle.

Access via Argyle Gardens or The Chase, both of which run south off St Mary's Lane (B187), with footpaths leading on to the reserve.

Upminster station is about 20 minutes walk. Bus 248 from Upminster station runs along St Mary's Lane.

Accessible at all times.

April and May for early flowers and birdsong; July and August for later flowers and insects.

Please keep dogs on leads near livestock and under control elsewhere.

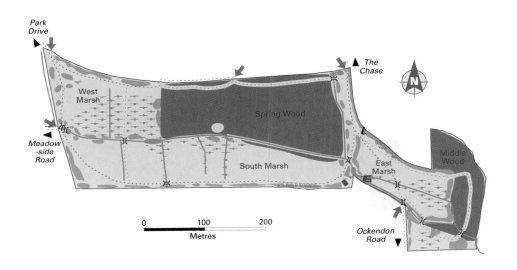

Curtismill Green

**Brentwood
Borough
Council**

119ac/48ha   *OS Ex175*   *TQ 517 965*   *SSSI*

An area of common land with Willow Cottage at its centre, with an open-air theatre nearby. Although the M25 is not far away, once there you could be in another age, when horses were the main form of transport.

In the north it is open grassland with clumps of dense scrub and scattered oaks, grazed by horses. The soils are a mixture of London clay and chalky boulder clay, in places damp, elsewhere dry, and as a result it supports some unusual plants, including betony, lesser spearwort, pepper saxifrage and sneezewort.

As you walk south the woodland becomes denser, consisting mainly of mature oaks with a scattering of hornbeam, hawthorn and holly, and with a brook running through it. In summer the woods are full of speckled wood butterflies.

Access via Albyns lane, which leaves the roundabout where Stapleford Road (B175) joins the A113, about a mile east of Abridge; or via footpaths and byroads from the minor road between Stapleford Abbotts and Navestock Heath. Parking is difficult, so either get someone to drop you off or walk or cycle in.

Accessible at all times

May for early flowers and birdsong in the woods; July–August for meadow flowers and insects.

The paths are used heavily by horses, so are pockmarked and rutted: wear good boots and beware wet patches in winter.

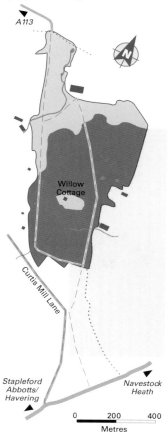

Corn bunting: resident;
its brief song sounds like jangling keys
David Harrison

East Ham

20ac/8ha   **OS Ex162**   **TQ 429 824**

The church of St Mary Magdalene in East Ham has the largest churchyard in London and Newham Council has turned this into a nature reserve. It has grassland, hedges, scrub, mature and young trees, a small raised pond and, of course, gravestones, a distinct microhabitat supporting mosses and lichens.

Here you will find a good selection of insects, reptiles such as slow worms, grass snakes and common lizards, and sometimes blackcap, whitethroat and other migrant birds stop off to nest.

Entrance on Norman Road, just north of the A13 near Beckton Alps.

District line to East Ham; DLR to Beckton; several bus services.

Open Tuesday to Friday 10am–5pm; Sundays 2pm–5pm (4pm in winter).

Disabled access to ground floor of visitor centre. Wheelchair trail with raised outdoor displays.

Guide dogs welcome, but other dogs strictly prohibited.

Phone 020 8470 4525.

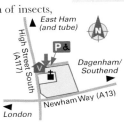

Fairlop Waters

100ac/40ha   **OS Ex174**   **TQ 460 905**

Fairlop Waters is on the site of the former spitfire base, RAF Fairlop, and the area has also been used for landfill. It has a large lake, used for sailing, a smaller one, used for angling, and a golf club. It also has a country park and a nature reserve, landscaped and planted up by Redbridge Council. These areas and the surrounding farmland form an important refuge for some of our declining birds, including skylarks, corn buntings and linnets, and also for brown hares.

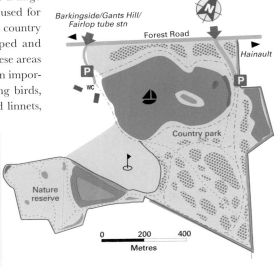

Off Forest Road, which runs from the Fulwell Cross roundabout in Barkingside south of Hainault to join the A1112.

Fairlop tube station is a short walk up Forest Road from the main entrance.

Accessible at all times.

Hainault Forest

What remains of Hainault Forest lies on the north-eastern boundary of Greater London on a miniature version of the ridge that forms Epping Forest – a cap of gravelly and sandy soils over London clay. Two small woodland Local Nature Reserves are close by.

Hainault Forest

291ac/118ha   **OS Ex174**   **TQ 475 938**   **SSSI**

WOODLAND TRUST

After it was 'disafforested' in 1851 most of Hainault Forest was destroyed for housing and farming. What remained, which runs across to the north of the present Hainault Forest Country Park, was managed as wood pasture until about 1900. Local commoners had lopping rights to the hornbeam and used to cut above head height to protect the new growth from cattle and other animals browsing on the forest floor. The limbs were cut before they grew above 10cm – the maximum size useable for charcoal burning and firewood in London. This means a cutting cycle of between 18 and 25 years. Pollarding stopped in the early part of this century as the markets for charcoal and firewood declined.

Now the woodland is being managed by the Woodland Trust, who are repollarding some of the old trees and also raising new trees for pollarding. Pollarding rejuvenates trees but after a long gap it is very risky. and better results can be obtained by starting afresh.

In time pollards form massive trees with a swollen head from which extend huge gnarled limbs. The ancient woodland to the east is dominated by hornbeam pollards and oak standards, with holly, bracken and bramble growing beneath them.

Much of the woodland floor is bare because of the dense shade cast by the overgrown pollards, but it has many damp areas and ditches that are greener and more varied, often lined with pendulous sedge. If you look around you will find unusual plants like wood speedwell, hartstongue fern, marsh pennywort and butcher's broom.

In the western part the woodland is very different. It has regenerated on sections that were cleared and is dominated by oak and birch with some aspen, poplar and ash.

In the north-west corner a small area of former heathland – a rare habitat in south Essex – is being restored by removing invading birch and scrub. It still has some heather and dwarf gorse which it is hoped will spread.

Chigwell Row Wood

39ac/15.6ha   **OS Ex174**   **TQ 463 929**   **LNR**

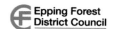
Epping Forest District Council

Once this fragment of woodland in Chigwell Row was part of the Royal Forest of Essex and later the Forest of Waltham, like Hainault Forest on the other side of Romford Road. It contains hundreds of veteran hornbeam pollards plus a number of ancient oaks. Like all ancient woodlands it is important for insects, and particularly those that depend on dead wood.

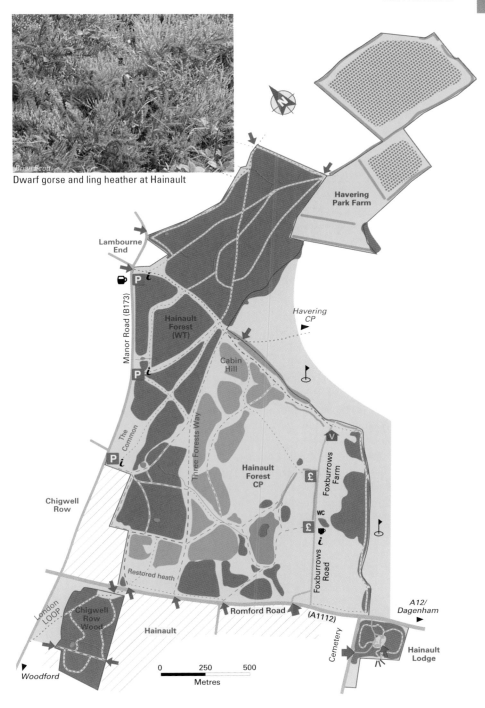

Dwarf gorse and ling heather at Hainault

Brian Ecott

Havering Park Farm

Lambourne End

Manor Road (B173)

P *i*

Hainault Forest (WT)

P *i*

Cabin Hill

Havering CP

The Common

P *i*

Three Forests Way

Chigwell Row

Hainault Forest CP

V

Foxburrows Farm

£

WC

£

i

Foxburrows Road

Restored heath

London LOOP

Chigwell Row Wood

Hainault

Romford Road

(A1112)

A12/ Dagenham

Woodford

Cemetery

Hainault Lodge

0 250 500

Metres

Hainault Forest Country Park

London Borough of **Redbridge**

247ac/100ha   OS Ex174   TQ 475 928

The area to the east and south of the ancient woodland was part of the Forest's 'plains' and therefore was treeless, but it has been invaded by birch and scrub since grazing ceased. The dense cover attracts many breeding birds including some that are scarce in Essex, such as spotted flycatchers.

The many areas of rough grassland sheltered by surrounding trees make good feeding territory for bats, which find roosting sites in the ancient trees. A number of different species can be seen feeding over the lake on warm evenings, including pipistrelles, noctules and daubenton's bats.

Off Romford Road (A1112), about one mile south of Chigwell Row. Enter the A1112 from the south via the A12 (London – Chelmsford) and from the north via the A113 (Woodford – Chelmsford).

The nearest stations are Ilford (Liverpool St line) and Hainault (Central line tube), from where buses run to the main entrance. Buses also run from Romford, Chadwell Heath and Barkingside.

Accessible at all times. The main (Foxburrows Road) car park is open every day from 7.00am to dusk; the small peripheral car parks on Manor Road, Chigwell Row are always open.

May for songbirds; or try a misty winter day to see the fantastic tree shapes in the ancient woodland.

The Forest is heavily visited, especially on holidays. The quietest time is early morning, accessing via the car parks off Manor Road along its northern edge.

Paths in the eastern part of the Forest are often very muddy.

Call the country park office on 020 8500 7353.

Havering Park Farm

WOODLAND
TRUST

54ac/22ha   OS Ex175   TQ 490 940

This farmland to the east of Hainault Forest was previously part of the mediæval deer park associated with the Palace of Havering nearby. It was acquired by the Woodland Trust in 2006 to create additional habitat.

Hainault Lodge

London Borough of **Redbridge**

14ac/6ha   OS Ex175   TQ 476 919   LNR

The site of an 18th-century hunting lodge, built on top of Hog Hill, now a Local Nature Reserve managed by Redbridge Council, supported by the Havering and Redbridge Wildlife and Countryside Group.

The former lodge and its grounds are surrounded by mature woodland including some massive oak and hornbeam pollards. New pollards of young trees are being created to eventually replace these. Woodland birds such as goldcrest and treecreeper nest in the reserve. A nature trail has been laid out.

On the corner of Forest Road and Romford Road, opposite Hainault Forest Country Park.

To gain access contact the country park office on 020 8500 7353.

Havering Country Park

150ac/60ha   *OS Ex175*   *TQ 500 924*

This country park, owned and managed by Havering Council, is mainly mature mixed woodland, including some ancient hazel coppice and one of the few established pine woodlands in this part of Essex, which attracts pine specialists such as goldcrests (which breed here) and coal tits. High on the ridge the soil is gravelly and here you find birch, gorse and bracken, while the damper, heavier clay soil of the valley to the south favours oak, hornbeam and bramble. The wildflower meadows are cut for hay in September. Agrimony, birdsfoot trefoil and ox-eye daisies grow here.

Access via Clockhouse Lane, which runs north from the roundabout in Collier Row where Collier Row Lane (B174 from Eastern Avenue, A12) meets Chase Cross Road. Pedestrian access also from Havering-atte-Bower along Wellingtonia Avenue.

Frequent buses run from Romford and terminate at the main (Clockhouse Lane) entrance.

Accessible at all times. Car parks open from dawn to dusk.

May for migrant songbirds and early flowers in the woodland; June–July for wild flowers in the meadows; autumn for tree colours.

Vehicle access to easy access trail from Wellingtonia Avenue via a radar key obtainable from Havering Council or from the Park Office (01708 720858).

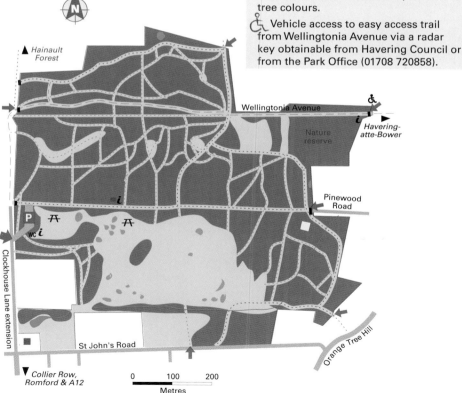

Ingrebourne Valley

This part of the Ingrebourne Valley, sandwiched between the built-up areas of Hornchuch and Rainham, has at its centre a prime wildlife site, the Ingrebourne Marshes SSSI, next to the former RAF Hornchurch, and surrounded by a number of areas of former landfill that have been landscaped. It is already a superb area for wildlife and can only get better.

Ingrebourne Marshes

371ac/150ha   **OS Ex175**   **TQ 535 848**   *SSSI (part), LNR*

This Local Nature Reserve (LNR) consists of Hornchurch Country Park and parts of the adjoining Ingrebourne Marshes SSSI, plus land adjoining the Ingrebourne both upstream and downstream.

Hornchurch Country Park was created in the early 1980s mainly on the site of an abandoned airfield, RAF Hornchurch. The airfield was first developed during World War I and during World War II squadrons of spitfires were based here that played a part in the Battle of Britain. Remnants of the airfield are still visible in the form of pillboxes and tett turrets. Thousands of trees have been planted and are creating an attractive landscape.

For wildlife, the highlight of the LNR is the Ingrebourne Marshes SSSI, a fine wetland next to the old airfield and further downstream alongside the River Ingrebourne. To protect it, Havering Council has raised water levels and reintroduced grazing. A wetland on this scale – with a huge reedbed alongside marsh and flood meadow – is very unusual anywhere, and especially so close to London.

Redshank, lapwing and yellow wagtail breed on this kind of wet tussocky grassland. Kingfishers make their nest holes in the steep banks of the river. Many sedge and reed warblers nest here, and also cetti's warblers, one of our few resident warbler species. Water rails can occasionally be seen prowling around in the tall vegetation. Our smallest duck, the teal, overwinters on the ponds and bearded tits, and occasionally bittern, in the reedbeds.

With such a variety of wet and dry habitats the area is valuable for insects too. Banded demoiselles can be seen all the way down the river and it also supports several rarities.

The London Loop long-distance footpath runs all the way down the valley to the Thames a mile or so to the south, at present diverting into South Hornchurch but planned eventually to follow the river all the way.

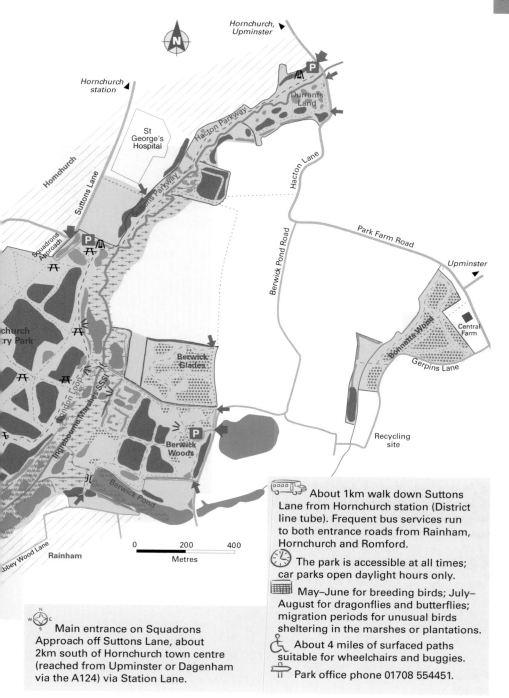

About 1km walk down Suttons Lane from Hornchurch station (District line tube). Frequent bus services run to both entrance roads from Rainham, Hornchurch and Romford.

The park is accessible at all times; car parks open daylight hours only.

May–June for breeding birds; July–August for dragonflies and butterflies; migration periods for unusual birds sheltering in the marshes or plantations.

About 4 miles of surfaced paths suitable for wheelchairs and buggies.

Park office phone 01708 554451.

Main entrance on Squadrons Approach off Suttons Lane, about 2km south of Hornchurch town centre (reached from Upminster or Dagenham via the A124) via Station Lane.

Ingrebourne Valley **Berwick Glades**

22ac/9ha **OS Ex175** *TQ 542 842*

Forestry Commission

Former farmland planted up by the Forestry Commission. To maintain the good views across the Ingrebourne marshes towards Hornchurch and Elm Park, large open glades have been left between pockets of new planting. Skylarks nest in these glades and in the surrounding fields.

Berwick Woods

50ac/20ha **OS Ex175** *TQ 542 837* **SSSI (part)**

Tarmac

Berwick Woods is a former gravel extraction site that has been restored by the gravel company, Tarmac. As well as newly planted woods and grassland, it has some established scrub and woodland around pits and ponds.

It borders Berwick Ponds, used partly for angling but also part of the Ingrebourne Marshes SSSI and surrounded by large stands of reed, and it overlooks the flood meadows alongside the Ingrebourne. With such a mix of habitats it supports a wide range of our commoner birds and also some rarities – cetti's warblers and water rail can be seen around Berwick Ponds.

It is also good for reptiles, supporting what is probably the largest population of adders in Greater London.

Access from Berwick Pond Road, which joins Hacton Lane, Hornchurch, to Warwick Lane, Rainham. Can also be reached from Hornchurch CP via the bridge across the Ingrebourne River.

Accessible at all times.

May for songbirds; high summer for butterflies and other insects.

Bonnetts Wood

42ac/17ha **OS Ex175** *TQ 555 845*

Forestry Commission

Former farmland planted up by the Forestry Commission in 2003. It is named after the Bonnett family who had farmed the land since the 1920s.

Access from Park Farm Road, across the road from the southern exit from Parklands, Upminster.

Accessible at all times.

Ingrebourne Hill

183ac/74ha **OS Ex175** *TQ 525 837*

Forestry Commission

A former gravel extraction site that has been landfilled and landscaped. Its main feature is the hill that gives it its name, from which there are good views across London and the Thames to the South Downs and where a mountain bike course is to be constructed.

Access from the south off Rainham Road (A125), north of Dovers Corner (junction with A1306); or from the north via Hornchurch country park.

Accessible at all times.

Nectar-feeders: bees and their mimics

Common carder bee (worker) on knapweed: nests in the surface thatch in rough grassland
Tony Gunton

Buff-tailed bumblebee (queen) on thistle: nests underground, entering via a tunnel
Tony Gunton

Leafcutter bee: cuts pieces of leaf to line its nest; there are several different species
Tony Gunton

Honey bee (worker) on hemp agrimony: important pollinators of food crops but also feed on wild plants
Tony Gunton

Bumblebee hoverfly: looks like a bee – to deter predators – but has only two wings and no sting
Tony Gunton

Red mason bee: one of our commonest bees, nests in hollow stems of bramble or hogweed
Peter Harvey

Lower Lea Valley Bow Creek

10ac/4ha   *OS Ex162*   *TQ 393 813*

This little gem in the East End was originally an osier bed, then became an ironworks, and has now been transformed into an ecology park.

As you enter, you have views over tidal mudflats fringing the river, where redshank often feed. Flocks of waders can also be seen commuting along the river as the tides change.

The path leads you past a stream and ponds fed from a borehole and small wildflower meadows, including a flood meadow kept wet via the stream. In summer you can expect to see butterflies, including small copper, orange-tip and green-veined white, and dragonflies such as the emperor.

Kestrels often hunt along the railway verges. Sand martin and kingfisher breeding banks have been created, so there is a chance of seeing them also. Reed buntings sometimes breed and in winter look out for grey wagtails.

East India Dock Basin

12ac/5ha   *OS Ex162*   *TQ 391 808*

First built in 1806, the East India Docks finally closed in 1967 and this basin is the only surviving remnant. It contains tidal brackish water and has mudflats with a small band of saltmarsh vegetation along its northern edge. This is dominated, unusually, by buttonweed, with sea milkwort and sea arrowgrass.

There are muddy and shingly islands within the basin and two nesting rafts, used every summer by a colony of common terns. In winter it attracts shelduck and flocks of teal and tufted duck. It is also a good place to see black redstart, a nationally rare breeding bird that has adapted to living on industrial sites in large urban centres like London.

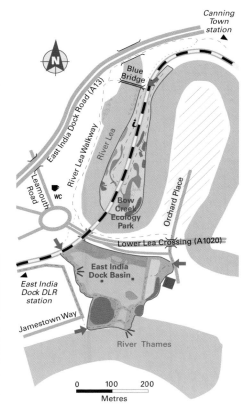

In Canning Town near where the River Lea enters the Thames, south of the East India Dock Road (A13) and just east of the Blackwall Tunnel.

Jubilee line tube or Docklands Light Railway to Canning Town station. Several bus services run to Canning Town also.

Accessible 9.15am to dusk.

Pot Kiln Wood

12ac/5ha   *OS Ex175*   *TQ 573 886*

WOODLAND
TRUST

Flower-rich horse pastures that have partly scrubbed over, with luxuriant hedgerows and a few patches of damp ground.

Some trees have been planted to screen the A127 to the north and horse grazing will continue to keep the flower-rich grassland open. A good selection of birds nest in the hedgerows and scrub.

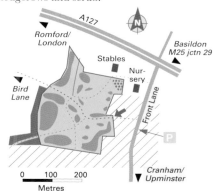

Reached via a footpath running east from Front Lane, Cranham. Front Lane can be entered from the A127 westbound about 1km beyond M25 junction 29 or from the B187 (St Mary's Lane) about 2km east of Upminster centre.

Bus 248 from Upminster station stops on Front Lane a short way from the entrance footpath.

Accessible at all times.

Green-veined white
Tony Gunton

Emperor dragonfly (male)
Tony Gunton

The Manor

174ac/70ha   *OS Ex175*   *TQ 551 928*   *LNR*

Dagnam Park was part of the former Manor of Dagnam. Across the centre is ancient parkland, sandwiched between two small ancient woodlands. It has a number of ponds in some of which great crested newts breed. The ancient grasslands in the east of the park are managed as hay meadows, and are rich in wild flowers and insects in summer. The many large patches of scrub and the ancient trees serve as nest sites for a variety of birds.

Duck Wood to the south is another ancient woodland. It has ten ponds, some open and surrounded by vegetation, others shady and overhung by shrubs and trees. Unusual aquatic plants such as starwort can found

here. It has carpets of bluebells in spring, and many other wild flowers including ancient woodland specialists: wood anemones, wood violets and others.

Many fallow deer visit, and it attracts a range of woodland birds, including hawfinches that sometimes visit in winter.

Off Settle Road in the north of Harold Hill. Turn off the A12 on to Gooshays Drive east of Gallows Corner, then turn right at the roundabout on to Dagnam Park Drive. Settle Road turns off on the left.

Bus services from Romford run along Dagnam Park Drive.

Accessible at all times.

May to August for birds, wild flowers and insects.

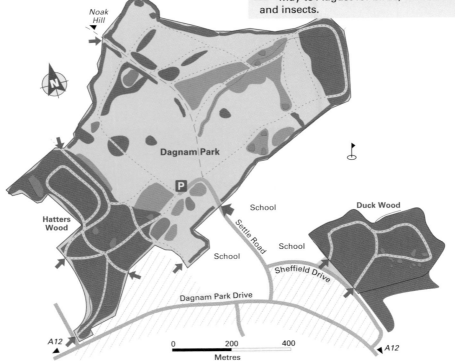

The Ripple

25ac/10ha   **OS Ex162**   **TQ 467 824**

Set among the industrial landscape of Barking Reach, the Ripple was once a dumping area for pulverised fuel ash, and shows how nature can reclaim industrial wasteland. Fuel ash creates a low-nutrient, alkaline soil and this in turn shapes the vegetation. Many pyramidal and southern marsh orchids can be seen dotted throughout the birch woodland in May and June, and the new meadow nearby has swathes of native wildflowers, attracting a wide range of butterflies and other insects in summer. Look out especially for flocks of goldfinches in summer and autumn.

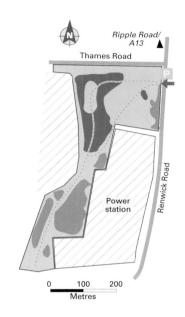

Next to Thamesmead Park City Farm at the junction of Thames Road and Renwick Road in Barking.

Tube or train to Barking, then bus to end of its route in Thames View estate.

May to June for orchids.

Tylers Common

Tylers Common, in the Metropolitan Green Belt between Harold Wood and the M25, is now surrounded by new Forestry Commission woodlands planted up as part of the Thames Chase Community Forest.

Tylers Common

69ac/28ha   **OS Ex175**   **TQ 563 907**

Tylers Common is the last remaining sizeable piece of common land left in Havering. Its name derives from the brick and tile industry that exploited the clay deposits around here from Saxon times onwards.

Parts are kept open by grazing by horses and parts have been invaded by scrub and trees. In summer the grassland is full of wild flowers, including agrimony, birdsfoot trefoil and knapweed. It also has some rarer plants, including sneezewort (in the damp south-east corner) and dwarf gorse, indicative of its heathland past.

Skylarks and meadow pipits breed here. The mix of scrub, tall hedges and open grassland also attracts declining seed-eating birds including yellowhammers, linnets and bullfinches.

Tylers Common Harold Court Woods

67ac/27ha   *OS Ex175*   *TQ 560 913*

A new Forestry Commission woodland surrounding Harold Court, which is now a riding stables. A flower meadow and pond have been created next to the railway and there is an established pond further south.

Pages Wood

183ac/74ha   *OS Ex175*   *TQ 561 894*

The largest of the Forestry Commission's new woodlands within Thames Chase, consisting of two former farms sloping down towards the River Ingrebourne, only a stream at this point.

The former Pages Farm has been extensively planted, but the grazing meadows of Mount Pleasant Farm lower down have been left in their original state and are rich in flowers and insects. The combination of these with the river, the young woodland and the rough grassland makes it a good area for birds at almost any time of the year.

Sculptures designed by local children add extra interest.

Tylers Wood

30ac/12ha   *OS Ex175*   *TQ 572 904*

Former arable land filling in the gap between Tylers Common and the M25, which runs across to the east on an embankment. Trees have been planted to screen the M25 and in patches elsewhere. Good views from the top and some flower-rich damp grassland as a bonus.

Folkes Lane Woodland

119ac/48ha   *OS Ex175*   *TQ 577 896*

Four former arable fields next to the M25, with a spectacular view towards Canary Wharf from the top.

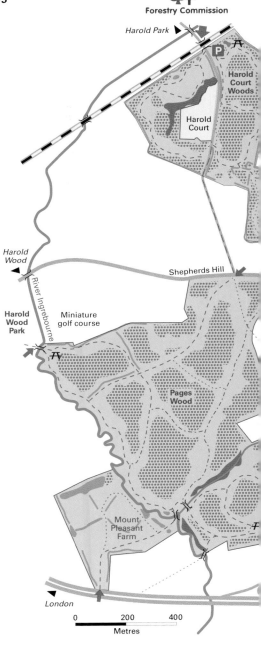

Harold Park

Harold Court Woods

Harold Court

Harold Wood

Shepherds Hill

Harold Wood Park

River Ingrebourne

Miniature golf course

Pages Wood

Mount Pleasant Farm

London

0   200   400
Metres

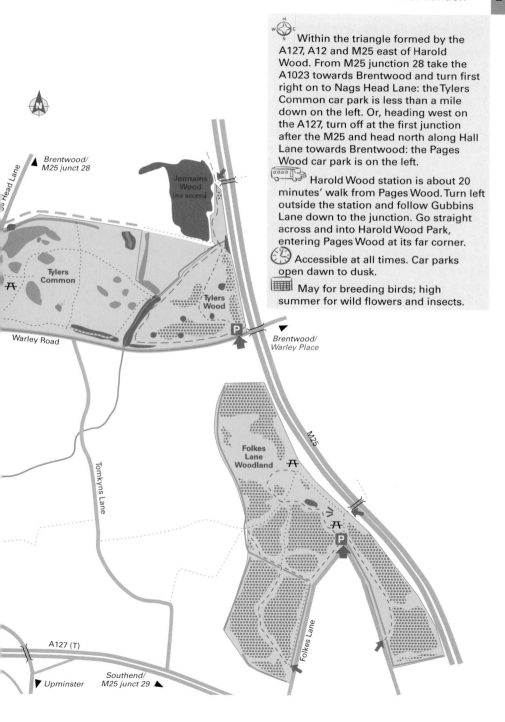

Within the triangle formed by the A127, A12 and M25 east of Harold Wood. From M25 junction 28 take the A1023 towards Brentwood and turn first right on to Nags Head Lane: the Tylers Common car park is less than a mile down on the left. Or, heading west on the A127, turn off at the first junction after the M25 and head north along Hall Lane towards Brentwood: the Pages Wood car park is on the left.

Harold Wood station is about 20 minutes' walk from Pages Wood. Turn left outside the station and follow Gubbins Lane down to the junction. Go straight across and into Harold Wood Park, entering Pages Wood at its far corner.

Accessible at all times. Car parks open dawn to dusk.

May for breeding birds; high summer for wild flowers and insects.

Brentwood/
M25 junct 28

Jermains Wood
(no access)

Tylers Common

Tylers Wood

Warley Road

Brentwood/
Warley Place

Folkes Lane Woodland

M25

Tomkyns Lane

Folkes Lane

A127 (T)

Upminster

Southend/
M25 junct 29

Wanstead Park

140ac/56ha   **OS Ex174**   **TQ 415 875**

CITY OF LONDON

Once the renowned 18th-century gardens of Wanstead House, Wanstead Park is managed now by the City of London as part of Epping Forest. It has several large lakes, with secluded inlets, islands and marshy areas. These are surrounded by a mixture of mature woodland, parkland and open acid grassland where harebells grow. The River Roding runs along its eastern boundary.

This combination makes for rich wildlife, despite the constant visitor pressure. Birdlife is particularly good, with kingfishers seen regularly throughout the year, wildfowl visiting the lakes in winter and hobbies in summer, and both water birds and migrant warblers nesting in summer.

South of the A12 (Eastern Avenue)/ M11 interchange. Can be reached from Wanstead Park Road to the east via an overbridge, from Woodlands Avenue/ Northumberland Avenue to the south and from Warren Road to the north-west. No parking on the site.

Central line tube to Wanstead. Several bus services run to this station also.

Accessible in daylight hours only.

Autumn/winter for visiting wildfowl; April/May for woodland flowers and birdsong.

A good network of surfaced paths.

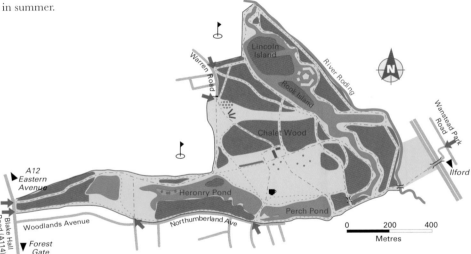

Brown hawker dragonfly and blue-tailed damselfly laying eggs at Wanstead Park

Tony Gunton

The south-west corner of Essex, mainly comprising Thurrock and Basildon, is heavily urbanised, but Basildon has the Langdon Hills and large areas of former plotland to the south of the new town, while Thurrock has the Mardyke Valley, a complex of ancient and new woodlands around Belhus, and the former chalk pits near Grays, now Chafford Gorges Nature Park. Along its southern fringe lie some of the best surviving marshlands of the Thames Estuary, the largest of which is the RSPB's Rainham Marshes reserve on the edge of Greater London.

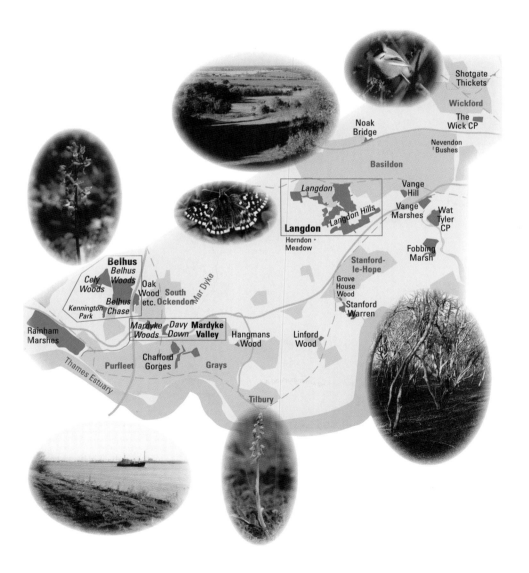

Shotgate Thickets

Wickford

Noak Bridge

The Wick CP

Nevendon Bushes

Basildon

Vange Hill

Langdon

Langdon Hills

Vange Marshes

Wat Tyler CP

Langdon

Horndon Meadow

Fobbing Marsh

Stanford-le-Hope

Belhus
Belhus Woods

Cely Woods

Oak Wood South Ockendon
etc.

Grove House Wood

Kennington Park

Belhus Chase

Mar Dyke

Stanford Warren

Rainham Marshes

Mardyke Woods

Davy Down

Mardyke Valley

Hangmans Wood

Linford Wood

Thames Estuary

Purfleet

Chafford Gorges

Grays

Tilbury

Belhus **Belhus Chase**

134ac/54ha   **OS Ex175**   **TQ 567 822**

WOODLAND
TRUST

This land to the south of Belhus Woods Country Park was acquired by the Woodland Trust in 1998 as part of its 'Woods on your Doorstep' project. Part has been planted with trees and part left as open meadows, to create a parkland atmosphere.

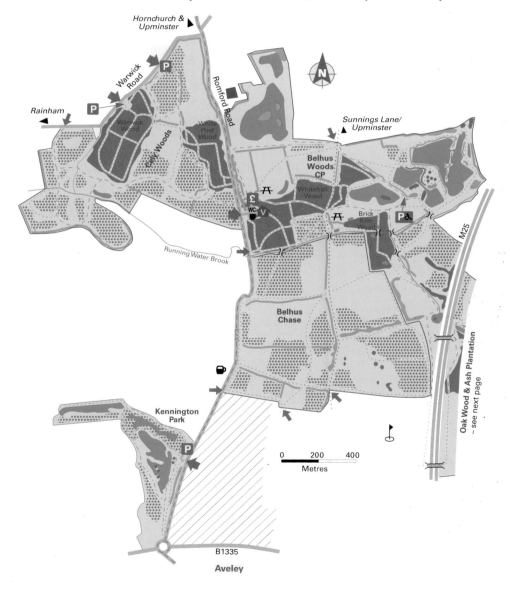

Belhus Woods Country Park

180ac/72ha   **OS Ex175**   **TQ 565 825**

Essex County Council

Belhus Woods was once a deer park, and was landscaped by Capability Brown in the mid-18th century. It is now a country park managed by Essex County Council. The main part, to the east of Romford Road, contains ancient woodland, grassland, and five lakes that were created by gravel extraction and added to the country park later. Two of these are used for fishing but the others are reserved for wildlife. There are two further small ancient woodlands on the other side of the road. More land surrounding the park has been added to it recently, some of which is being planted with trees and some kept as hay meadows.

With such a variety of habitats the park is rich in wildlife. Brick Kiln wood with its streams and ponds, dug to extract clay for brickmaking, is alive with insects in summer, as are the meadows nearby. The hazel in Running Water Wood is coppiced to produce timber for thatching and hurdle-making, and the clearings are full of wild flowers, including early purple orchids and ragged robin.

Cely Woods

141ac/57ha   **OS Ex175**   **TQ 560 828**

Forestry Commission

In 2001/2 the Forestry Commission acquired farmland surrounding the ancient woodlands of Warwick and White Post Woods and planted parts of it with trees. Open meadows have been left between the woods and north of White Post Wood and natural regeneration from the woods is being encouraged. Running Water Brook crosses the site and a small wetland has been created nearby.

The name Cely refers to an Essex merchant family that owned land here in the Middle Ages.

Kennington Park

99ac/40ha   **OS Ex175**   **TQ 560 812**

waste recycling group

A restored former clay pit near Aveley. A network of paths leads around several lakes, some of which are used for angling. Wetland birds breed in the dense vegetation around the lakes and it is a good place for dragonflies in summer.

Access from Romford Road north of Aveley. From Upminster follow Corbets Tey Road (B1421) south, turn right on to Harwood Hall Lane at the Huntsman & Hounds PH, then first left on to Aveley Road which runs straight on into Romford Road.

Half-hourly service from Upminster station to Grays runs along Romford Road.

Belhus Woods open 8am until dusk all the year round. Visitor centre open 10am–5pm at weekends and 1pm–4pm on Wednesdays from April to October. Other sites and public footpaths accessible at all times.

May–July for birdsong, butterflies and dragonflies. Choose a day with a westerly breeze to carry away the noise from the nearby M25.

Parking area for disabled near the Belhus Woods lakes.

Call the Belhus Woods ranger on 01708 865628 for more information or details of activities.

Belhus Oak Wood & Ash Plantation

62ac/25ha   *OS Ex175*   *TQ 577 816*

THURROCK ◆ COUNCIL

Part of the former gardens of Belhus House, which were designed by Capability Brown. It consists of two woodlands separated by part of the Long Pond, now truncated by the M25 motorway. The open grassland between the woods and the M25 contains some plants that are unusual in Essex, including harebells and subterranean clover.

Access from Hamble Lane and Humber Avenue in South Ockendon or from Belhus Woods via the footbridge across the M25.

Accessible at all times.

Surfaced path loop suitable for wheelchairs.

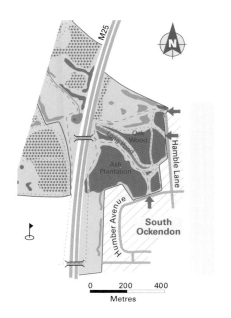

Pyramidal orchid: flowers mid-June–August

Alan Sadgrove

Kidney vetch: flowers April–September

Tony Gunton

Chafford Gorges Nature Park

163ac/66ha   **OS Ex162**   *TQ 597 795*   **SSSI (part)**

ESSEX
Wildlife Trust

Chafford Gorges Nature Park lies at the heart of the Chafford Hundred housing development in Grays Thurrock, near the Lakeside Shopping Centre. It consists of former chalk quarries known as Warren Gorge, Lion Gorge and Grays Gorge, together with connecting land.

Much of it has chalky soil and as a result it has a great number of plants that like alkaline conditions, including kidney vetch, bladder campion and many orchids. As well as chalky soil, it has some sandy and gravelly areas and these support a large number of unusual insects. The large lakes, the woodland and the chalk cliffs provide habitats for a wide range of other animals, including great crested newts, bats, kingfishers and sand martins.

Warren Gorge

This is the largest gorge and can be viewed and accessed from Essex Wildlife Trust's visitor centre that overlooks it and from the cycle path that runs around most of its perimeter.

Much of the meadow in the base of the gorge has been translocated from chalk meadows on land near Chafford Hundred station that has now been developed. It is managed to encourage the rare plants likely to be in the seed bank in the soil. In summer you can see pyramidal and common spotted orchids, yellow rattle and kidney vetch.

In summer you may hear reed and cetti's warblers singing in the reeds, or see kingfishers, hobbies or house martins feeding in or above the lake. In winter the gorge is visited by birds such as siskin, redpoll, pintail and pochard.

Lion Gorge

The large lake supports a variety of species of fish, including tench, rudd, pike and bream. A community-led fishing club has been set up to help manage these waters.

This gorge is also important for bats: four different species have been recorded here and they make a spectacular show feeding over the lake on warm summer nights. A grille has been fitted over the entrance to the tunnel leading to Warren Gorge to protect the bats that roost inside.

The cliffs at the southern end have important Pleistocene Thames deposits containing many fossils.

Accessed from the A1012 to Grays via Devonshire Road and Drake Road. The A1012 can be reached from the A13 east of where it meets the M25 at junction 30.

Nearest train stations are Grays and Chafford Hundred with regular bus services from both: nearest bus stop is opposite medical centre on Drake Road. Half-hourly bus service from Upminster station to Grays: get off opposite the supermarket and follow the footpath round Warren Gorge to the visitor centre.

Nature park accessible at all times. Visitor centre open daily except Mondays, 9am to 5pm.

Something of interest at all times of the year, but come in June or July for a spectacular display of wild flowers, later in the summer for butterflies and dragonflies, or on warm summer evenings to watch bats over the lakes.

Dogs on leads in Lion Gorge please.

Good surfaced paths in Warren Gorge and Lion Gorge but some steep inclines to negotiate.

For more information contact the visitor centre on 01375 484016.

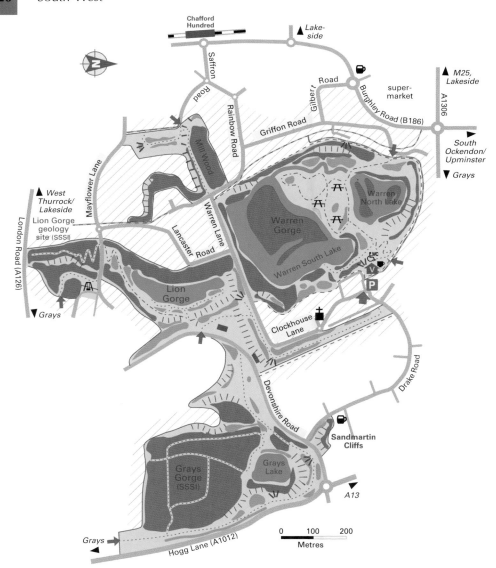

Grays Gorge

This gorge is well known locally for its great range of wild flowers, including nine different species of orchid. Other unusual plants that grow here include common milkwort, fairy flax and autumn gentian. It is important also for butterflies, including green hairstreak and holly blue, and a number of nationally important species of bee, wasp and beetle.

A path runs around the top of the gorge and along here you can see good numbers of pyramidal and man orchids in June. The meadow at the far end has adderstongue fern and is a good spot to see marbled white butterflies, flying from late June to mid-August.

Fobbing Marsh

187ac/76ha   *OS Ex175*   *TQ 716 845*   *SSSI (part)*

ESSEX
Wildlife Trust

One of the few remaining Thameside grazing marshes, set on the north-west edge of Fobbing Creek, part of which was dammed in the aftermath of the 1953 floods. As well as the grazing meadows it has areas of rough grassland (the largest of which is the bed of the dammed creek), saltmarsh, seawalls and an adjoining small reedbed.

Its flowering plants are typical of Thameside marshes, including hairy buttercup, knotted hedge parsley, slender hare's-ear and sea barley, together with the normal range of saltmarsh plants and, in early summer, large colourful patches of vetches and tares. It also supports corn chervil and the nationally rare least lettuce.

In summer there are many dragonflies and damselflies along the borrow dykes. The rank grass along the seawalls is a haven for grass-hoppers and bush-crickets.

Corn bunting and yellow wagtail breed regularly, and the marsh is used by wintering raptors, wildfowl and waders. Visiting passage migrants include wheatear and whinchat.

Down Marsh Lane, 800m north of Fobbing Church and about a mile from the A13. Park in Fobbing High Road near the top of Marsh Lane. Please leave the entrance to Marsh Lane clear as it is used by wide farm machinery. Walk down Marsh Lane and at the bottom take the left-hand fork and follow the track until you see the reserve noticeboard – this is almost a mile from the High Road.

A bus service from Basildon and Stanford-le-Hope stops at Marsh Lane.

Accessible at all times

December and January to see raptors and waders; March, April and September for birds on passage; summer for insects and wild flowers.

Please do not walk along the top of the seawalls as this disturbs and frightens away the wildlife.

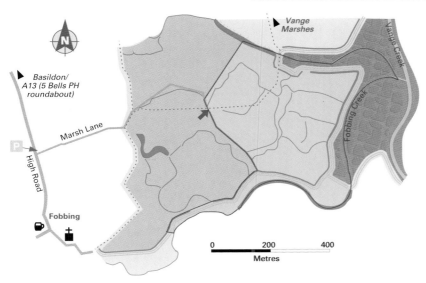

Grove House Wood

6ac/2.4ha   *OS Ex163/175*   *TQ 686 818*   *LNR*

A small wood in Stanford-le-Hope, owned by Thurrock Council and managed by Essex Wildlife Trust. It adjoins the River Hassenbrooke, here lined with reeds and marshy areas. It supports the usual woodland birds and its dead elms provide nesting sites for woodpeckers.

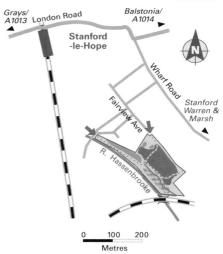

Entrance from Fairview Avenue, Stanford-le-Hope. On-street parking.

Stanford railway station is a few minutes' walk away.

Accessible at all times

Hangman's Wood

THURROCK ◆ COUNCIL

12ac/5ha   *OS Ex162/175*   *TQ 630 793*   *SSSI*

A fragment of ancient woodland in Little Thurrock, in the eastern part of Grays. It has a number of deneholes – caves which are the remains of mediæval chalk mines – which are used by bats for hibernation and roosting. (These are not accessible to the public.)

Accessed via a public footpath which runs from the western end of Stanford Road (A1013), near the roundabout where it joins Lodge Lane.

Accessible at all times

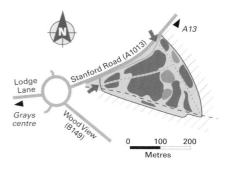

Horndon Meadow

2ac/1ha   *OS Ex175*   *TQ 672 851*

ESSEX
Wildlife Trust

A small unimproved hay meadow on clay soil, which has probably never been ploughed. It is important primarily for its wild flowers, containing about 80 species. The highlight is a fine display of several hundred spikes of green-winged orchids in early May, when patches of adderstongue fern can also be seen. These are followed by yellow rattle in profusion, several patches of musk mallow, and the prominent spikes of black knapweed, which attract the reserve's butterflies.

On the B1007 from Horndon-on-the-Hill to Basildon, about 2km from Horndon village. The entrance is at Tyelands Farm, from where a track leads to a gate on the right opening into the meadow. Park considerately by the track and take care when pulling out on to the main road afterwards.

Accessible at all times

April to July for wild flowers (early May for orchids in particular).

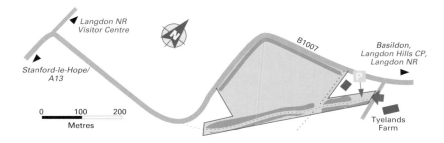

Yellow rattle: flowers May–September

Tony Gunton

Musk mallow: flowers July–August

Tony Gunton

Langdon

Just south of Basildon lies a crescent-shaped hilly ridge more than 100m high, extending from the former plotland township of Dunton in the west to Vange in the east and giving tremendous views over the Thames estuary and into east London. Its name, Langdon, means 'long hill' and much of its land is set aside for wildlife and for recreation, with Essex Wildlife Trust's Langdon nature reserve to the north and west, partnered by Langdon Hills country park, managed by Thurrock Council's Ranger Service, to the south and east.

Langdon nature reserve

520ac/211ha   **OS Ex175**   **TQ 659 874**

This is Essex Wildlife Trust's largest inland reserve, more than 500 acres of flower-rich meadows, ponds, ancient and secondary woodland, and hundreds of former plotland gardens.

Between the A127 and the A13 4.5 miles east of M25 junction 29. Signposted from the north from the B148 turning off the A127 and from the south from the A13 – follow the brown-and-white duck signs.

Laindon station on the Fenchurch Street–Southend line is less than 800m from the reserve. Frequent bus services run from Basildon town centre to Laindon station, to Langdon Hills and to Highview Avenue.

Reserve accessible at all times. Visitor centre open 9am - 5pm except Mondays.

Something of interest all the year round: spring for breeding birds and early flowers such as primroses; summer for orchids and other flowers, and for birdsong, autumn for fruit and berries and for late butterflies; winter to see huge flocks of migrant thrushes and perhaps a long-eared owl.

Call the Centre on 01268 419095 for more information and for details of events and activities for young and old.

Its importance lies not in its rarities but in the abundance of wildlife once common in our countryside but now threatened by intensive farming and urban spread. To date 29 species of butterfly and over 350 flowering plants have been recorded, and the list still grows. Badgers, foxes and weasels thrive in 'unimproved' meadows and orchids can be counted in their thousands.

Langdon Visitor Centre is the gateway to people's understanding of the social and natural history of this fascinating reserve, enabling thousands of visitors each year to explore what lies on their doorstep.

The original reserve consisted of four sections: from west to east these are Dunton, Lincewood, Marks Hill and Willow Park. In 2007 the reserve was extended to include a large lake and some meadows immediately north of Dunton called (unsurprisingly) 'Langdon Lake & Meadows'.

David Corke

Grizzled skipper: flies May –June

Langdon Lake & Meadows: view from the hillside

Mick Coulson

Langdon Nature Reserve (continued)

Langdon Lake & Meadows

A recent addition to the Langdon nature reserve, this is former plotlands and agricultural land on the west side of the Langdon Hills ridge.

It has a large lake, meadows and broadleaved woodland. The meadows are unimproved and have a variety of flowers and butterflies, but are particularly important as a habitat of the grizzled skipper butterfly. The bottom meadow will continue to be grazed and cut for hay. The top meadow will be managed to maintain a mosaic of scrub compartments and rides of varying widths and grass heights, to suit the grizzled skipper.

It also attracts a variety of birds, including raptors such as hobby, kestrel and sparrowhawk, and little grebe, wigeon, and common tern on the lake.

Four different species of bat have been recorded, feeding over the lake.

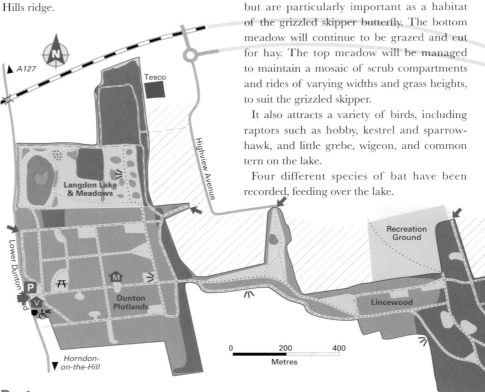

Dunton

Dunton today consists of the remains of plotland homes and gardens, wide grassy avenues bordered by hawthorn scrub, and glades where wild grassland species compete with garden perennials. This patchwork of habitats is superb for butterflies. Old orchards with pear, apple, plum and damson trees attract people and animals alike in autumn and the plotland ruins offer many basking sites for snakes and lizards. The Visitor Centre and the adjacent picnic area make Dunton an ideal starting point for your visit to the reserve.

Lincewood

The derelict plotland roads in Lincewood are accompanied by ancient and secondary woodland on higher ground, making it a good spot to look out for all three woodpecker species. Bluebells carpet the woodland floor in spring and a riot of garden escapes flower throughout the summer - goats rue, old roses and many others. An adjacent recreation ground has thousands of green-winged orchids in May.

Marks Hill

Marks Hill is a patchwork of ancient and secondary woodland, meadows and deserted plotlands. Stands of oak, ash and hornbeam have been brought back into a coppice cycle to enhance the rich diversity of flowering plants. In spring there is an impressive display of bluebells, wood anemones and primrose. The grassland supports a large number of

Willow Park

Willow Park was once a mediæval deer park. The unimproved hay meadows are bordered by ancient hedgerows and more recent mixed plantations, planted by the Commission for New Towns in the 1980s. The meadows and rough grassland are home to many flowering plants, including several species of orchid, and to the grizzled skipper butterfly. Seven ponds of varying sizes attract a wide range of dragonflies and damselflies.

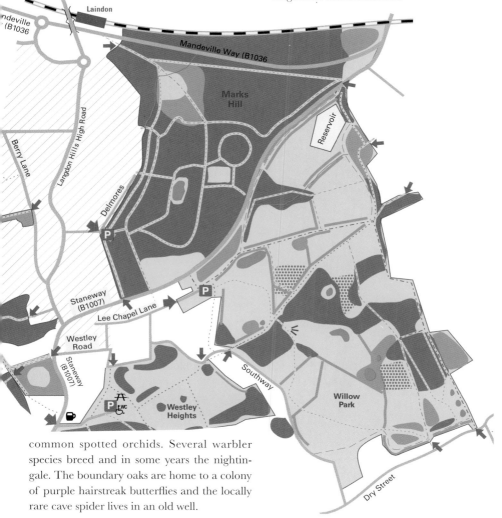

common spotted orchids. Several warbler species breed and in some years the nightingale. The boundary oaks are home to a colony of purple hairstreak butterflies and the locally rare cave spider lives in an old well.

Langdon Langdon Hills Country Park

400ac/162ha   *OS Ex175*   *TQ 697 861*   *SSSI (part)*   **THURROCK ◆ COUNCIL**

This mixture of ancient and more recent woodland and flower-rich meadows was bought by Essex County Council in the 1930s under the Green Belt scheme and designated a country park in 1973.

Northlands, Martinhole and Hall Wood are all ancient in origin, and dominated by oak, hornbeam and ash trees. Northlands Wood also has a large number of wild service trees, a reliable sign of an ancient wood, while Hall Wood to the west has an unusual concentration of wild cherry along its western and

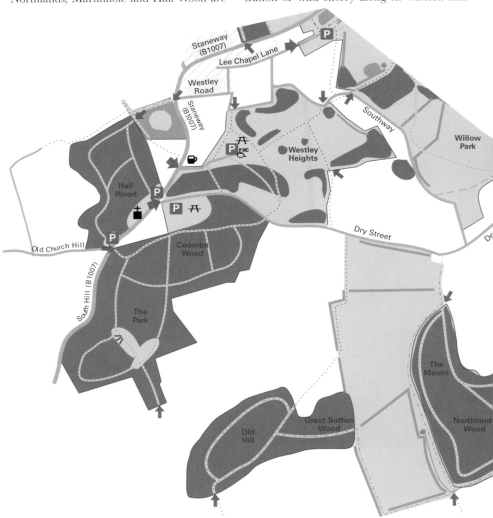

southern fringes. Coombe Wood and The Park are former parkland, while the others are secondary woods that have grown up on former farmland.

The meadows around One Tree Hill are either cut for hay or grazed to keep their diversity of plants. Two of them, east of One Tree Hill, are good enough to qualify as Sites of Special Scientific Interest and are covered in green-winged orchids: be sure to visit before the hay cut, usually in July.

One Tree Hill is signposted from the Five Bells roundabout (A176 junction) on the A13. Westley Heights can be reached from there via Dry Street (left turn off A176) or via the B1007 (Stanford-le-Hope–Basildon). It is behind the Harvester at the top of the hill.

Every day from 8am until dusk.

May for bluebells and birdsong in the woods; June for meadow flowers.

For more information contact the Rangers on 01268 542066.

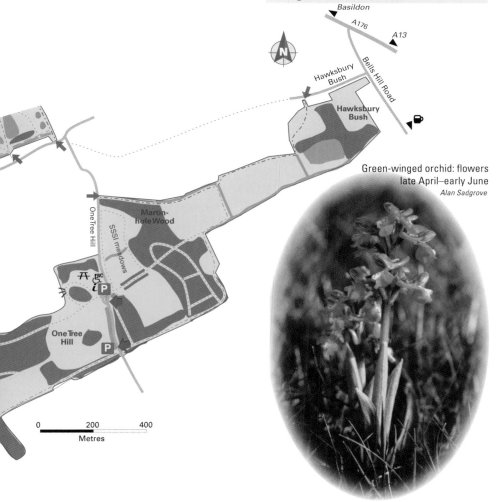

Green-winged orchid: flowers late April–early June
Alan Sadgrove

Linford Wood

21ac/9ha   *OS Ex163*   *TQ 676 797*   *LNR*

ESSEX
Wildlife Trust

This wet woodland close to Linford consists of an ancient hedge, a mixed willow plantation, ditches and an open area. It is surrounded by arable farmland. It supports tawny owls, great spotted and green woodpeckers and is an oasis for migrant birds in spring and autumn.

Entrance from East Tilbury Road, Linford, next to Merrie Lotts Farm.

A few minutes' walk from East Tilbury station.

Accessible at all times.

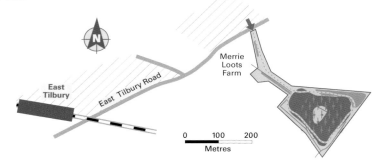

East Tilbury

East Tilbury Road

Merrie Loots Farm

0   100   200
Metres

Mardyke Valley Davy Down

ESSEX & SUFFOLK WATER

32ac/13ha   *OS Ex162*   *TQ 588 803*

THURROCK COUNCIL

Former farmland in the Mardyke valley that has been planted and landscaped by Thurrock Council and Essex & Suffolk Water, supported by local volunteers and the Thames Chase Community Forest team. It also includes a pumping station containing huge diesel pumps, now disused, and is overlooked by an impressive railway viaduct dating from 1892.

It has meadows running along the Mar Dyke, maturing woodland, ponds and a small wetland, and is a particularly good place to see water voles, both in the ponds and along the Mardyke.

Davy Down is on the B186 (Pilgrims Lane) between South Ockendon and Chafford Hundred. Leave the A13(T) or the M25 at their junction and head east on the A1306 towards Chafford Hundred/Grays, turning right where it crosses the B186. The entry is on the left about 200m up. Mardyke Woods can be reached via Davy Down or from Stifford Road (B1335) in South Ockendon.

Bus services from Romford to Lakeside run along Pilgrims Lane.

Accessible at all times.

Surfaced paths run all round Davy Down.

Mardyke Woods

62ac/25ha   *OS Ex162/175*   *TQ 585 803*

Forestry Commission

A group of mainly ancient woods on a hillside overlooking the Mardyke, acquired by the Forestry Commission in 2002. The woods are quite diverse in terms of tree species and there are good views across the flood plain of the Mardyke.

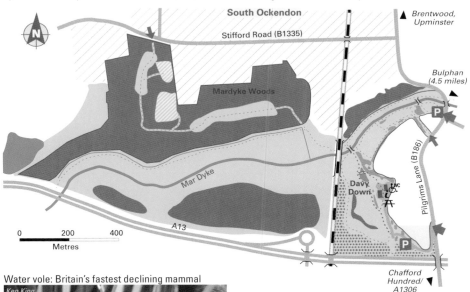

Water vole: Britain's fastest declining mammal

Ken King

Green woodpecker: resident

Alan Williams

Nevendon Bushes

15ac/6ha   **OS Ex175**   *TQ 735 898*

A fragment of old woodland within the Felmore district of Basildon. It has a woodbank near its eastern edge and some wild

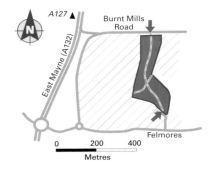

service trees, suggesting that it is ancient (pre-1600). It is mainly oak and coppice ash with a dense understorey of hawthorn, blackthorn, wild rose and field maple. It has a large pond.

Wood anemones and early purple orchids flower in spring. It supports woodpeckers and migrant warblers such as blackcap, white-throat and willow warbler.

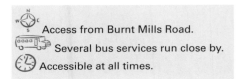

Access from Burnt Mills Road.

Several bus services run close by.

Accessible at all times.

Noak Bridge nature reserve

20ac/8ha   **OS Ex175**   *TQ 696 904*

A former plotland area that has scrubbed over and is now in the care of Basildon Council, supported by the Noak Bridge Nature Reserve Society.

The woodland is mainly hawthorn scrub with some mature oak and ash, a few wild service trees and – showing its plotland past – some cultivated fruit trees.

With its open flower meadows and many ponds it is excellent for butterflies, dragonflies and damselflies in summer. In spring visiting warblers join the resident woodpeckers to nest. The ponds and damp ditches support frogs, great crested newts and grass snakes.

Access via footpath from Eastfield Road. Leave the A127 at its junction with the A176 and at the roundabout and take the exit (signposted Noak Bridge) to South Wash Road: Eastfield Road is the second turning on the right.

Regular buses from Chelmsford to Lakeside run through Noak Bridge.

Accessible at all times.

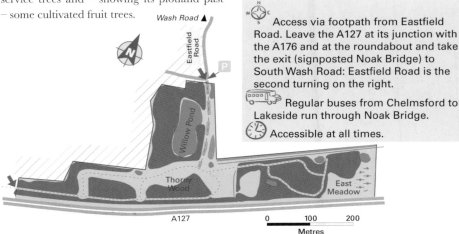

Commoner damselflies

Banded demoiselle (male): flies June–September

Banded demoiselle (female): flies June–September

Common blue damselfly (male): flies May–August

Large red damselfly (male): flies May–July

Red-eyed damselfly (male): flies June–July

Emerald damselfly (female): flies July–September

Rainham Marshes

870ac/352ha **OS Ex162** **TQ 552 792** **SSSI**

In 2000 the RSPB acquired Aveley and Wennington Marshes, formerly used by the Ministry of Defence as a firing range and a substantial part of the Inner Thames Marshes SSSI, and has developed it into a superb nature reserve.

Habitat work has concentrated on water management. Some 20km of ditch have been restored and sluices have been installed to control water levels across the reserve. New scrapes – areas of shallow water – have been constructed and are managed to provide habitat for breeding waders and wintering waterfowl. The ditches also act as wet fences so that the grassland can be grazed by sheep and cattle without intrusive fencing.

Such a large area of grazing marsh adjacent to the Thames Estuary is very important in wildlife terms and particularly (but not only) for its birds. Large numbers of wildfowl winter here, with wigeon regularly reaching 1,000 and teal up to 3,500. The reserve also supports important numbers of breeding reed bunting, little grebe, meadow pipit and skylark, with stonechat, barn owl, grasshopper warbler and water rail also breeding. On the Thames nearby, large numbers of dunlin and black-tailed godwits winter, along with curlew, grey plover and turnstone.

The reserve also has a large population of water voles and many unusual plants and invertebrates. Its noisiest resident is the marsh frog, introduced into Kent from mainland Europe in the 1930s and now spreading across southern England.

The Environment and Education centre contains a café and shop and provides good views across the marshes and River Thames. It has been built to high environmental standards, with features such as solar panels, rainwater harvesting, natural light and ventilation and a ground source heat exchange system.

Stonechat: resident

Alan Williams

Reed bunting: resident

Alan Williams

Take the M25 or A13 to junction 30, then head west along the A13 to its junction with the A1306 and follow the A1306 south towards Purfleet. At the traffic lights turn right on to New Tank Hill Road, signposted Purfleet and RSPB. The entrance is signposted approximately 300 metres along this road, on the right.

Nearest rail station is Purfleet, with a regular service from London Fenchurch Street, Grays and Southend. Turn right outside the station and follow the road to 'The Royal', on the left, then head down to the Thames and join the Riverside Path.

This crosses the Mardyke River at a small bridge, after which turn left and follow the pavement around to the centre.

Open 9.30am to 4.30pm daily. Free access to RSPB members and residents of Havering and Thurrock; otherwise £2.50/adult, £1/child.

Something of interest at all times of the year: highlights are large movements of migrating birds in autumn and large flocks of wildfowl and waders in winter.

Paths and trails are suitable for wheelchairs.

Web www.rspb.org.uk or phone 01708 899840.

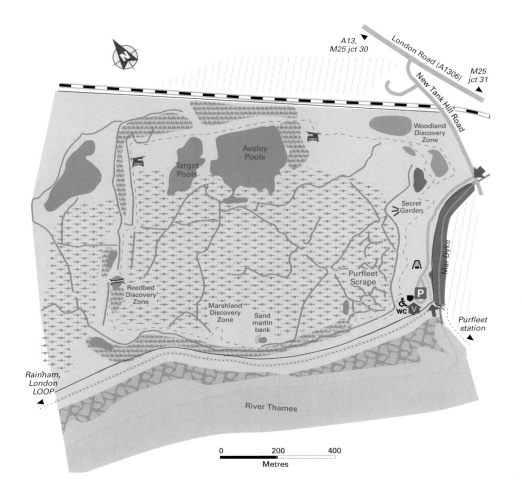

Shotgate Thickets

8ac/3ha   *OS Ex183*   *TQ 765 939*

ESSEX
Wildlife Trust

This Essex Wildlife Trust nature reserve is situated on the north bank of the tidal River Crouch, which is narrow at this point. It consists of thorn thickets, rough grassland and large ponds. With the adjoining river banks and railway embankment this small area has a surprising diversity of habitats and, consequently, of wildlife.

Well over 100 plant species can be found, including golden dock and dyer's green-weed. More than 70 species of bird have been recorded, about half of which breed on or near the reserve. This includes all three species of woodpecker, and a good selection of finches and warblers.

The ponds teem with life and eleven species of dragonfly have been identified, including the emerald damselfly and black-tailed skimmer. Butterflies are numerous. Among the other insects roesel's bush-cricket is found in good numbers.

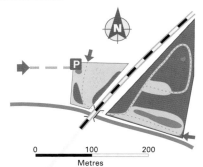

0   100   200
Metres

800m north-east of Wickford. Access is either through Southlands farm (parking at far end of the farm road) or west along the river bank from Battlesbridge, starting close to the Hawk public house.

Runwell/Wickford   A132

Rettendon Turnpike/ A130

Southlands Farm

P

River Crouch

Battles-bridge

Frequent buses along the A129 or train to Battlesbridge.

Accessible at all times.

At its best in mid-to-late spring when scrub and wood resound with birdsong.

The large pond has steep banks and deep water.

Roesel's bush-cricket
Tony Gunton

Stanford Warren

41ac/17ha   OS Ex163/175   TQ 687 812   SSSI

ESSEX
Wildlife Trust

A Thames-side reserve consisting of one of the largest reedbeds in Essex, created by gravel extraction in the 1920s, together with areas of marsh and rough grassland.

In spring and summer the reedbeds are full of birds fussing around, including reed buntings, reed warblers and sedge warblers, all of which breed. Cuckoos regularly use the warblers as hosts for their eggs. Water rail breed here too, but you will be lucky to see them because they are very shy, creeping quietly around in the reeds.

Winter brings in bearded tits, grey wagtail and snipe – best seen along the Hassenbrooke, a small river that bisects the reserve and crosses under the footpath.

Common lizard, grass snake and adder frequent the rough grassland, and harvest mice nest among the reeds.

Access from London Road in Stanford-le-Hope – off the A1013, which runs alongside the A13. Turn south down Butts Lane then left into Mucking Wharf Road. Please park considerately by the former church at the start of the footpath.

About 20 minutes' walk from Stanford station. Turn right outside the station then right down Wharf Road. You meet the footpath after crossing under the railway.

Accessible at all times.

Late spring/summer for breeding birds and flowering plants; winter for visiting birds such as bearded tits.

Please keep to the marked footpaths, which provide good views over the whole area.

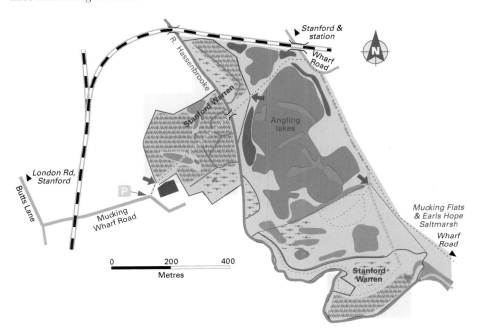

The Wick country park

50ac/20ha   **OS Ex175**   **TQ 755 919**

A new country park on the south-east fringe of Wickford, created on former agricultural land and opened in 2003. It is surrounded by old hedgerows, and has a large lake with reedbeds, several ponds, a small wetland that you cross on a boardwalk and a sizeable area of rough grassland and scrub that is developing a rich flora. The North Benfleet Brook crosses the site.

Off Tresco Way, on the southern fringe of Wickford. From the first roundabout on the A132 north of the A127, follow Cranfield Park Road east across three roundabouts into Tresco Way. The country park is signposted on the right just past a roundabout.

Open 9am until dusk

Over 2km of easy access trail.

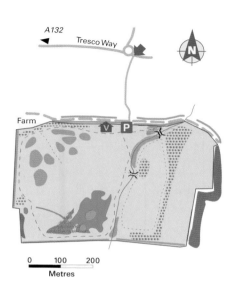

Flowers of damp grassland

Ragged robin: flowers June to August

Tony Gunton

Southern marsh orchid: flowers June to July

Tony Gunton

Vange Hill

30ac/12ha   *OS Ex175*   *TQ 720 875*   *LNR*

Basildon **Council**
BASILDON · BILLERICAY · WICKFORD

A former plotlands area that is now an informal open space of grassland and scrub woodland. At the foot of the hill is a large drainage ditch built to prevent Vange from flooding and now surrounded by trees and scrub. From the top there are commanding views across the south Essex marshland and over the River Thames into Kent.

The soil here is free-draining, and the south-facing slopes in particular are warm and dry, which makes them particularly valuable for insects such as butterflies and bees. Large numbers of the commoner butterflies can be seen in summer, and also some rarities such as the marbled white.

Notable among its flowering plants are pale flax and fairy flax.

Access from Vange Hill Drive. Follow London Road (B1464) from the roundabout on the A176 just north of its junction with the A13. Vange Hill Drive turns off on the left about 1 mile down.

Several bus services run along Vange Hill Drive.

Accessible at all times.

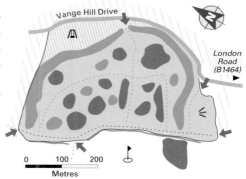

Bugle: flowers April to June
Tony Gunton

Cuckoo flower or lady's smock: flowers April–June
Tony Gunton

Vange Marshes

272ac/110ha   **OS Ex175**   **TQ 731 871**   **SSSI (part)**

Vange Marshes is a new RSPB reserve south of Pitsea. It has a large freshwater lagoon with islands and a smaller saltwater lagoon, plus extensive reed beds and some grassland with patches of scrub.

Avocet, lapwing, little ringed plover and redshank breed on the marshes and lagoons. Large numbers of reed and sedge warblers and a few cetti's warblers nest in the reedbeds, as do reed buntings. The boundary hedgerows and scattered scrub in the grassland are good habitat for yellowhammers and corn buntings.

Wigeon, teal, shoveler and snipe visit in winter, and sometimes large flocks of godwits, curlews or gulls. The reedbeds attract good numbers of bearded tits in the winter and it is possible to get close views of these birds.

The site is good for insects also. It has small heath and marbled white butterflies, and scarce emerald damselflies. Water voles frequent the ditches and the drier grassland has a population of adders.

RSPB is maximising the wildlife value of the reserve by controlling water levels and by grazing with cattle to create a sward of varying heights.

Accessible via a public footpath that leaves Pitsea Hall Lane right opposite the exit from Pitsea station. A footpath link direct from Wat Tyler country park is planned. From the roundabout in Pitsea where the A132 joins the A13 follow Pitsea Hall Lane south and park either at the station or in Wat Tyler country park.

Train to Pitsea and walk straight down the exit road. Cross the road at the T-junction and continue straight ahead along the footpath, following it across the railway line and into the reserve.

Accessible at all times.

May for breeding birds; winter for over-wintering waders, gulls and wildfowl, and for bearded tits in the reedbeds.

Bearded tit (male): resident
Gerald Downey

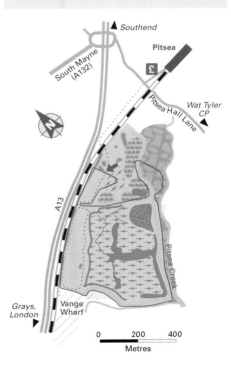

Wat Tyler country park

125ac/51ha   *OS Ex175*   *TQ 739 867*   *SSSI*

Basildon**Council**
BASILDON · BILLERICAY · WICKFORD

Wat Tyler country park is named after the leader of the Peasants' Revolt of 1381 against the poll tax, and does indeed have a chequered past. Originally part of the Pitsea Hall estate, it was grazed until the late 1800s, then taken over by the British Explosive Syndicate and later the Nobel Explosive Company, to make and store ammunition. In the 1930s and 1940s it was used by the War Department to store materials, and after that for industry. In the 1980s Basildon Council embarked on its plan that has produced the present country park.

The past industrial use of the site has created some strikingly unusual habitats – nowhere else in Essex can you see mature woodland consisting almost entirely of hawthorn, for example, which normally plays second fiddle to larger trees like oaks. The hawthorn hedges planted many years ago have spread to dominate the site, crowding other shrubs such as blackthorn, dogwood, elder and wild rose out to the margins. In places the hawthorn has formed a dense canopy under which very little else grows except for fungi in autumn. Elsewhere it has been coppiced to ground level, and in other parts forms impenetrable cover that is good for many songbirds.

There are many ponds, ditches and creeks both within and around the park and consequently in summer dragonflies are everywhere, including the scarce emerald damselfly.

The clearings and the broad rides are rich in wild flowers including blue fleabane, brookweed, yellowwort and vervain – because of the poor soil they are able to compete with more aggressive grasses. On sunny days these open areas are crowded with grassland butterflies such as the skippers and common blue, and day-flying moths including the six-spot burnet. Hobby and long-eared owl have nested here.

Three hides overlook the saltmarsh and mudflats of Timbermans Creek. Wading birds and ducks often feed on the mudflats, especially when driven off the estuary by the rising tide. Sparrowhawks and other birds of prey can sometimes be seen hunting over the rough ground beyond. Further hides overlook Pitseahall Fleet, frequented by bearded tits, and the scrape on the landfill site beyond the fleet (where **RSPB** has placed a live webcam: www.southendrspb.co.uk/serspbcam/webcam.htm).

Hawthorn woodland at Wat Tyler

Tony Gunton

From the roundabout in Pitsea where the A132 joins the A13 follow Pitsea Hall Lane south across the railway.

Train to Pitsea, then walk south 800m down Wat Tyler Way.

8am to dusk all the year round. Visitor centre open daily except Saturdays but may be closed when warden is out on site.

May–June for birdsong and early flowers; July for flying insects; migration periods and winter for visiting birds.

Easy access trail all round the site. Wheelchair access to hides.

RSPB helps to man the centre and runs events from there. For more information visit the Southend RSPB website at www.southendrspb.co.uk.

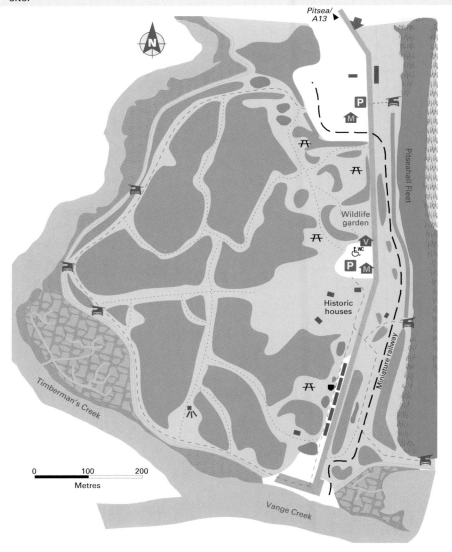

The Southend conurbation extends almost unbroken along the north bank of the Thames estuary, but south of the housing, Two Tree Island and Southend's foreshore are both great places for wildlife and especially for birds.

Castle Point to the west still has a fringe of coastal marshland and at its heart a superb group of ancient woods, while Hockley Woods to the north is certainly the largest unbroken expanse of ancient woods in Essex, and perhaps the greatest.

To the north, extending up to the Crouch Estuary, is the Roach Valley and the farmland of Rochford, with just a few nature reserves, the largest of which is Lion Creek.

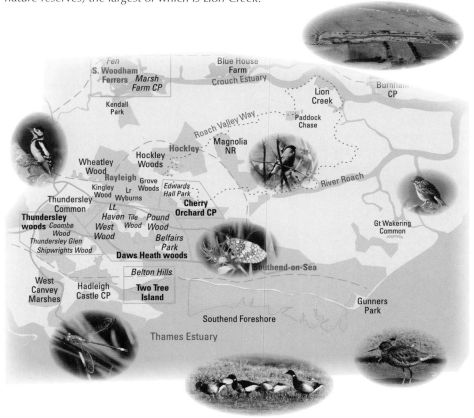

Fen
S. Woodham
Ferrers
Marsh Farm CP

Blue House Farm
Crouch Estuary

Lion Creek

Burnham CP

Kendall Park

Roach Valley Way

Paddock Chase

Hockley

Magnolia NR

Wheatley Wood

Hockley Woods

Rayleigh

Kingley Wood

Grove Woods

Lr Wyburns

Edwards Hall Park

River Roach

Thundersley Common

Lt. Haven

Tile Wood

Cherry Orchard CP

Thundersley woods Coombe Wood
West Wood

Pound Wood

Gt Wakering Common

Thundersley Glen
Shipwrights Wood

Belfairs Park

Daws Heath woods

Southend-on-Sea

Belton Hills

West Canvey Marshes

Hadleigh Castle CP

Two Tree Island

Gunners Park

Southend Foreshore

Thames Estuary

Cherry Orchard Jubilee Country Park

100ac/40ha   **OS Ex175**   **TQ 845 897**

Rochford District Council

Anew country park created by Rochford Council on former farmland in the attractive setting of the rolling countryside of the Roach Valley. It has three plantations of native trees, a large lake and some open grassland, with a network of connecting paths and bridleways. The existing hedgerows have many fine mature trees and an attractive stream runs along its northern boundary.

Wildlife is already moving in and the park can only improve as its habitats mature.

Edwards Hall Park is at the top of Bosworth Road, Eastwood – off Rayleigh Road (A1015). For Cherry Orchard, walk across the park to Flemings Farm Road and follow the bridleway from there. Footpath access also from Gusted Hall Lane, Cherry Orchard Way (B1013) or Blatches Chase, off Western Approach.

Regular bus services along Rayleigh Road.

Accessible at all times.

Paths can be muddy in wet weather.

Edwards Hall Park

Southend-on-Sea Borough Council

32ac/13ha   **OS Ex175**   **TQ 836 896**

Four meadows, formerly part of the farm at Upper Edwards Hall, surrounded by ancient hedges and with a long-established pond. The meadows were last ploughed in the 19th century and now they are cut for hay in summer every year. As a result they are rich in wild flowers and attract butterflies and other flying insects in summer. A variety of birds nest in the trees and hedges, and in winter it is a good place to see large flocks of redwings and fieldfares, visiting from Scandinavia.

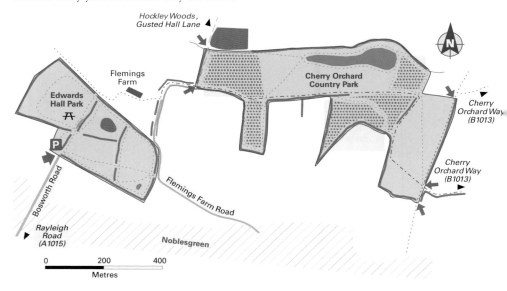

Daws Heath woods

The ancient woodlands in and around Daws Heath have much in common. They are all 'working woods', coppiced for centuries to supply wood for a range of purposes, and they all occupy land that was unattractive for agriculture – gravelly slopes or plateaux of infertile soil, running down into damp stream valleys. Yet they are also very different from one another, showing what effect man's treatment of a wood can have on its wild-life and character, even many decades after.

Belfairs Park

Southend-on-Sea
Borough Council

447ac/181ha   **OS Ex175**   *TQ 820 875*   *LNR, SSSI (part)*

Belfairs Park contains two large areas of ancient woodland that were part of a large stretch of woodland in the southern part of Rayleigh Hills, like Hockley Woods to the north. In the 1930s Hadleigh Great Wood was saved from destruction for housing following a campaign led by South Essex Natural History Society. Belfairs Wood to the east was not so fortunate, because in 1938 fairways were bull-dozed through it to construct a golf course.

Hadleigh Great Wood (also known as Belfairs Nature Reserve) has a history of many centuries of uninterrupted coppicing. As a result a wide range of flowers and shrubs grow amongst the trees, including sheets of wood anemones, and it attracts a wide range of birds and butterflies. The canopy trees in the wood are mainly oak and sweet chestnut. It also has significant numbers of wild service trees and alder buckthorn, foodplant of the brimstone butterfly. Here and there you can see patches of ling heather.

In 1997 it was chosen as a reintroduction site for the heath fritillary butterfly, which had become extinct in Essex. This butter-fly depends on open glades within wood-land where the food plant for its caterpillars, common cow-wheat, can be found. With the ending of coppicing in the 1940s many wood-lands became unsuitable and as a result it disappeared. The reintroduction has been a great success and large numbers of heath fritillaries can normally be seen in flight in late June and early July.

Belfairs Wood has not had the same level of management and the effects of this are obvious. While still an attractive woodland, it is more heavily shaded and its populations of plants and birds are much poorer. It is a good place to see nuthatch and also has many woodpeckers. You have to be careful to dodge golf balls when crossing the fairways but it has many paths and small clearings and is well worth exploring.

The main entrance is in Eastwood Road North, which can be reached from the A13 via Eastwood Road and from the A127 westbound via The Fairway.

Regular bus services between Basildon and Southend run along the A13 to the south. Leigh-on-Sea station is about 30 minutes' walk via Belton Hills, Salisbury Road and Eastwood Road.

Accessible at all times. Car park open dawn to dusk.

Something of interest at all times of the year, but especially May for woodland flowers and birdsong; mid-June to mid-July for heath fritillaries.

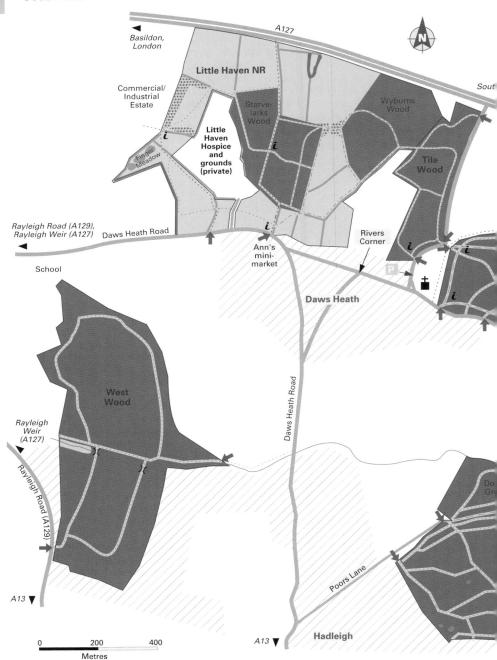

A127

*Basildon,
London*

Little Haven NR

Commercial/
Industrial
Estate

Starve-
larks
Wood

Wyburns
Wood

Sout

Little
Haven
Hospice
and
grounds
(private)

Finger
Meadow

Tile
Wood

*Rayleigh Road (A129),
Rayleigh Weir (A127)*

Daws Heath Road

Ann's
mini-
market

Rivers
Corner

School

Daws Heath

West
Wood

*Rayleigh
Weir
(A127)*

Daws Heath Road

Rayleigh Road (A129)

Do
Gr

A13 ▼

Poors Lane

0   200   400
Metres

A13 ▼   Hadleigh

Daws Heath woods West Wood

castlepoint
benfleet | canvey | hadleigh | thundersley

79.4ac/32ha   **OS Ex175**   **TQ 805 880**

W est Wood has been managed as coppice woodland for at least two hundred years, except that a large area of the northern part was clear felled in the 1930s, removing the standards as well as the coppice. It is owned by the Church Commissioners and is is managed as a public open space by Castle Point Council.

Accessible from Rayleigh Road (A129), which runs south from the Rayleigh Weir roundabout on the A127 to join the A13 in Hadleigh. You can also walk in via a footpath from Daws Heath Road.

Frequent bus services along Rayleigh Road.

Accessible at all times.

April to June for spring flowers and woodland birdsong.

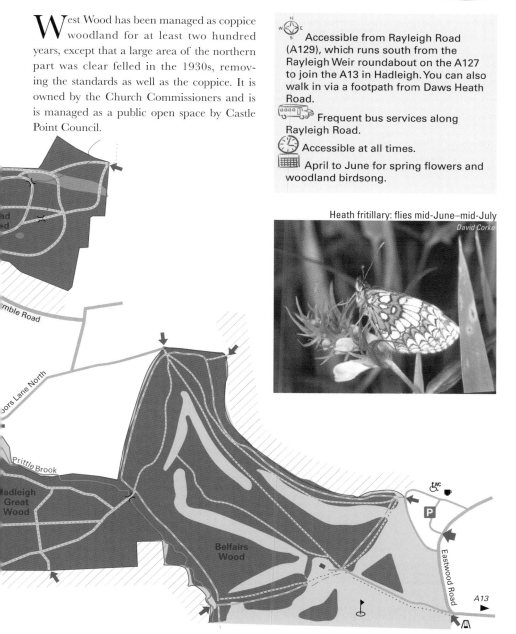

Heath fritillary: flies mid-June–mid-July
David Corke

Daws Heath woods **Little Haven**

104ac/42ha   **OS Ex175**   **TQ 811 889**

ESSEX
Wildlife Trust

This nature reserve surrounding Little Haven Children's Hospice was formerly part of Lower Wyburns Farm. It comprises 14 meadows, a network of fine old hedgerows and two woods.

Starvelarks Wood is mainly sweet chestnut and is probably a 19th century plantation that has been under coppice management.

Wyburns Wood contains a complex range of tree and plant species, indicating its ancient origins. It is very damp in places and here it supports a rare type of woodland known as plateau alder wood, which has a ground flora of male fern and pendulous sedge.

Pound Wood

55ac/22ha   **OS Ex175**   **TQ 816 888**

ESSEX
Wildlife Trust

Pound Wood was acquired by Essex Wildlife Trust in 1993 following a public appeal. Its complex geology gives it a great variation in woodland types. Sweet chestnut and birch occur on the plateaux and ridges, hornbeam and holly on the slopes, and hornbeam, ash, willow, aspen and hazel in the three stream valleys. In places there are many wild service trees. The oaks are mostly sessile, with pedunculate in the valleys. The south-west section is very old secondary woodland, almost indistinguishable from the ancient woodland.

There are fine early mediæval woodbanks, several ponds and many dells. Bramble, bracken and bluebell dominate the woodland floor, with common cow-wheat, yellow archangel, wood spurge and figwort where light can penetrate this once neglected wood.

Heath fritillaries can be seen in the more open woodland beneath the power cables.

Tile Wood

16ac/6ha   **OS Ex175**   **TQ 816 890**

One of the earliest ancient woods to have been recorded in south-east Essex, being mentioned in anglo-saxon times. The tree species are predominately sessile oak, hornbeam and sweet chestnut, with some wild service. It is particularly rich in ancient woodland plants, including wood sorrel, bluebell and wood-rush, and has many wood ants.

Turn south off the A127 at Rayleigh Weir on to Rayleigh Road (A129) and turn left on to Daws Heath Road at the Woodmans Arms mini-roundabout. Or join the A129 from the A13 and turn right on to Daws Heath Road. Park on local streets with consideration for residents.

Hourly bus service exc. Sundays serves Daws Heath Road. More frequent services run along Rayleigh Road and pass Woodmans Arms PH (400m to west via Daws Heath Road).

Accessible at all times.

April to June for spring flowers and woodland birdsong

Wheelchair access gate to Little Haven opposite Ann's mini-market.

Please keep dogs on leads when there is livestock on Little Haven.

To minimise disturbance to wildlife, please keep to the designated paths.

from dispensers in the reserves or from Essex Wildlife Trust visitor centres.

Great Wakering Common

**Great Wakering
Parish Council**

22ac/8.85ha   **OS Ex176**   **TQ 952 878**

A long stretch of common land consisting of rough open grassland and wetland, plus a recently planted woodland of native trees. It may originally have been a tidal creek, cut off when the seawall was built.

An attractive pond fringed by black poplar trees supports great crested newts. Corn buntings are often seen here and in the winter you may catch sight of snipe or redshank feeding around the margins of the pond.

From the A13, follow the B1017 to Great Wakering and turn left on to Common Road at the end of the High Street.

Accessible at all times.

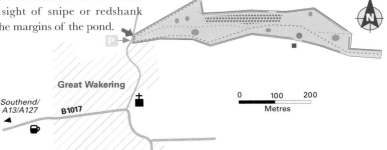

Grove Woods

Rochford
District Council

2ac/1ha   **OS Ex175**   **TQ 825 901**

This fragment of woodland between Rayleigh and Eastwood developed after a 'plotlands' settlement was abandoned in the 1940s. The original plotland roads can still be seen and also the hawthorn hedges planted to mark out the plots. The remaining area has been colonised mainly by hawthorn and oak, but there are also some large cherry and ash trees, patches of open grassland and a couple of small ponds, possibly in bomb craters.

To the north of Eastwood Road (A1015), roughly midway between Rayleigh and Eastwood. From the A127, turn north at the Rayleigh Weir roundabout on to the A129: Eastwood Road turns off right after about a mile.

Accessible at all times.

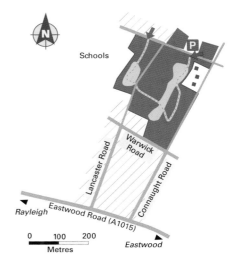

Butterflies of woodland and hedgerow

Brimstone (on knapweed): breeds on buckthorn; flies April–June and August–November

Roger Jiggins

Comma (on hemp agrimony): breeds on hop, nettle and elm; flies in April, July and autumn

Tony Gunton

Purple hairstreak: spends most of its time in the treetops drinking honeydew; flies July–August

Iris Newbery

Green-veined white: breeds on crucifers such as cuckoo flower; flies April–September

Tony Gunton

Ringlet: found along woodland rides and in glades; breeds on native grasses; flies July–August

Ken Wooldridge

Speckled wood: frequents shady woods and hedgerows; flies April–September

Tony Gunton

Gunners Park

17ac/7ha　　*OS Ex176*　　*TQ 933 849*　　*LNR*

Southend-on-Sea
Borough Council

This is all that remains of a large area of common and rough grazing stretching from Southend to Shoebury, consisting of a barrier beach and spit backed in some places by marshland. It used to be part of the MoD rifle ranges and therefore is untouched by agriculture.

It is mainly grassland, divided by ditches and dykes lined with reed, and with patches of dense scrub and clumps of trees. This combination makes for good bird and insect life in summer. Goldfinches, linnets and whitethroats nest in the scrub, and kestrels and barn owls hunt over the grassland. It is also a good place to see unusual passage migrants in autumn and spring.

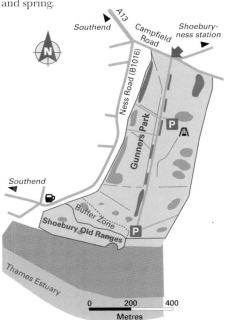

Entrance in Campfield Road, Shoeburyness, just beyond the end of the A13.

A short walk from Shoeburyness station. Buses run from Southend centre.

Access to Gunners Park at all times. Vegetation in Shoebury Old Ranges is fragile, so access only by arrangement with Essex Wildlife Trust: call 01621 862960.

May to August for birdsong and insects; autumn for passage migrants.

Shoebury Old Ranges

22ac/9ha　　*OS Ex176*　　*TQ 931 841*　　*SSSI*

ESSEX
Wildlife Trust

An old common area that has never been ploughed, together with a buffer zone. It contains fossil coastal features such as shell banks and sand dunes with wetter slacks between. The vegetation is mainly short species-rich turf, closely grazed by rabbits and with lichens predominating in small areas.

The area was saved as a nature reserve because of its botanical richness. It contains local and regional rarities such as meadow saxifrage, yellow horned-poppy, suffocated clover, fenugreek, dune fescue and bulbous meadow-grass.

It is one of the richest areas for invertebrates in Essex as well, holding species once much more widespread in this south-eastern corner of the county.

The buffer zone is reclaimed saltmarsh that has been allowed to develop into scrub and rough grassland for the benefit of wildlife.

Hadleigh Castle Country Park

300ac/121ha   *OS Ex175*   *TQ 799 870*

Essex County Council

This country park is hillside running down, steeply in places, to grazing marsh, seawall and a narrow strip of saltmarsh alongside Benfleet Creek.

From the open areas on the hillside there are views of industrial Canvey on the other side of Benfleet Creek, but these are quickly forgotten as you explore the mosaic of grassland, scrub and light woodland on the hillside. The hay meadows and rides are full of flowering plants such as rest-harrow, trefoils and self-heal. On a sunny summer day butterflies such as comma, speckled wood and skippers flutter along the rides, and adders slither out to sun themselves. The grassland also supports some unusual plants, including deptford pink, bithynian vetch and wild catmint.

At the foot of the hill you emerge into a pastoral landscape where cattle graze the marshland behind the seawall. In summer pipits and skylarks nest in the grazing marsh and it is alive with insects, including the scarce emerald damselfly, once thought to be extinct in Essex, and the shrill carder bee, a rare species selected for priority conservation action. Little grebes and reed warblers breed among the dykes and ponds. Unusual migrant birds are often seen here, and merlins occasionally come to hunt in winter.

The main entrance is via Chapel Lane, which leaves the A13 by the Morrison's supermarket in Hadleigh. It can also be reached from the footpath running along the seawall between Benfleet and Leigh.

Benfleet station (Fenchurch St–Southend line) is a short walk from the western arm of the park. A number of bus services run along the A13 through Hadleigh and to Benfleet station.

Open from 8am until dusk all year round.

Mid-summer for wild flowers, butterflies and other insects; winter (for the hardy) for birds, ideally at high tide when they are closest.

Unsuitable because of the steep terrain.

Three waymarked trails of different lengths start from the Chapel Lane car park.

Call the Rangers on 01702 551072.

Essex Way (B1014)

St Mary's Road

Station Road

Benfleet station

Benfleet Downs

Canvey Island ▼

0   250   500

Metres

Shrill carder bee
Peter Harvey

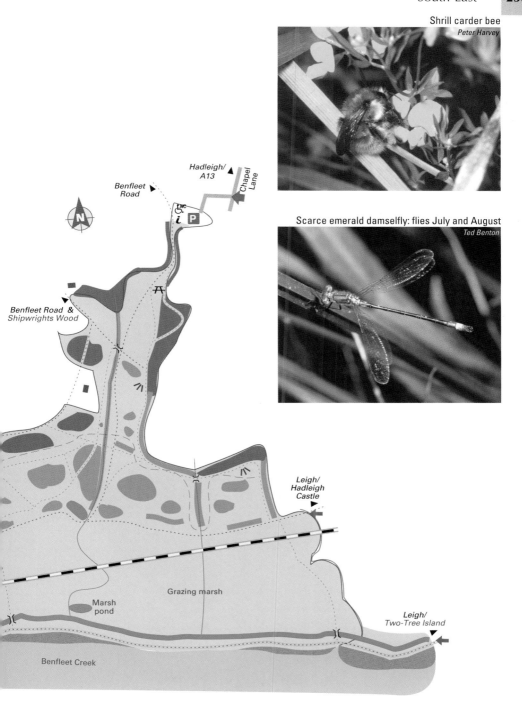

Scarce emerald damselfly: flies July and August
Ted Benton

Hadleigh/
A13

Chapel
Lane

Benfleet
Road

N

Benfleet Road &
Shipwrights Wood

Leigh/
Hadleigh
Castle

Leigh/
Two-Tree Island

Grazing marsh

Marsh
pond

Benfleet Creek

Hockley Woods

270ac/109ha   OS Ex175/6   TQ 833 924   SSSI

Rochford District Council

If you only had time to visit one ancient coppiced woodland then Hockley Woods might be the place to choose. It is the largest continuous (unlike Epping Forest, which is divided by roads) native woodland not only in Essex, but in the whole of eastern England. It consists of a group of half-a-dozen ancient woods, mostly owned by Rochford Council and virtually intact except for a few bits lost around the fringes. It is not as rich in wild flowers as some of the northern Essex woods, but has a wide variety of woodland types all on one site and many ancient woodland plants.

The ground falls steeply from the car park with a variety of trees on the upper slopes including oak, sweet chestnut, ash and rowan. These give way to hornbeam on the heavier and wetter soils lower down.

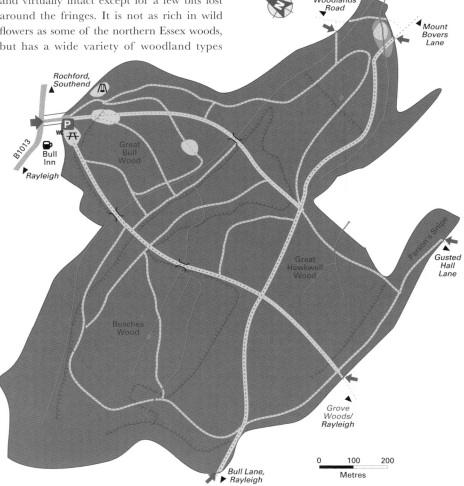

The woods are criss-crossed by woodbanks, the earliest dating from the Middle Ages. Woodbanks were used both to keep grazing animals out of coppice woods and to show where ownership changed. The earliest banks show boundaries between manors and later ones those between farms as well. (The map shows only the main banks.)

Large patches of common cow-wheat are scattered through the woods. This is not a striking plant, having small yellow flowers similar to snapdragon, but it is very important as the only foodplant (in eastern England) of the heath fritillary butterfly. This butterfly is now very rare throughout Britain and had died out in Essex until it was reintroduced to these and several other woods, including Hadleigh Great Wood (Belfairs Park, p. 245) and Thrift Wood (p. 144). The best time to see it is from mid-June to early July.

South of the B1013 Rayleigh-to-Rochford road, just west of Hockley. The Bull Inn is right next to the entrance road. You can also reach the woods from the south, by walking through farmland and several small woods starting from the car park on Grove Road.

Hockley station is about 20 minutes' walk. Bus services from Rayleigh and Southend run past the main entrance.

Accessible at all times.

May for early flowers; July for butterflies; October for fungi.

Call Rochford Council on 01702 546366.

Kendall Park

7ac/2.7ha   *OS Ex175*   *TQ 808 954*   *LNR*

Rochford District Council

Grassland and woodland with hedges and ditches in Hullbridge. It overlooks the intertidal area of Hullbridge Creek, in the Crouch Estuary, looking across to Marsh Farm Country Park on the northern bank.

Accessed from The Promenade which runs west alongside the estuary from Ferry Road, Hullbridge.

Accessible at all times.

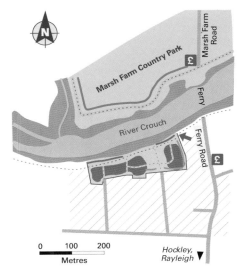

Kingley Wood

4ac/1.7ha   *OS Ex175*   *TQ 794 900*

A fragment of ancient woodland on a steep slope beside the A127. It is mainly oak and hornbeam, but at the top are two huge sweet chestnut trees and it also has rowan, hazel and elm.

It is surrounded on three sides by wood-banks, traditionally used to mark woodland boundaries. Bluebells, wood anemones and common cow-wheat occur throughout.

Access from Western Road, Hollytree Gardens or Weir Farm Road in the estate just north of the Rayleigh Weir roundabout on the A127. From there take the A129 north and turn off first or second left. On-street parking.

Accessible at all times.

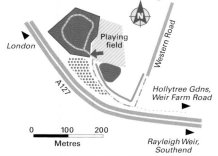

Lion Creek & Lower Raypits

161ac/65ha   *OS Ex176*   *TQ 923 948*   *SSSI*

This former creek on the southern shore of the Crouch estuary was acquired by Essex Wildlife Trust in 1986. It was cut off from the estuary by a new seawall, and is bounded on three sides by the old one. The creek contains brackish water and in late summer has an attractive border of salt-marsh plants such as sea lavender, golden samphire and sea spurrey.

Above the zone affected by salt water, sea couch and false oat are the dominant grasses, with a mixture of tall herbs. Where the grass is shorter, smaller plants can be found, including the localised slender birds-foot trefoil and, on the seawall, sea clover.

Among its insects are essex skipper and brown argus butterflies, and roesel's and short-winged conehead bush-crickets.

The water margins attract a variety of wading birds, and in winter birds of prey such as hen harrier and short-eared owl

hunt over the grassland and seawalls.

The meadow alongside the creek was added to the reserve later, and supports a range of plants and insects including the shrill carder bee, a national priority species.

Lower Raypits can be reached via the seawall path. It consists of saltmarsh, permanent pasture and seawalls. Most of it lies within the Crouch and Roach Estuaries SSSI, an important complex of saltmarsh, intertidal and grazing habitats that serves as a notable feeding and roosting area for wildfowl and waders, including brent geese.

The seawall was damaged in 2007 and a section has been rebuilt, and at the same time a scrape, featuring special water vole islands, and a small saline lagoon were created.

Dykes and seawalls support nationally scarce plants, including beaked tasselweed, sea barley, curved hard-grass and grass vetchling, plus a wealth of invertebrates.

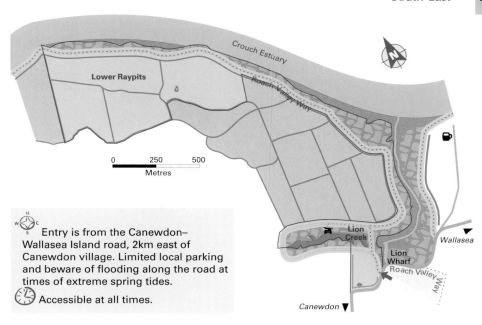

Entry is from the Canewdon–
Wallasea Island road, 2km east of
Canewdon village. Limited local parking
and beware of flooding along the road at
times of extreme spring tides.

🕑 Accessible at all times.

Lower Wyburns

8ac/3.4ha   *OS Ex175*   *TQ 812 895*

WOODLAND
TRUST

A young woodland in Rayleigh, just
north of the A127, planted originally
by Rochford District Council and given by
them to the Woodland Trust in 1995, which
completed the planting.

Mature oaks grow along the northern
boundary, bordering a small stream. A wide
grassy ride allows access to the whole site.

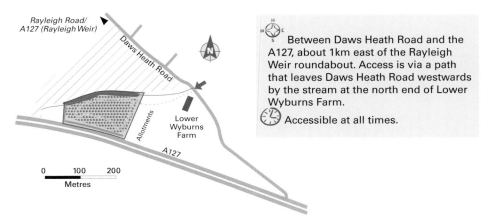

Between Daws Heath Road and the
A127, about 1km east of the Rayleigh
Weir roundabout. Access is via a path
that leaves Daws Heath Road westwards
by the stream at the north end of Lower
Wyburns Farm.

🕑 Accessible at all times.

Magnolia Nature Reserve

22ac/9ha   *OS Ex175*   *TQ 860 923*   *LNR*

This former brickworks on the border between Ashingdon and Hawkwell has developed into an attractive nature reserve with a variety of habitats, alongside relics of its industrial past. Managed by Hawkwell Parish Council, it has flower-rich meadows, marshy areas, a long pond, patches of scrub and a patch of light woodland, mainly hawthorn.

It is particularly good for birds, with greatest numbers in the breeding season but in winter it often attracts bullfinches, which are increasingly scarce elsewhere.

On Rectory Road, which runs from Hall Road, Hawkwell (B1013) to Ashingdon Road, Ashingdon. Turn off just beyond (east of) the railway.

Accessible at all times.

A surfaced bridleway runs the length of the reserve.

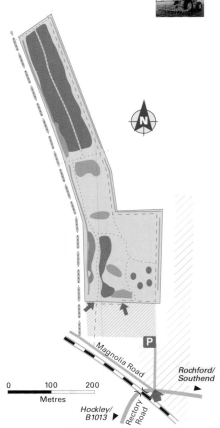

Bullfinch: resident
Alan Williams

Alder buckthorn
David Corke

Paddock Copse

3ac/1ha   **OS Ex175/176**   **TQ 905 946**

WOODLAND
TRUST

This small 'Woods-on-your-Doorstep' site near Canewdon has been planted up mainly with oak, ash, field maple and wild cherry.

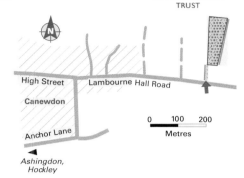

Access via a path that leaves Lambourne Hall Road northwards at the east side of the property called 'The Paddock' about 200m east of Canewdon.

Accessible at all times.

Thundersley Common

34ac/13.7ha   **OS Ex175**   **TQ 798 896**   **SSSI**

castlepoint
benfleet | canvey | hadleigh | thundersley

Thundersley Common packs great variety and interest into a relatively small area. Like most commons it was used by local people to graze their animals, collect firewood and so on. When these practices stopped it was invaded by trees and scrub, but most of this was cleared in 1972 and some of the original heathland plants reappeared.

The northern slope has many heathland plants in the uncut islands of heather and gorse in the grassland, including milkwort, cross-leaved heath and common cow-wheat.

The woodland in the central section is dominated by oak, hornbeam and hawthorn, but there is also alder buckthorn, food plant of the brimstone butterfly, and, on the western boundary, a pollarded wild service tree.

The southern plateau has some marshy pools with lesser spearwort and on the drier ground you will find tormentil and a small patch of heather.

On Kingsley Lane, the first turning on the right off Rayleigh Road (A129) just south of the Rayleigh Weir roundabout on the A127 Southend Arterial Road.

Regular bus service serving Rayleigh station and Southend bus station via the A13; get off at Sainsbury's.

Accessible at all times.

June–August for flowers and insects.

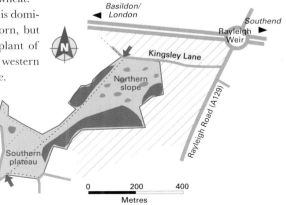

Thundersley woods

Castle Point Council looks after three contrasting woods in Thundersley.

Coombe Wood

20ac/8ha   *OS Ex175*   *TQ 783 883*

An old coppice woodland north of Bread & Cheese Hill in Thundersley, containing a deep valley and a pond. In 2007 it was granted Village Green status to protect it as a public open space.

The dominant trees are oak but it has a variety of other species including dogwood and wild cherry. The flowering plants are concentrated along the edges and paths, and include bluebells, dog violets and – unusual in Essex because it prefers alkaline soils – spurge laurel. Ferns and lesser celandine grow alongside the stream.

Good for migrant warblers in summer and woodpeckers all year.

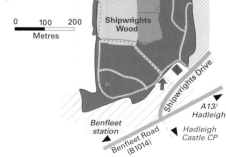

Spurge laurel
Adrian Knowles

Access to Coombe Wood and Thundersley Glen from the A13 in Thundersley, with parking in local streets. For Shipwrights Wood, park at Hadleigh Castle CP (p.252) and walk in from there, or on Shipwrights Drive.

Regular bus services between Basildon and Southend along the A13.

Accessible at all times.

April–May for woodland flowers and birdsong.

Thundersley Glen

27ac/11ha   *OS Ex175*   *TQ 787 878*

A former plotland area on a south-facing slope alongside the A13 in Thundersley that has 'tumbled down' to woodland and scrub. This is mainly hawthorn and oak with a scattering of birch and hornbeam, but it also has a patch of ancient woodland, near the south-west corner, with coppiced hornbeam trees, bluebells and lesser celandine.

With its large pond and some sunny clearings and marshy hollows, it attracts a variety of resident and migrant birds and is a good place for insects in summer.

Shipwrights Wood

30ac/12ha   *OS Ex175*   *TQ 795 871*

What is now called Shipwrights Wood in fact comprises two pieces of ancient woodland. The original Shipwrights Wood forms roughly the southern half and the eastern section to the north is part of Jervis Wood, which formerly extended west all the way to Thundersley Glen. The remainder is more recent woodland and a flower-rich meadow.

The topography is complex, with many ridges, slopes and marshy hollows, and this makes for very varied vegetation. It has a mixture of trees, including oak, hornbeam, ash (some of it coppiced), sweet chestnut and wild cherry. Along the ancient woodbank on the western boundary are some large wild service trees.

Woodland birds

Nuthatch: resident

David Harrison

Great spotted woopecker (male): resident

Alan Williams

Blackcap (male): summer visitor

Alan Williams

Birds seen around the coast in summer

Shelduck, Britain's largest duck: resident

Alan Williams

Oystercatchers: resident

Gerald Downey

Southend Foreshore

Southend-on-Sea 🏛️
Borough Council

2688ac/1088ha OS Ex175   *TQ 911 837*   *LNR, SSSI, SPA*

Stretching more than eight miles from Leigh-on-Sea to Shoeburyness, Southend's foreshore – the area lying between normal high and low tide marks, also known as the intertidal zone – is internationally important for migrating birds, and for that reason has been declared a Local Nature Reserve.

In winter, its mudflats serve as a feeding ground for large numbers of birds that migrate to the Essex estuaries from their less hospitable breeding grounds further north. The sheer numbers of birds and their movement as they retreat before the advancing tide make for a tremendous spectacle. You can expect to see flocks of waders such as knot or dunlin wheeling and circling, along with lapwing, curlew, redshank and grey plover. Ducks that feed here include teal, mallard, wigeon and shelduck.

There are fewer birds in summer, some resident like shelduck, oystercatchers, ringed plovers and redshanks, and others, like the common and little terns, that arrive here in spring and stay on to breed.

Southend pier is a good vantage point for watching terns plunge diving for food in summer, and on cold days in the winter you may see a variety of divers, grebes and other sea birds out on the estuary, and possibly purple sandpipers around the pier itself.

If you don't have your own binoculars or telescope, you can use telescopes positioned all along the seafront and on the pier.

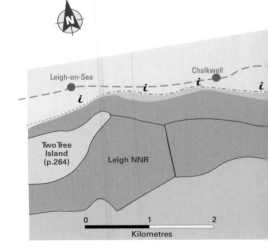

Ringed plover: resident

Redshank: resident

David Harrison

Common tern with chicks: summer visitor

Gerald Downey

Viewable from many points along the seafront from Leigh-on-Sea to Shoeburyness, and from Southend pier.

Train to Southend Central or Shoeburyness, then work back along the front as the tide drives the birds westwards towards Two-Tree Island, returning from one of the other stations.

Accessible at all times.

Winter for large numbers of birds feeding on the mudflats – best viewed when the tide is low, so check tide tables before you visit.

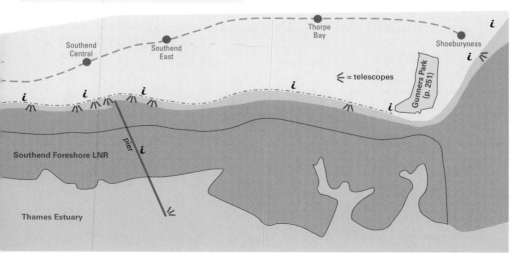

Thorpe Bay

Southend Central

Southend East

Shoeburyness

Gunners Park (p. 251)

⇐ = telescopes

pier

Southend Foreshore LNR

Thames Estuary

Two Tree Island

641ac/260ha   **OS Ex175**   **TQ 824 852**   **SSSI, NNR**

Two Tree Island typifies the history of many Essex coastal sites. It was reclaimed from the sea in the 18th century when a sea-wall was built around saltmarsh, and was used for rough grazing until 1910 when a sewage farm was built on its eastern tip. In 1936 Southend Council acquired the whole island and used it as a rubbish tip until the 1970s. Now it is leased to Essex Wildlife Trust as a nature reserve.

Turn south off the A13 down to Leigh station, then cross the bridge over the railway and follow the road past the golf range and over the bridge on to the island. There is a car park immediately over the bridge.

Twenty minutes' walk from Leigh station (Fenchurch St line), which is also served by a number of bus services.

Accessible at all times.

Migration periods and winter for birds – the brent geese are normally present from late September to mid-November; July for saltmarsh colours and butterflies.

To avoid disturbing the birds, please keep strictly to the marked footpaths in the eastern section.

The island itself consists of grassland, scrub, reedbed and lagoons, and supports a number of interesting plants and 'escapes'. A wide variety of birds is seen, and particularly migrants. Kestrels hover over the grassland and short-eared owls visit during the winter, hunting for field voles, and large numbers of little egrets roost here. Water vole, kingfisher, water rail, reed and sedge warblers may be seen in the lagoons and reedbed, while adder, slow worm and common lizard frequent the grassland. Insects of note include the marbled white butterfly, roesel's bush-cricket, the house cricket and the lesser marsh grasshopper.

The western section has a network of surfaced paths. At its western tip is a lagoon with a bird hide, from which you can see birds such as redshank and heron feeding. Recently avocets have started to nest here also.

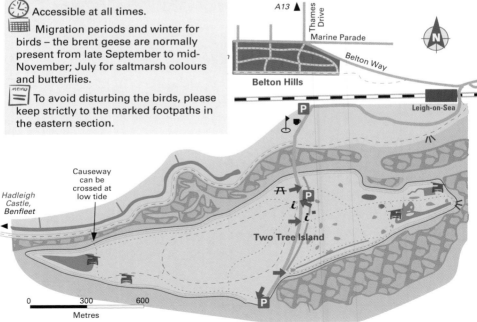

The eastern section is part of Leigh National Nature Reserve, along with the adjoining saltmarsh and a large area of intertidal mudflats. The saltmarsh, along the southern shore of the island, is one of the best surviving in the Thames estuary. Among many typical saltmarsh plants it has golden samphire, sea wormwood, sea purslane, common and lax-flowered sea lavenders and sea aster.

The mudflats support dense beds of eel grass and provide a valuable feeding ground for wildfowl and waders, and especially the dark-bellied brent goose. The concentration of thousands of these birds arriving on their autumn migration is of international importance. Waders such as curlew, dunlin, redshank, grey plover and knot occur in significant numbers outside the breeding season.

The Leigh cockle sheds nearby bring winter flocks of turnstone close inshore and attract some of the rarer gull species.

Belton Hills

49ac/20ha   **OS Ex175**   **TQ 825 860**   **LNR**   Southend-on-Sea
Borough Council

A steep hillside overlooking the Thames estuary at Leigh-on-Sea that has covered over with scrub and small trees.

In summer birds sing from almost every thicket – whitethroats, blackcaps and other migrants as well as residents such as yellowhammers and linnets. Paths have been cut through the scrub and these are lined with wild flowers and frequented by butterflies, including the marbled white – one of the few places in Essex where it can still be seen.

Some characteristic coastal plants that are rare in Essex grow here, including deptford pink (flowering June–August) and bithynian vetch (flowering May–June).

> South of Marine Parade, Leigh-on-Sea. Turn off the A13 on to Tattersall Gardens or Thames Drive, which lead down to Marine Parade.
>
> Leigh station is 10 minutes' walk via Belton Way.
>
> Accessible at all times.
>
> May/June for birdsong; summer for butterflies (mid-June to mid-July for the marbled white).

West Canvey Marshes

635ac/257ha   **OS Ex175**   **TQ 770 845**

A cquired by RSPB in 2006, this large area of coastal grazing marsh is managed principally for breeding waders such as lapwings and redshanks, using a mix of cattle grazing and hay cutting, plus control of water levels.

The saltmarsh alongside Benfleet Creek already has the highest density of breeding redshanks in Essex. The north and west sides of the reserve are bounded by tidal creeks where oystercatchers, knots, dunlins, godwits and sandpipers can be found. The wide fleet, with its open water and fringe of reeds, attracts good numbers of feeding little egrets. The drier grassland is good for breeding skylarks. The scrubby areas attract linnets and whitethroats.

Water voles and a large great crested newt colony occupy the freshwater ditches.

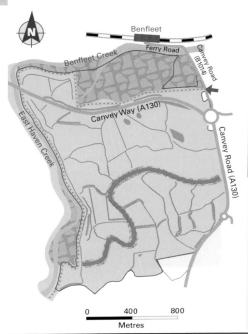

Little egret: recent colonist and now resident

Alan Williams

South of Benfleet. Park in Benfleet or at the station and follow Ferry Road past the station and over the bridge. The seawall path leaves the road on the right.

Benfleet station is a short walk.

Accessible at all times via the seawall footpath. For the latest visiting arrangements check the RSPB website www.rspb.org.uk.

Wheatley Wood

84ac/34ha   **OS Ex175**   **TQ 788 914**

WOODLAND
TRUST

Former farmland given to the Woodland Trust by Rochford Council and planted up as part of the Trust's 'Woods on your Doorstep' millennium project. The trees include oak, ash, hornbeam and willow, and shrubs such as hawthorn and guelder rose. The meadow areas are cut for hay.

Reached via Little Wheatley Chase, a turning on the right 600m past the roundabout where the A129 Wickford–Rayleigh road meets the A1245.

Rayleigh station (Liverpool Street to Southend) is about 10 minutes' walk.

Accessible at all times.

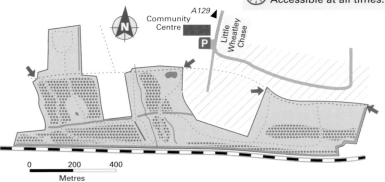

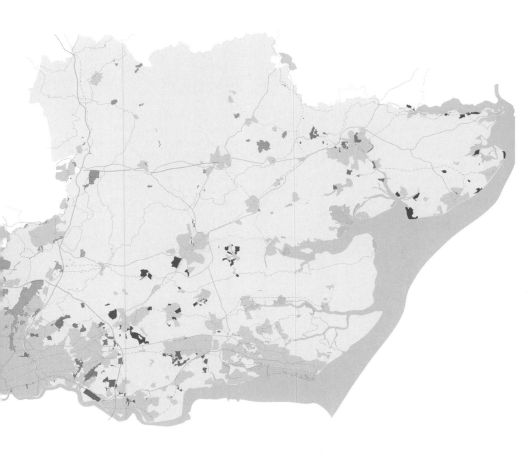

Alan Williams

Tony Gunton

Index of sites and summary of facilities

Index of sites (continued)

Index of species photographs

The Nature of Essex series

For more information or to order contact Lopinga Books on (01799) 599 643 or go to the Lopinga website at www.lopinga.com.